Python Without Fear

Python Without Fear

A Beginner's Guide That Makes You Feel Smart

Brian Overland

✦ Addison-Wesley

Boston • Columbus • Indianapolis • New York • San Francisco • Amsterdam • Cape Town
Dubai • London • Madrid • Milan • Munich • Paris • Montreal • Toronto • Delhi • Mexico City
São Paulo • Sydney • Hong Kong • Seoul • Singapore • Taipei • Tokyo

Visit us on the Web: informit.com/aw

Library of Congress Catalog Number: 2017946292

ISBN-13: 978-0-13-468747-6
ISBN-10: 0-13-468747-7
1   17

For all my beloved four-legged friends:
Skyler, Orlando, Madison, Cleo, and Pogo.

Contents

Chapter 5   *Python Lists*   77

Chapter 6   *List Comprehension and Enumeration*   101

Chapter 7 · *Python Strings* · 125

Chapter 8 · *Single-Character Ops* · 147

Chapter 13   *Matrixes: 2-D Lists*   249

Chapter 14   *Winning at Tic-Tac-Toe*   271

Chapter 15   *Classes and Objects 1*   295

Preface

There's a lot of free programming instruction out there, and much of it's about Python. So for a book to be worth your while, it's got to be good…it's got to be really, really, *really* good.

I wrote this book because it's the book I wish was around when I was first learning Python a few years back. Like everybody else, I conquered one concept at a time by looking at almost a dozen different books and consulting dozens of web sites.

But this is Python, and *it's not supposed to be difficult!*

The problem is that not all learning is as easy or fast as it should be. And not all books or learning sites are *fun*. You can, for example, go from site to site just trying to find the explanation that really works.

Here's what this book does that I wish I'd had when I started learning.

Steering Around the "Gotchas"

Many things are relatively easy to do in Python, but a few things that ought to be easy are harder than they'd be in other languages. This is especially true if you have any prior background in programming. The "Python way" of doing things is often so different from the approach you'd use in any other language, you can stare at the screen for hours until someone points out the easy solution.

Or you can buy this book.

How to Think "Pythonically"

Closely related to the issue of "gotchas" is the understanding of how to *think* in Python. Until you understand Python's unique way of modeling the world, you might end up writing a program the way a C programmer would. It runs, but it doesn't use any of the features that make Python such a fast development tool.

```
a_list = ['Don\'t', 'do', 'this', 'the' ,'C', 'way']
for x in a_list:
    print(x, end=' ')
```

This little snippet prints

```
Don't do this the C way
```

Intermediate and Advanced Features

Again, although Python is generally easier than other languages, that's not universally true. Some of the important intermediate features of Python are difficult to understand unless well explained. This book pays a lot of attention to intermediate and even advanced features, including list comprehension, generators, multidimensional lists (matrixes), and decorators.

Learning in Many Different Styles

In this book, I present a more varied teaching style than you'll likely find elsewhere. I make heavy use of examples, of course, but sometimes it's the right conceptual figure or analogy that makes all the difference. Or sometimes it's working on exercises that challenge you to do variations on what's just been taught. But all of the book's teaching styles reinforce the same ideas.

What's Going on "Under the Hood"

Although this book is for people who may be new to programming altogether, it also caters to people who want to know how Python works and how it's fundamentally different "under the hood." That is, how does Python carry out the operations internally? If you want more than just a simplistic introduction, this book is for you.

Why Python?

Of course, if you're trying to decide between programming languages, you'll want to know why you should be using Python in the first place.

Python is quickly taking over much of the programming world. There are some things that still require the low-level capabilities of C or C++, but you'll find that Python is a *rapid application development tool*; it multiplies the effort of the programmer. Often, in a few lines of code, you'll be able to do amazing things.

More specifically, a program that might take 100 lines in Python could potentially take 1,000 or 2,000 lines to write in C. You can use Python as "proof of concept": write a Python program in an afternoon to see whether it fulfills the needs of your project; then after you're convinced the program is useful, you can rewrite it in C or C++, if desired, to make more efficient use of computer resources.

With that in mind, I'll hope you'll join me on this fun, exciting, entertaining journey. And remember this:

```
x = ['Python', 'is', 'cool']
print(' '.join(x))
```

Acknowledgments

It's customary for authors to write an acknowledgments page, but in this case, there's a particularly good reason for one. There is no chapter in this book that wasn't strongly influenced by one of the collaborators: retired Microsoft programmer (and software development engineer) John Bennett.

John, who has used Python for a number of years—frequently to help implement his own high-level script languages—was particularly helpful in pointing out that this book should showcase "the Python way of doing things." So the book covers not just how to transcribe a Python version of a C++ solution but rather how to take full advantage of Python concepts—that is, how to "think in Python."

I should also note that this book exists largely because of the moral support of two fine acquisition editors: Kim Boedigheimer, who championed the project early on, and Greg Doench, whom she handed the project off to.

Developmental and technical editors Michael Thurston and John Wargo made important suggestions that improved the product. My thanks go to them, as well as the editorial team that so smoothly and cheerfully saw the manuscript through its final phases: Julie Nahil, Kim Wimpsett, Angela Urquhart, and Andrea Archer.

Author Bio

At one time or another, Brian Overland was in charge of, or at least influential in, documenting all the languages that Microsoft Corporation ever sold: Macro Assembler, FORTRAN, COBOL, Pascal, Visual Basic, C, and C++. Unlike some people, he wrote a lot of code in all these languages. He'd never document a language he couldn't write decent programs in.

For years, he was Microsoft's "go to" man for writing up the use of utilities needed to support new technologies, such as RISC processing, linker extensions, and exception handling.

The Python language first grabbed his attention a few years ago, when he realized that he could write many of his favorite applications—the Game of Life, for example, or a Reverse Polish Notation interpreter—in a smaller space than any computer language he'd ever seen.

When he's not exploring new computer languages, he does a lot of other things, many of them involving writing. He's an enthusiastic reviewer of films and writer of fiction. He's twice been a finalist in the Pacific Northwest Literary Contest.

Meet the Python

What if I told you there's a computer language that's easier to learn, easier to get started with, and easier to accomplish a great deal with, using only a few lines of code, than other computer languages?

In the opinion of millions, Python is that language. Derived from a language called ABC (as in "simple as ABC"), it's gained a massive worldwide following over the last two decades. So many programmers have joined the Python community that there are more than 100,000 free packages that work with the basic Python setup.

Come join the Python stampede. In this book I show you how to get started even if you have limited programming experience. I also steer you around the "gotchas"—the things Python does so differently that they trip up experienced programmers. This book is for new programmers as well as experienced programmers alike, and it discusses what goes on under the covers.

A Brief History of Python

Python was invented in 1991 by Dutch programmer Guido van Rossum, who derived much of it from the ABC language (not to be confused with C).

ABC had many features that exist today in Python. Van Rossum, whose title in the Python world is Benevolent Dictator for Life (BDFL), also incorporated elements of the Modula-3 language.

Van Rossum named the language after the BBC comedy series *Monty Python's Flying Circus*, so the connection to pythons is indirect, although troupe member John Cleese originally came up with "Python" as suggesting something "slithering and slimy" (source: Wikipedia.org). So there you have it—there is a connection to reptiles after all.

Since then, several versions of Python have been developed, adding important capabilities, the latest of which is Python 3.0. This book uses Python 3.0, although it includes notes about adapting examples to Python 2.0.

How Python Is Different

The first thing to know about Python is that Python is free.

Many Python extensions are free and come with the basic download. These modules offer features such as math, date/time, fractions, randomization, and tkinter, which supports a graphical user interface that runs across multiple platforms. Again, all are free.

Python's built-in numeric support is impressive, as it includes complex numbers, floating-point, fractions (from the Fractions module), and "infinite integers."

Python has attracted an extraordinary following. Many developers provide libraries—called *packages*—to their fellow Python programmers, mostly free of charge. You can get gain access by searching for *Python Package Index* in your Internet browser and then going to the site. As of this writing, the site offers access to more than 107,000 packages.

At first glance, a Python program may look something like code in other languages, but a close look reveals major differences.

- Unlike most languages, Python has no "begin block" or "end block" syntax— all relationships are based on indentation! Although this might seem risky to a C programmer, it enforces a consistent look that's more comprehensible to beginners.

- Python has no variable declarations. You create variables by assigning values to them. This goes a long way toward simplifying the language syntactically, but it also creates hidden "gotchas" at a deep level. This book will steer you around them.

- Python is built heavily on the idea of *iteration*, which means looping through sequences. This concept is built deeply into high-level structures (lists, dictionaries, and sets). Use them well, and you'll be able to get a great deal done in a small space.

Python is often considered a "prototyping" or "rapid application development" language because of these abilities. You can write a program quickly in Python. If you later want to improve machine-level efficiency, you can later rewrite the program in C or C++.

How This Book Works

I believe strongly in learning by example as well as by theory. The plan of this book is to teach the basics of Python (as well as some intermediate and advanced features) by doing the following:

▶ Introducing a Python feature, using syntax diagrams and short examples

▶ Showing a major example that demonstrates the practical application of the feature

▶ Including a "How It Works" section that deconstructs the example code line by line

▶ Listing a set of exercises that challenge you to do variations on the example

Because Python has an interactive development environment, IDLE, I often invite you to follow along with the shorter examples, as well.

This book uses a number of icons in the margin to help give you additional visual cues.

These sections describe some basic rule of Python syntax. Anything meant to be entered at the keyboard precisely as shown (such as a keyword or punctuation) is in bold. Meanwhile, placeholders, which contain text you supply yourself, are in italics. For example, in the syntax for the **global** statement, the keyword itself is in bold, while the name of the variable—which you supply—is in italics.

global *variable_name*

This icon indicates a block of pseudocode, which systematically describes each step of a program purely in English, not Python-ese. However, because Python statements are often not so far from English, I don't always need to use pseudocode. It can still be helpful, on occasion, for summarizing program design.

This icon indicates a section that deconstructs every line of a major example, or at least every line that isn't already trivial.

This icon indicates a section that provides exercises based on the preceding example. You'll learn Python much faster if you try at least some of the exercises.

This icon precedes a section that shows how to revise or greatly improve an example. These are not included for every example. Where this book does use them, it's because the example used the more obvious way to do something; the "optimized" approach will then show how the more experienced, sophisticated Python programmer would handle the job.

Installing Python

The steps for installing Python are essentially the same regardless of whether you have a Windows-based system, Macintosh, or any other system that Python supports. Here are the basic steps:

1 Go to the Python home page: **python.org**.

2 Open the Downloads menu.

3 If a Downloads for Windows screen appears, click the Python 3.6.1 button. If your system does not run Windows, you'll need to select another operating system by examining all the choices in the Downloads menu.

4 Click the Save File button.

5 Find the file you just saved; any system will generally have a place that it puts downloads. This saved file contains the Python installer. Double-click the name of this saved file and follow the instructions.

If all goes well, Python is installed on your computer with all the basic modules, tkinter (GUI development) included. Now you have a choice to make. To start using Python, you can use "basic interactive mode"—which is functional but nothing special—or you can use IDLE, the interactive development environment.

I strongly recommend the latter. IDLE does everything the basic interactive mode does, and a great deal more. In the next section, I describe some ways of using IDLE that can save you a lot of time later.

Here's what basic interactive mode looks like. It offers only rudimentary editing and no support for loading programs from text files.

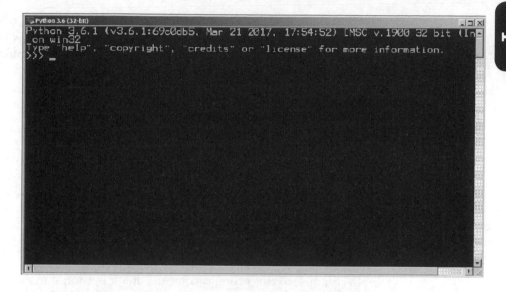

Here's what IDLE looks like. Notice all the menus it provides. You can do a great deal more—including loading programs from text files and debugging them—than you can with the basic interactive mode.

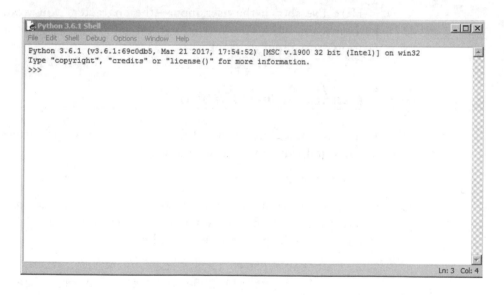

From within Windows, you should find the basic interactive-mode application right on the Start menu. But this is not the Python you want. It's well worth your while to select Programs, select Python, and then finally select IDLE.

With Mac systems (assuming you have downloaded Python, including IDLE), you may need to get to IDLE by opening Finder and selecting Applications; then select Python and finally select IDLE. Your download may or may not even have basic mode.

Begin Using Python with IDLE

Start IDLE, the interactive development environment. I advise you to make this your home base, the place you'll want to spend most of your time while learning Python. You should use your system to put the icon on your desktop so that you can easily start IDLE any time you want.

As soon as you start IDLE, you'll see a prompt, like this:

```
>>>
```

In response to this prompt, you can enter a Python statement or expression. You can also get help by typing the **help** command followed by a type name, like this:

```
>>>help(str)
```

Here I've shown the user input—the characters you would enter at the keyboard—in bold; output from Python is in normal font. I follow this convention throughout the book.

Correcting Mistakes from Within IDLE

One of the best features of IDLE is that it makes error correction easy. Let's say you sit down and enter the following:

```
>>>x = z
```

As you'll learn in upcoming chapters, this assignment statement produces an error if the variable z has not already been assigned a value. The environment responds by printing a message like this:

```
Traceback (most recent call last):
  File "<pyshell#205>", line 1, in <module>
    x = z
NameError: name 'z' is not defined
```

In this case, it's easy to reenter the offending statement. But suppose you have a much longer block of code that is erroneous and you don't want to retype the whole thing. Here's an example:

```
def print_nums(n):
    i = 1
    while i <= n:
        print(i, end='\t')
        i +++= 1
```

The problem with this block of code is that it ends with the line i +++= i instead of i += i. There was supposed to be only one plus sign (+).

You'd like to fix this error but don't want to retype all those statements. Fortunately, Python makes error correction easy. Just do the following:

1 Position the cursor on any line in the block of code. (If the block of code is only one line, make sure the cursor is at the end of the line.)

2 Press the Enter key.

Voilà! The entire block of code magically reappears, with the cursor positioned at the end; you can then fix whatever you need to fix. Use the arrow keys to go back to any statement and then make your corrections. Finally, to resubmit a block of code, place the cursor at the end of the last line again and press Enter twice.

Remember this technique. It will save you many hours of work.

Dealing with Ends of Lines

Because of the way in which Python interprets lines, you cannot freely cross physical-line borders as you can in C. But what if you need to enter an exceptionally long line?

The end of a physical line usually terminates a Python statement, because there is no statement-terminator syntax as in C. However, an open parenthesis, curly brace, or bracket automatically continues the virtual line to the next physical line. Here's an example:

```
total_amount = (this_amount + that_amount
    + a_big_number + count + even_more amounts )
```

The open parenthesis, (, on the top line creates a situation in which you can freely continue the statement onto other lines, until this parenthesis is matched. This is one case in which indentation doesn't matter but is only for readability. (Usually, Python forces indentation to be consistent.)

Occasionally, you may not be able to rely on this technique. If you really need to continue a physical line and have no alternative, you can use a backslash.

```
>>>my_str = 'I am typing a very long \
line of code.'
```

This example raises a question: How would you type a literal backslash in quoted string? The answer is that you'd use a double backslash, \\, to represent a literal backslash.

```
>>>my_str = 'I am typing a backslash: \\ \
in a long line of code.'
```

Chapter 7, "Python Strings," will get into the details of creating quoted strings in much greater detail.

In the last few pages, I've given you some Python survival skills. Now, if you're ready, it's time to go on a Python safari.

Additional Help: Online Sources

In this chapter, I've strongly suggested you download Python 3.0 or newer. If you are using an older version of Python 2.0, most of the code in this book will work, but you may need to make some adjustments. Although I've included some version notes, you can find additional help on the following websites:

wiki.python.org/moin/Python2orPython3

wiki.python.org/moin/PortingToPy3k/BilingualQuickRef

Although many chapters in this book feature examples that are relatively short and therefore easy to type in yourself, some of the later chapters feature longer program listings. You may find it helpful to download the code. You can find the code listings at this site:

brianoverland.com/books

2 A Python Safari: Numbers

Now that you've installed Python (you did install it, didn't you?), you're ready to go. The IDLE interactive environment is your starting point for Python safaris. But it's not just for beginners; for a long time, you should find it useful as a learning device as you advance.

But now—let's start! This chapter covers the following:

▶ Python "infinite" integers

▶ Integer vs. floating-point operations

▶ How variables are used in Python

Python and Numbers

Start IDLE. Up should come a prompt, although you may have to hit Enter one time to get it to appear.

```
>>>
```

Type in your favorite number and press Enter again. Let's say it's five.

```
>>>5
5
```

Here I use bold—as I will throughout most of this book—to show user input. Entering **5** and getting 5 in response is not that exciting. But let's do a calculation.

```
>>>10 + 15
25
```

So…interactive Python is a handy calculator! It's obvious what + does. But as with other programming languages, we can throw in subtraction (–) and multiplication (*).

```
>>>25 - 5 * 2
15
```

There's an issue of *precedence* here. If you subtract first, you get a final result of 40. But standard conventions of math say you multiply first, so 15 is correct. We could've used parentheses to get a different result.

```
>>>(25 - 5) * 5
40
```

So far, Python just appears to be a convenient one-line calculator. But wait. The next thing I want to show you is that Python—almost (but not quite) uniquely among programming languages—can handle extraordinarily large numbers.

The easiest way to generate super-large numbers is to use the exponent operator. This operator consists of two asterisks (**) in a row. For example, taking 3 to the 4th power gives us 3 times 3 times 3 times 3, or 81.

```
>>>3 ** 4
81
```

Eighty-one isn't that big, but 9 to the 30th power is 30 factors of 9 multiplied together…and that's a pretty big number.

```
>>>9 ** 30
42391158275216203514294433201
```

You might be tempted to say, "I've used floating-point numbers, and they can get bigger than this, so what's so impressive?"

In Python, as in most other programming languages, integers are absolutely precise, which means that no matter how high they get, adding 1 always creates a new value. That is not true of floating-point numbers, as you'll see.

For example, enter **10**40** and **10**40+1** and see what happens.

```
>>>10 ** 40
10000000000000000000000000000000000000000
>>>10 ** 40 + 1
10000000000000000000000000000000000000001
```

You should be able to see that these two numbers are distinct; they are not equal. Just look at the last digit in each number and compare. If you apply the test-for-equality operator, you can verify this directly in Python.

Test-for-equality (==) is an operator you'll probably use a great deal in Python programming. This operator produces the value **True** or **False**, which are special reserved words, called *keywords*. That means they have a special predefined meaning to the Python language.

If the two expressions produce indistinguishable results, then this operator will produce **True**.

```
>>>10 ** 40 == 10 ** 40 + 1
False
```

The result, **False**, means that Python recognizes that the results on either side of the equal signs (==) are not equal. So, adding 1 does produce a truly distinct number.

That, in turn, is amazing, because it shows the usefulness of super-large integers; they never lose their precision. Even if you're counting a very large population, one item at a time, you can rest assured that each time you add 1, you get a distinct value.

This Python "infinite integer" feature is impressive. You even can handle—with absolute precision—some legendary large numbers. For example, you may have heard of the term *google* (also spelled *googol*). In math, a google (or googol) is 10 to the 100th power, an almost unimaginably large number.

But it's a piece of cake to handle this number in Python.

```
>>>10 ** 100
10000000000000000000000000000000000000000000000000000000
0000000000000000000000000000000000000000000000
```

You can start with this number and then count forward one at a time. As before, adding 1 produces a distinct number, because there's no loss of precision.

```
>>>10 ** 100 + 1
10000000000000000000000000000000000000000000000000000000
0000000000000000000000000000000000000000000001
```

By the way, there is a subtlety here. In the absence of parentheses, the exponent operator is applied before addition. There is a definite precedence to Python operators, as listed in Appendix A.

Interlude

Why Doesn't C++ Support Infinite Integers?

Among programming languages in wide use today, Python is the only language that supports "infinite integers" in its standard form. Why doesn't C++ support this feature?

▼ *continued on next page*

Interlude

▼ *continued*

Using the class feature of C++, which is very powerful, you could in fact create an infinite-integer class for yourself. My book *C++ Without Fear* doesn't discuss how to do that exactly, but by using all the tools in that book, you could figure it out.

But it would not be easy. Creating a super-integer class that supports addition and subtraction would not be so difficult, but multiplication and division are tough. The Python integer type was created by math specialists who understand optimal ways to multiply and divide exceptionally large numbers. The good news is that when you use Python, all these problems have been solved for you.

Although Python's integer capacity is impressive, there is ultimately a limitation—imposed not by Python but by the computer's hardware capabilities. This is a fuzzy limitation, admittedly. You can go much bigger than a google, specifying (for example) 10 to the 200th power.

```
>>>10 ** 200
100000000000000000000000000000000000000000000000000000
000000000000000000000000000000000000000000000000000000
000000000000000000000000000000000000000000000000000000
0000000000000000000000000000000000
```

This is a number so large it is beyond the ability of the human mind to grasp. Yet Python can handle this number.

Mathematicians can think of far higher numbers still. A *google-plex* is 10 raised to the power of a google. This is easy enough to specify.

```
10 ** (10 ** 100)
```

But as they say on television, don't try this at home! Printing out such a number would be *1 followed by a google zeros!* Just the number of zeroes the computer would have to print would be larger than the number of atoms in the universe, and that far exceeds the ability of your computer to print zeroes.

Before we leave "the google" altogether, consider that we can use the abilities in this section to solve problems *not even solvable in most programming languages*—that is, not without great difficulty. Consider the problem of taking the number google plus 1 and then determining whether it is divisible by 7.

The remainder operator (%), which has the same precedence as multiplication and division, comes to our aid here. This operator produces the remainder after division; if a number is evenly divisible by 7, then—after division by 7—it will produce a remainder of 0. Let's try this.

```
>>>(10 ** 100 + 1) % 7
5
```

What did we just learn? The first number bigger than a google (which is a google plus 1) yields a remainder of 5 if you divide by 7. It is therefore not a multiple of 7. With a little mathematical reasoning, you can quickly infer that the smallest integer bigger than a google, which is a multiple of 7, is a google plus 3.

That is a fact that would be difficult or impossible to determine with other programming languages.

EXERCISES

Exercise 2.1.1. Would you expect the power operator (**) to take precedence over multiplication? Try a calculation to test your guess.

Exercise 2.1.2. Use Python to generate the result of 7 to the 40th power.

Exercise 2.1.3. How big, precisely, is the address space of a 64-bit architecture computer? Bear in mind that for each additional bit, the address space doubles. Use Python to generate this number.

Exercise 2.1.4. Use Python to help determine the first number bigger than a google that is divisible by 13. You may need to use a little trial and error, but you shouldn't need too much.

Interlude

How Big Is a Google?

The best estimates by scientists now say the number of elementary particles in our physical universe—counting all electrons, protons, neutrons, and so on—is around 10 to the 80th power.

The number of grains of sand on our planet has been estimated at a "mere" 7.5 times 10 to the 18th power. Therefore, the number of particles in the universe is (no surprise!) incomprehensibly larger.

Although 10 to the 80th is pretty big, it still falls short of a google by 10 to the 20th, and 10 to the 20th is 1 followed by 20 zeroes. That number itself is not so small.

10,000,000,000,000,000,000,000

That is to say, 10,000 times a billion times another billion. What Carl Sagan called "billions and billions." So, if every universe was like our own, it would take all the particles *in that many universes* to equal a google!

▼ *continued on next page*

Interlude

▼ *continued*

The base number here—10 to the 80th power—is just a few powers of 10 short of the estimated size of the physical universe in cubic centimeters. This follows from the estimate that the diameter of the physical universe is 10 to the 26th meters across.

But as far as mathematicians are concerned, we've hardly gotten started. The number called a *google-plex* can be expressed as 1 *followed* by a google's worth of zeroes. Therefore, just to write out the number using standard notation would be 1 followed by so many zeroes they could not fit into the universe, if each 0 was written on its own little block a 10th of a meter (roughly 3 inches) in diameter.

It would take "billions and billions" of physical universes like our own just to find space to write down all the zeroes in a google-plex!

Fortunately, scientific notation and substitution makes it possible to write down these figures, even though they are so large as to be far beyond corresponding to anything in the universe.

```
google = 10 ** 100
google-plex = 10 ** google
```

As I've shown in this chapter, Python is good at handling numbers in the range of a google or even a google squared—which would be 1 followed by 200 zeroes. Even division between two such quantities is fast and efficient. But don't ask Python to try to deal with a google-plex, which is far beyond the ability of Python to handle. It's really only comprehensible as a theoretical notion.

Oh, and the physical constant that comes closest to a google? That would be the density of the universe (in kilograms per cubic meter) at the time of the Big Bang—or rather one unit of Planck time immediately after the Big Bang. That number is 10 to the 96th power, and it still comes up short.

Python and Floating-Point Numbers

Another operation, of course, is division. Division is special, because even though you use two integers (an integer being a number with no fractional portion), division has the possibility of producing a fractional result; if it is fractional, it will be stored in floating-point format.

```
>>>15 / 2
7.5
```

Unfortunately, here is where version differences raise their ugly head. This is the result you can expect to see with Python version 3.*x*. With version 2.*x*, if two integers are involved in division, the result is automatically rounded down to the nearest integer. To get the same effect with version 3.*x*, use integer division (//).

```
>>>15 // 2
7
```

This looks like the remainder is being thrown away. Indeed it is. But you can always use the remainder-division operator (%) to get that quantity.

```
>>>15 % 2
1
```

Version ▶ In version 2.*x*, all division between two integer operands is interpreted as integer, or rather "ground" division. That is to say, if both operands are integers, division will throw fractional portions away. Sadly, Python 3.*x* is not 100 percent backward compatible, and integer division is one of those areas in which there is a significant difference.

With version 2.*x*, to force division to be precise, you'd need to promote one of the operands to floating point, either by specifying it in floating-point format (such as "2.0") or by using a **float** conversion.

```
>>>15 / float(2)
7.5
```

◀ **Version**

For the most part, you don't need to worry about the details of how the computer carries out floating-point math. However, there are a few things you do need to know.

First, floating-point numbers have the capacity to represent fractions. For that reason, there are many situations in which you'll want to use floating point.

Second, to specify floating-point format, just use a decimal point. The following numbers are both considered floating point by Python, even though the second case contains a zero fractional portion:

```
>>>1.75
1.75
>>>9.0
9.0
```

The third thing to understand about floating-point format is that you can freely combine integer and floating-point expressions. Python will happily promote an integer expression to floating point so that the numbers can be freely combined.

```
>>>1 + 2.5
3.5
```

Floating-point numbers, unlike integers, have limited precision. This means that very large floating-point numbers lose the ability to distinguish between one number and the next. Consider the following number, formed by taking 9 to the 30th power—but doing so with floating-point math, not integer:

```
>>>9.0 ** 30
4.23911582752162e+28
```

We used a decimal point in 9.0, so the expression is treated as floating point, not integer. With large floating-point numbers (or tiny amounts extremely close to 0.0), Python switches to scientific notation. The number shown here is approximately 4.239 times 10 to the 28th power.

If you now add 1 (either floating-point or integer) to this result, you'll see that there's a limited precision. The following produces a result that isn't distinguishable from the previous result:

```
>>>9.0 ** 30 + 1
4.23911582752162e+28
```

There are cases where you might want to use this number in counting, and in such cases, it's critical that adding 1 produces a new number. So if we test the two quantities for equality (==), we should get **False**. But look what happens:

```
>>>9.0 ** 30 == 9.0 ** 30 + 1.0
True
```

In other words, we added 1 to the quantity 9.0 ** 30 and failed to get a new number.

Think about what this means. We added 1 to a number, which should produce a different number not equal to the first! Yet Python says they are equal. This means either that Python doesn't understand math or that there was a rounding error because of loss of precision.

As we saw in the previous section, adding 1 to the quantity 9 ** 30 (which is an integer expression, not floating point) *does* produce a new number. That's because integers, unlike floating-point numbers, are always precise.

The moral of the story is, if you have a number that's used for counting or indexing purposes, it should be an integer.

EXERCISES

Exercise 2.2.1.   Describe in English the meaning of the expression
5.23911582752162e+22.

Exercise 2.2.2.   Based on how the expressions were evaluated in the previous examples, what would you say is the precedence of test-for-equality (==) relative to arithmetic operators (+, −, /, *, **)?

Assigning Numbers to Variables

So far, we've been using Python as a super-powered calculator, able to handle numbers such as a google.

But programming requires variables. A variable is simply a name to which we assign a data value. In Python, any variable can refer to any type of data at any time. That's because Python variables have no type; only data objects do. I'll get into the consequences of that fact later.

It's easy to start using variables in Python. For example, you can enter the following:

```
>>>a = 1
>>>b = 2
>>>a + b
3
```

If you've used any other programming language before—or even if you haven't—what happened here should be clear. Even if this is your first attempt at programming, this should still be easy to understand. Here's what we did:

1 Associate the variable name a with the value 1.

2 Associate the variable name b with the value 2.

3 Add a and b together, which represent 1 and 2, respectively. Python responds as if **1 + 2** were entered.

Although Python may seem lax, there are restrictions. The third statement in this example used a + b on the right side of the assignment; but this was valid only because a and b had already been created. Here is the general rule, and it's the most fundamental rule in Python:

✱   **A variable must be created before being used, but an assignment (=) creates a variable if it does not already exist.**

One upshot of this rule is that—with few exceptions—a variable must appear on the *left* side of an assignment before it appears on the right.

For example, you can create a variable named my_amount, but if a new variable appears on the *right* of the assignment, that's an error. Here, the use of x on the right side causes an error:

```
my_amount = x            # Error! x not yet created.
```

The problem was that this statement used x, even though x didn't represent anything. The solution is to create x first, by assigning it a value. Only then can x be used in any other context.

```
>>>x = 10
>>>my_amount = x
```

Python has no trouble with these statements now. The effect in this case is to associate both of the names, x and my_amount, with the data value, 10.

What happens if we assign a value to a variable a second time? The answer is

▶ First, the value on the right is fully calculated.

▶ Second, any previous association the variable had is now canceled.

▶ The variable is now associated with the value on the right side of the equal sign (=).

Once again, it doesn't matter whether the variable previously referred to integer or floating-point data; the variable becomes associated with the new value. Here's an example:

```
>>>x = 7.59
>>>x
7.59
>>>x = 2
>>>x
2
```

A variable may appear on *both* sides of an assignment—but only if it was previously created by another assignment. The old value is used in the calculation of the new. Here's an example:

```
>>>n = 5
>>>n = n + 1
>>>n
6
```

Another rule is that every name in the Python language is case-sensitive. Consequently, the following produces 101, not 200!

```
>>>a = 1
>>>A = 100
>>>a + A
101
```

Assignment, in Python, is a statement. That means there's a strict syntax that determines how you can use it. With some exceptions we'll cover later, this is how you use assignment:

```
variable_name = expression
```

Remember that a single equal sign (=) is used here, not double (==), which differentiates assignment from test-for-equality.

As for variable names, rules are as follows:

▶ The first letter in a variable (or other symbolic name) must be an underscore (_) or a letter.

▶ The other characters may be any combination of underscores, letters, and numerals.

The expression on the right can be a single value, or it can be more complex. Here's an example:

```
>>>my_num1 = 7
>>>my_num2 = my_num1 + (3.0 / 2)
>>>my_num2
8.5
```

The first line here creates the variable my_num1, through assignment. The second statement creates the variable my_num2 while using my_num1 on the right; this usage of my_num1 is valid because my_num1 was already created. The next line is just the name my_num2. When you are in the interactive environment (IDLE) and you enter a variable name by itself, Python prints its value.

Once we get to script programming, you'll find variables to be essential. But we can use variables now to build complex expressions.

For example, consider the problem of using the quadratic formula, which is as follows:

$$x = \frac{-b \pm \sqrt{b^2 - 4ac}}{2a}$$

Taking a square root is the same operation as raising it to the power of one half (0.5). We therefore have all the tools we need to use this formula.

As you may recall from high school, the quadratic formula solves an equation of the following form:

```
0 = ax² + bx + c
```

One quadratic I've always been fascinated with is the one that determines the golden ratio, in which A/B equals (A + B)/A. One of the properties is that the square of this number is 1 more than the number itself.

$$x^2 = x + 1$$

This gives us a quadratic equation like this:

$$0 = x^2 - x - 1$$

This gives us values for a, b, and c, which we can enter into Python.

```
>>>a = 1
>>>b = -1
>>>c = -1
```

Now let's apply the quadratic formula. First, let's get the determinant, which is the portion of the formula under the square root sign. I'll abbreviate this value as determ to make for less typing.

```
>>>determ = (b * b - 4 * a * c) ** 0.5
```

Again, assignment creates a variable, in this case, determ. As always, we can get the value of this variable by entering it alone on a line.

```
>>>determ
2.23606797749979
```

Looking back at the full quadratic formula, it's not too hard to plug this into the rest of the formula to get the final answer or, rather, one of them.

```
>>>x = (-b + determ) / (2 * a)
```

This statement creates x as a variable by assigning a value to it, and now we can get its value.

```
>>>x
1.618033988749895
```

This result is indeed the golden ratio, to a high degree of precision!

EXERCISES

Exercise 2.3.1. If you look closely at the quadratic formula and the steps we took to get a value, you should see that there is another value possible for x. Using a statement similar to the one we just entered, get this second value for x. (Hint: if you turn a few pages back, you'll see that the formula uses a plus-or-minus sign, indicating that there are two different solutions.)

Exercise 2.3.2. What is the problem, if any, with the following series of Python statements?

```
he_loves = 10
she_loves = -10
Love = 2
they_love = he_loves * she_loves + love
```

Exercise 2.3.3. Which of the following are valid names for variables?

```
amount
amount55
_amount
1x
y1
2y
n2
```

What Do Python Assignments Really Do?

For C, C++, and BASIC, the way I usually define a *variable* is as a named location that stores a value. In other words, a variable is like a little box that has a name on it, into which you can put any value you want as long as it is in the right format.

Such "little boxes," it should be noted, have a series of attributes in C++. A variable, or "box," is declared to only be able to hold certain kinds of data. If I try to put any other data in there, the result is an error.

But Python does things differently. This difference may seem trivial right now. But later in the book, it will matter greatly.

Consider how things are done in other languages. Again, most variables can be viewed as little boxes that contain values for as long as you want them to:

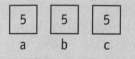

Python instead treats every variable as a *reference*. A reference, in turn, has some similarities to C pointers or to Windows handles. The key point is that when multiple variables are references (that is, refer to) the same value, they do not store the value separately. Let's say several variables are assigned the value 5.

▼ *continued on next page*

Interlude

▼ *continued*

```
>>>a = 5
>>>b = 5
>>>c = 5
```

Here's the result in memory, in which the lines indicate a "refer to" relationship:

All of these variables now refer to just one value, 5, which is stored at a single location in memory. But note that as soon as one of the variables is assigned a new value, it refers to a new location.

```
>>>c = 10
```

The variable c now refers to a new location and a new value (data object). So, c no longer refers to the same place in memory that a and b do.

Yet the following statement still does exactly what you'd expect.

```
>>> b + c
15
```

So, it may not be easy at first to see how the difference matters, because at this point, there seems to be no difference in the results.

One of the most important consequences is that because Python uses this mechanism, a variable can be assigned a new value with a different type. One moment it's storing an integer; the next moment, it's storing a floating-point value.

Although you can do that to your heart's content, it's almost always bad programming practice to use the same name to refer to different kinds of data. Ideally, names should be chosen that remind the programmer of the kind of data being named. Most letters—i, j, and k, in particular—are usually used to name integers, while x, y, and z usually are used to name floating-point data.

Variable-Naming Conventions in This Book

Remember that, in Python, there are no variable declarations, only assignments. That makes simple programs simpler, but it also means that for more complex applications, you don't have the option of looking up a variable's type. You can determine type by using the built-in **type()** function (which is particularly helpful within the interactive development environment), but you can't determine type by seeing how a variable is declared in the program.

I have found that, with Python, programming code is far more readable if you stick to variable-naming conventions. As a result, you can tell what kind of data you're dealing with just by looking at the name. Although there are occasional exceptions, I mostly stick to the following plan:

NAME	USED FOR
*xxx*_`str`, or any name with `str` in it; also `s`, `s1`, `s2`, and so on	Text strings
*xxx*_`list`, or any name with `list` in it	Python lists (introduced in Chapter 5)
`x`, `y`, `z`	Floating-point numbers
Most other letters, but especially `i`, `j`, `k`, and `m`	Integers

If a variable name does not fit into one of these categories, it's usually an integer.

Finally, when you get to the use of functions, remember that functions are usually known through their use of active verbs in the name, for example, `convert_to_centigrade()`.

Some Python Shortcuts

When it comes to numeric manipulation and assignment, Python has some slick shortcuts. Some of them resemble shortcuts from the C and C++ languages.

One of the slickest conveniences is the multiple-assignment technique. The following statement creates five variables and initializes them all to 0:

```
>>>a = b = c = d = e = 0
```

You can now use any of these variables and/or get their value.

```
>>>a
0
```

But—and this is a caution primarily for C and C++ programmers—this is a limited technique. In C, for example, multiple assignments work because an assignment is really an expression and, in those languages, can be included in larger expressions.

```
b = (7 + (a = 10));    // This is a C/C++ statement.
```

In C, this would assign 10 to a, and 17 to b. This does not work in Python.

But in Python, you can use multiple assignments to assign any one value you want. For example, I could've initialized all the variables to 50.77.

```
>>>a = b = c = d = e = 50.77
```

Python has some tricks of its own. One of the most impressive (and useful) is serial assignment, also called *tuple* assignment. Let's say I want to create three variables, i, j, and k, and give them all different values. I can do this by putting comma-separated groups on either side of the equal sign.

```
>>>i, j, k = -100, 123, 456
>>>i
-100
>>>j
123
>>>k
456
```

You can also display multiple values efficiently. In this case, the three data values named by i, j, and k are displayed as a *tuple*—which is like an array but is immutable; its values cannot be altered.

```
>>>i, j, k
(-100, 123, 456)
```

Here is another, though related, shortcut. Assuming a and b already exist (because they've previously been the target of assignments), you can do operations such as the following:

```
>>>a, b = a + b, a
```

This kind of assignment is difficult to express in other languages, because the timing of assignments is an issue. You'd need several statements involving a "temp" variable. But with Python, a gets the old value of a + b, and b gets the old value of a, *simultaneously*, without the need for temporary variables.

One last shortcut we'll explore combines addition and assignment. Consider how common it is to increment a variable, as in the following statement:

```
amount = amount + 1
```

As you might imagine, incrementing a variable is an extremely common operation. Python provides a shortcut to carry this out. The following statement increments the variable named `amount` by 1; it is equivalent to the previous statement, `amount = amount + 1`.

```
amount += 1
```

The next statement increments `amount` by another 5.

```
amount += 5
```

Remember that none of these statements is valid until the variable, `amount`, has been initialized by means of a standard assignment statement.

```
amount = 0
```

Python supports a whole series of operators that carry out an operation and store the results in the variable on the left.

OPERATOR	EXAMPLE	MEANING
+=	n += 1	n = n + 1
−=	n −= 1	n = n − 1
*=	n *= amt	n = n * amt
/=	n /= 2	n = n / 2
**=	n **= 2	n = n ** 2

None of these operators, it should be remembered, forms an expression. Rather, each of these operators defines a complete statement, as in the following syntax:

```
value1 += value2
```

The values, in this case, are added together, and the result is put in *value1*. It is roughly equivalent to the following:

```
value1 = value1 + value2
```

Two C/C++ shortcuts that do *not* work are increment (++) and decrement (--) operators. If you come from the land of C programming, this is a particularly treacherous "gotcha" because it will not produce a syntax error, but it will have no effect at run time, which can make for particularly insidious, difficult-to-track-down bugs.

The issue arises because Python supports unary + and − operators. The minus sign changes the sign of the operand, but the plus sign doesn't do anything at all.

```
>>>n = 5
>>>-n
-5
>>>+n
5
```

Consider the expression ++n. Python evaluates this as follows:

    +(+n)

This says, "Do nothing to n and then do nothing again."

Likewise, --n says, "Take the negative of n and then take the negative of that result," which, of course, gets you back to n without change, because a negative times a negative is a positive.

    -(-n)

Remember that the assignment operators (such as += and *=) do work in Python, but they cannot be used within larger expressions. And they require that the variable being operated on already exists.

EXERCISES

Exercise 2.4.1.   Create a set of variables, a1, a2, and a3, initializing them all to 10.

Exercise 2.4.2.   Create a set of variables, tt, ty, and tz, initializing them to 10, 20, and 30, respectively.

Exercise 2.4.3.   Assume you assign the variable xx a floating-point value. Then you assign a new value to it, and this new value is an integer value. What type would you expect xx to have now?

Chapter 2   *Summary*

Here are the important points of Chapter 2:

▶ The +, −, *, /, //, and ** operators are all supported in Python version 3.*x*. / signifies division, // signifies ground division (rounding down), and ** is the exponent operator.

▶ The exponent operator (**) can be used to create integers of fantastic sizes. (An integer is a number with no fractional portion.) The only limitations are those imposed by the size and speed of the computer itself. But you can easily specify a google (or googol), for example.

```
>>>10 ** 100
```

▶ A number with a decimal point is automatically stored internally in floating-point format, even if it has a 0 after the decimal point. Floating-point numbers have large ranges, as well as the ability to store fractional portions, but they also have limited precision.

```
>>>9.0
```

▶ A variable is a name associated with a particular value in Python. Assignment, which uses just one equal sign (=), associates the variable with the value on the right. Also, an assignment will create a variable if it does not already exist.

```
>>>x = 2.5
```

▶ If a variable does not yet exist, it is illegal to use it on the right of an assignment or in any other context. Therefore, you must first assign a value to a variable before using it.

▶ If a variable already exists (because it was previously the target of an assignment) and then it's assigned *another* value, Python makes no objection. The effect is that the old association is broken, and the variable takes on the type, format, and data of the new value on the right side.

```
>>>x = 88        # x now associated with 88, an integer
```

▶ Python has some slick shortcuts. The following statement assigns values to four variables. The effect of this statement is to associate all the variables with the value 0.

```
>>>a = b = c = d = e = 200
```

▶ Another slick shortcut is list assignment.

```
>>>x, y, z = 10, 20, 30
```

▶ Python has a set of operators that combine assignment with some other operation, including +=, −=, *=, etc. Here's an example:

```
>>>x += 1        # Increment x by 1 (x = x + 1).
```

▶ Remember that names and keywords are case-sensitive in Python.

▶ Remember, also, that a variable name must begin with a letter or underscore (_) but may be made up of letters, underscores, and digits throughout the remainder of the variable name.

3 *Your First Programs*

Programming is like writing a script, creating a predetermined list of words and actions for actors to perform night after night. A Python function is not so different. From within the interactive environment, you can execute a function as often as you like, and it will execute the same predefined "script." (The term *script* can also refer to an entire program.)

Within the Python interactive development environment (IDLE), writing functions is the beginning of true programming. In this chapter, I explore how to write functions, including the following:

▶ Using functions to calculate formulas

▶ Getting string and numeric input

▶ Writing formatted output

Temperatures Rising?

I happen to live in the Northwest corner of the United States, and I have Canadian relatives. When they discuss the weather, they're always talking Celsius. They might say, "Temperature's all the way up to 25 degrees. Gettin' pretty warm, eh?"

For people accustomed to the Fahrenheit scale, 25 is cold enough to freeze your proverbial hockey stick. So I have to mentally run a conversion.

```
fahr = cels * 1.8 + 32
```

If you have the Python interactive environment running, this is an easy calculation. I can convert 20 degrees in my head, but what about 25? Let's use Python! The following statements assign a value to the name `cels` (a *variable*), use that value to assign another value to the name `fahr`, and then finally display what the `fahr` value is.

```
>>>cels = 25
>>>fahr = cels * 1.8 + 32
>>>fahr
77.0
```

So, 25 "Canadian" degrees are 77.0 degrees on the "real" (that is, the American) temperature scale. That's comfortably warm, isn't it? For those living north of the border, it's practically blistering.

Python prints the answer with a decimal point: 77.0. That's because when the interactive environment combined my input with the floating-point value 1.8, it promoted all the data to floating-point format.

Let's try another one. What is the Fahrenheit value of 32 degrees Celsius? Actually, there's a faster way to do this calculation. We don't have to use variables unless we want to do so.

```
>>>32 * 1.8 + 32.0
89.6
```

Thirty-two degrees on the Celsius scale is 89.6 Fahrenheit. For a Canadian, that's practically burning up.

But I'd like to make this calculation even easier. What I'd really like to do is just enter a function name followed by a value to convert.

```
>>>convert(32)
89.6
```

And—here is the critical part—if this function worked generally, as if it were part of Python, I could use it to convert any number from Celsius to Fahrenheit. All I'd have to do is enter a different argument.

```
>>>convert(10)
50.0
>>>convert(20)
68.0
>>>convert(22.5)
72.5
```

But Python lets me create my own such function. This is what the **def** keyword does: define a new function. We could write it this way from within the interactive environment:

```
>>>def convert(fahr):
    cels = fahr * 1.8 + 32.0
    return cels

>>>
```

Notice that these statements by themselves don't seem to do anything. Actually, they do quite a bit. They associate the symbolic name `convert` with something referred to as a *callable* in Python, that is, a function.

If you display the "value" of the function, by itself, you get a cryptic message.

```
>>>convert
<function convert at 0x1040667b8>
```

This message tells you that `convert` has been successfully associated with a function. There were no syntax errors; however, runtime errors are always possible.

Not until we execute `convert` do we know whether it runs without errors. But this is easy. To execute a function, just follow it with parentheses—enclosing any *arguments*, if any.

```
>>>convert(5)
41.0
```

So, 5 degrees Celsius is actually 41.0 Fahrenheit…cool but not quite freezing.

If you enter this example as shown—using the bold font to indicate what you should type as opposed to what Python prints—and if everything goes right, then congrats, you've just written your first Python function!

If instead you get a syntax error, remember that you can easily edit a function by 1) moving the cursor to any line of the function and 2) pressing Enter. The entire function definition will reappear, and you can edit it by moving the cursor up and down. Finally, you can reenter it again. (To reenter, put your cursor on the end of the last line and press Enter twice.)

Before resubmitting the function definition, review the following rules:

▶ The definition of `convert` is followed by parentheses and the name of an *argument*. This name stands in for the value to be converted. In this case, the argument name is `fahr`.

▶ You must type a colon (:) at the end of the first line.

▶ The environment then automatically indents the next lines. Use this indentation. Don't try to modify it—at least not yet.

▶ The `return` statement determines what value the function produces.

▶ Remember that in Python all names are case-sensitive.

▶ In the interactive environment, you terminate the function by typing an extra blank line after you're done.

Note ▶ From within the interactive environment, you should use whatever indentations the environment creates for you. Doing otherwise may cause Python to report errors and fail to run the program.

However, when you write Python scripts in separate text files, the preferred convention is to use four spaces (and no tab characters). This is somewhat arbitrary, because almost any indentation scheme works if you hold to it consistently. But four spaces is the style preferred according to the PEP-8 standard that is observed by many Python programmers.

As much as possible, this book tries to hold to this PEP-8 standard. You can read more about this typographic standard for Python programming by searching for *PEP-8* online.

◀ Note

Let's take another example. Let's define another function and this time give it the name `inch_to_cent`. This function is even simpler than the `convert` function: it changes inches to centimeters, according to the formula 1 inch = 2.54 centimeters.

```
>>>def inch_to_cent(inches):
    cent = inches * 2.54
    return cent

>>>
```

As with the earlier function, entering a syntactically correct definition doesn't immediately do anything, but it does create a *callable* that you can then use to perform the inches-to-centimeter conversion whenever you want.

Here's an example:

```
>>>inch_to_cent(10)
25.4
>>>inch_to_cent(7.5)
19.05
```

Note that the `inch_to_cent` function definition uses its own variable—a local variable—named `cent`. Because it is local, it doesn't affect what happens to any variable named `cent` outside of the function.

But the use of this variable in this case isn't really necessary. You could define the same function more succinctly, as follows. But the effect is the same in either case.

```
>>>def inch_to_cent(x):
    return x * 2.54

>>>
```

You can conceptualize the action of a function call as follows. Each call to the `inch_to_cent` function passes a particular value in parentheses. This value is passed to the name `x` inside the function definition, and the return statement produces the output after operating on the `x` value passed to it.

Here's an illustration of how this works:

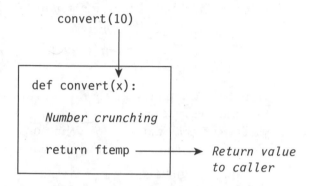

Remember, a function must be defined before a call to that function is executed.

Python's Use of Indentation

Syntactically, Python is fundamentally different from all the languages in the C-language family—including C++, Java, and C#—as well as other languages such as BASIC. The single biggest difference is that spacing matters, particularly indentation.

In the interactive environment, Python automatically indents statements inside a control structure, such as a **def**, **if**, or **while** statement block. Until you terminate that block, you should accept the indentation and not try to "fix" it.

When you learn later in this chapter to compose text files as Python scripts, you can indent any number of spaces you want, but you must do it consistently. If the first statement within a block of statements is indented four spaces, the next statement must be indented four spaces as well—no more, no less.

Note that the PEP-8 specification states that four-space indentation is the preferred standard.

A pitfall awaits you in the form of invisible tab characters. You can use tabs, but the danger is that a tab may look like four blank spaces when in fact it is only one character. And if you indent with a tab on one line and use spaces to indent on the next, Python gets confused and issues a syntax error.

▼ continued on next page

▼ *continued*

If possible, then, always use either one technique or the other: a single tab or multiple blank spaces. The safest policy is to have your text editor follow the rule of replacing a tab with blank spaces.

Indentation is an area in which C++ programmers are bound to feel superior. Take the following Python function:

```python
def  convert_temp(x):
    cels = x * 1.8 + 32.0
    return cels
```

In Python, you must indent this way or Python gets horribly confused. In C and C++, you are freed from spacing issues for the most part, because statement blocks and function definitions are controlled by curly braces. Here's how you might write this function in C++:

```cpp
float convert_temp(float x) {
    float cels = x * 1.8 + 32.0;
    return cels;
}
```

There are similarities between these two versions—the Python and the C/C++ version—but the latter gives you a lot more freedom to space things as you choose.

```cpp
float convert_temp(float x)
{cels = x * 1.8 + 32.0; return cels; }
```

With a little optimization, you can even put all the code on a single line.

```cpp
float convert_temp(float x){return x * 1.8 + 32.0;}
```

What C and C++ programmers tend to like about this is that the compiler is largely indifferent to spacing issues—as long as some whitespace appears where needed to separate variable names and keywords. C++ will never complain because you intended three spaces rather than four, which to a C++ programmer seems fussy, if not petty.

But the Python way has its own advantages. To beginning and intermediate programmers especially, Python indentation allows you to see how "deep" you are in the program. It makes relationships between different statements more obvious. And it closely echoes the indentation of pseudocode I use throughout this book.

Once you get used to Python's reliance on indented statements, you'll love it. Just be careful that your text editor doesn't let you confuse tab characters with blank spaces.

Putting in a Print Message

What if I want the function to not just return a number but to instead print out a user-friendly message such as the following:

```
7.5 inches are equal to 19.05 centimeters.
```

I can easily do that in Python. All I need to do is add a call to the built-in **print** function. Because **print** is a built-in function of Python, it's one that you do not define yourself; it's already defined for you. Here's a sample of this function in action:

```
>>>print('My name is Brian O.')
My name is Brian O.
```

Version ▶ Python version 2.0 features a version of **print** that does not expect parentheses around the argument list, because it is not a function. Starting with Python version 3.0, **print** becomes a function and therefore requires the parentheses.

```
print 'My name is Brian O.'  # Python 2.0 version
```

◀ Version

Why did I place single-quotation marks around the message to be printed? I did that because this information is text, not numeric data or Python code; it indicates that the words are to be printed out exactly as shown. Here are some more examples:

```
>>>print('To be or not to be.')
To be or not to be.
>>>print('When we are born, we cry,')
When we are born, we cry,
>>>print('That we are come'
    ' to this great stage of fools.')
That we are come to this great stage of fools.
```

The ability to use **print** pays off in a number of ways: I can intermix text—words placed in quotation marks—with variables.

```
>>>x = 5
>>>y = 25
>>>print('The value of', x, 'squared is', y)
The value of 5 squared is 25
```

By default, the **print** function inserts an extra blank space between one item and the next. Also, after a call to the **print** function is finished, then by default it prints a newline character, which causes the terminal to advance to the next line.

Now let's combine the printing ability with the power to define functions.

```
>>>def convert(x):
    c = x * 2.54
    print(x, 'inches equal', c, 'centimeters.')

>>>convert(5)
5 inches equal 12.2 centimeters.
>>>convert(10)
10 inches equal 25.4 centimeters.
```

Do you now see why the **print** function is useful? I can call this built-in function from within a definition of one of my functions; that enables my functions to print nice output messages rather than just producing a number.

Syntax Summaries

Throughout this book I use summaries to summarize parts of Python syntax. These are the grammatical rules of the language, and—although they are generally easier and more natural than syntax rules for human language—they must be followed precisely. If you're required to use a colon at the end of the line, you must not forget it.

Here is the syntax summary for function definitions:

```
def function_name(argument) :
    indented_statements
```

There actually is more to function syntax than this, as you'll see in Chapters 9 and 10. As I'll show later in this chapter, you can have more than one *argument*; if you do, use commas to separate them.

In a syntax display—such as the one shown previously—items in bold must be typed in as shown; the items in italics are items you supply, such as names.

Here's another example you can compare to the syntax summary:

```
>>>def print_age(n):
    print('Happy birthday.')
    print('I see that you are', n)
    print('years old.')

>>>
```

Remember, as always, that to end the statement block from within the interactive environment, type an extra blank line at the end.

Remember, also, that certain errors are not detected until the function is executed. Suppose a function does not contain syntax errors, but it tries to refer to a variable that is not yet recognized. Executing the function will generate an error unless the variable is created before the function is executed.

For a variable to be recognized, one of several things must happen.

▶ The function creates a variable by assigning it a value during an assignment (=).

▶ The variable must already exist because of an earlier assignment.

▶ Or, the variable exists because it represents a value passed to the function (for example, n in the previous function-definition example).

Here's a sample session that executes the print_age function. It assumes that this function has already been defined through the use of a **def** statement, as shown earlier.

```
>>>print_age(29)
Happy birthday.
I see that you are 29
years old.
```

Here is the same function, this time called with the value 45 rather than 29:

```
>>>print_age(45)
Happy birthday.
I see that you are 45
years old.
```

The built-in **print** function has a simple syntax—although there are some special features I'll introduce later.

print(_items_**)**

When **print** is executed, it displays the items on the console, with an extra blank space used to separate one item from the next.

During the call to **print**, you use commas to separate arguments if there is more than one.

```
>>>i = 10
>>>j = 5
>>>print(i, 'is greater than', j)
10 is greater than 5
```

Example 3.1.   *Quadratic Equation as a Function*

Now let's do something a little more interesting: take the quadratic formula example from Chapter 2 and place it in a function definition, by using the **def** keyword.

The quadratic formula computes the value of x, given the following relationship to arguments a, b, and c.

$$0 = ax^2 + bx + c$$

The following interactive session defines quad as a function taking three arguments and returning a value, which is the solution for x.

```
>>>def quad(a, b, c):
    determ = (b * b - 4 * a * c) ** 0.5
    x = (-b + determ) / (2 * a)
    return x

>>>
```

With this definition entered into the environment, you can then call the quad function with any values you like. For example, a simple quadratic equation is as follows:

$$0 = x^2 + 2x + 1$$

In this statement, a, b, and c correspond to the values 1, 2, and 1, respectively. Therefore, by giving the values 1, 2, and 1 as arguments to the quad function, we will get the value of x that satisfies the equation.

```
>>>quad(1, 2, 1)
-1.0
```

This means that we should be able to plug the value –1.0 in for x and get the quadratic equation to come out right. Let's try it.

$$0 = (-1)^2 + 2(-1) + 1$$
$$= 1 - 2 + 1$$

It works! Everything checks out nicely, because plugging –1.0 in for x does indeed produce 0. But a more interesting equation involves the numbers 1, –1, and –1, which give us the golden ratio. That ratio has the following property:

$$x/1 = (x + 1)/x,$$

That equation, in turn, implies the following:

$$x^2 = x + 1$$

This in turn yields a quadratic equation, as shown here:

$$0 = x^2 - x - 1$$

Finally, that gives us values for a, b, and c of 1, −1, and −1, which we can evaluate with the quad function. Let's try it!

```
>>>quad(1, -1, -1)
1.618033988749895
```

And this turns out to be correct to the 15th decimal place. This is the special number "phi." One of its many special properties is phi squared minus 1 produces phi itself. This is the golden ratio.

You can verify it this way:

```
>>>phi = quad(1, -1, -1)
>>>phi
1.618033988749895
>>>phi * phi - 1
1.618033988749895
```

A-ha! Phi squared, minus 1, gives us phi again! This is indeed the golden ratio or, rather, a close approximation of it.

How It Works

Although the quad function may look more complicated than the other, more elementary examples in this chapter, at the bottom it's doing the same thing: taking in some input, doing some number crunching, and returning a result. The one true innovation in this example is that here I've introduced the use of *three* arguments rather than just one.

The order of arguments is significant. Because the quad definition takes three arguments, a, b, and c, each call to quad must specify three values, and these are passed to those variable names: a, b, and c, in that order.

The following illustration shows how this works for the function call quad(1, 2, 1), assigning 1, 2, and 1 to the values a, b, and c:

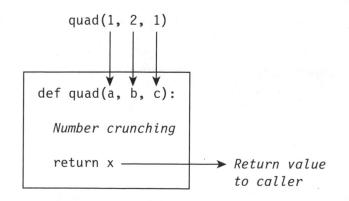

Now it's simply a matter of doing the correct number crunching to get an answer, and that means applying the quadratic formula.

$$x = \frac{-b \pm \sqrt{b^2 - 4ac}}{2a}$$

We can use pseudocode to express what this function does. A pseudocode description of a program or function uses sentences that are very close to human language but lists the steps explicitly.

Here is the pseudocode description of the quad function:

For inputs a, b, and c:

    Set determ equal to the square root of (b * b) – (4 * a * c).

    Set x equal to (–b + determ) divided by (2 * a).

    Return the value x.

The quadratic formula actually produces two answers, not one. The plus or minus sign indicates that –b plus the determinant (the quantity under the radical sign) divided by 2a is one answer; but –b *minus* the determinant divided by 2a is the other answer. In Example 3.1, the function returns only the first answer.

EXERCISES

Exercise 3.1.1.   Revise the quad function by replacing the name determ with the name dt and by replacing the name x with the name x1; then verify that the function still works.

Exercise 3.1.2.   Revise the quad function so that instead of returning a value, it prints two values using the Python **print** statement in a user-friendly manner: "The x1 value is…" and "The x2 value is…" (Hint: The use of the plus/minus sign in the quadratic formula indicates what these two—not one—values should be. Review this formula closely if you need to do so.) Print each answer out on a separate line.

Exercise 3.1.3.   The mathematical number "phi" represents the golden ratio, more specifically, the ratio of the long side of a golden rectangle to the short side. Try to predict what the reciprocal (1/phi) is; then use the Python interactive environment to see whether you're right. How would you express the relationship between phi and 1/phi?

Getting String Input

Before you can finally write "real programs," you'll need to be able to write scripts that can query the user for more information. Fortunately, Python includes a powerful built-in function, the **input** function, which makes this easy.

I'll give you the syntax first and then show examples.

string_var = **input(***prompt_string***)**

Version ▶ If you're using Python 2.0, use the function name **raw_input** instead of **input**. In 2.0, the **input** function works, but it does something different: it evaluates the string input as a Python statement rather than just passing it back as a string.

◀ Version

The essence of this syntax is that the built-in **input** statement both takes and produces a text string. In one way, the concept of text string is easy to understand; it's just "words" for the most part—or more accurately, letters and other characters.

For example, we might write a function, main, which we're going to use as a script.

```
>>>def main():
    name1_str = input('Enter your name: ')
    name2_str = input('Enter another: ')
    name3_str = input('And another: ')
    print('Here are all the candidates: ')
    print(name1_str, name2_str, name3_str)

>>>main()
Enter your name: Brian
Enter another: Hillary
And another: Donald
Here are all the candidates:
Brian Hillary Donald
```

This by itself is not a very exciting program. It takes some text and displays it on the console. But this little program demonstrates an important ability of Python: the ability to prompt the user for a text string and then assign it to a variable.

While other variables up until now have referred to numeric values, these variables—name1, name2, and name3—all refer to text strings in this case.

What exactly can go into a text string? Basically, anything you can type can go in a text string. Here's an example:

```
>>>in_str = input('Enter input line: ')
Enter input line: When I'm 64...
>>>in_str
'When I'm 64...'
```

As you can see, text strings can contain numerals (digit characters). But until they're converted, they're just numerals. They are text-string representations of numbers, not numbers you can perform arithmetic on.

If this isn't obvious, just remember that the *numeral* 5 is just a character on a keyboard or on the screen. But the *number* 5 can be doubled or tripled to produce 10 or 15 and has little to do with characters on a keyboard.

Here's an example:

```
in_str = '55'
```

But assigning 55 with no quote marks around it does something different.

```
n = 55
```

The difference is that 55 is an actual number, meaning that you can add, subtract, multiply, and divide it. But when enclosed in quotation marks, '55' is a text string. That means it is a string consisting of two numerals, each a 5, strung together.

A simple program should help illustrate the difference.

```
>>>def main():
    in_str = input('Enter your age: ')
    print ('Next year you'll be', in_str + 1)

>>>main()
Enter your age: 29
Error! Incompatible types.
```

Oops! What happened? The characters 29 were entered at the prompt and stored as a text string, that is, a numeral 2 followed by a numeral 9—a string two characters long. But that's not the same as a number, even though it looks like one.

Python complains as soon as you try to add a text string to a number.

```
in_str + 1
```

No error is reported until you execute the function. Python variables don't have types; only data objects do. Consequently, Python syntax seems lax at first. But the types of data objects—which are not checked for syntax errors, as there are no "declarations"—are checked whenever a Python statement is actually executed.

This means, among other things, that you cannot perform arithmetic on a string of numerals such as 100, until that string is first converted to numeric format. If this doesn't make sense now, don't worry; it will make sense when you read the next section.

The next section shows how to get input and store it as a number rather than text string.

Getting Numeric Input

As the previous section demonstrated, if you write a program that takes numeric input and does number crunching on it, you need to first convert to a numeric format.

To do that, use one of the following statements, depending on whether you are dealing with integer (**int**) or floating-point data (**float**):

```
var_name = int(input(prompt_message))
var_name = float(input(prompt_message))
```

These statements combine the input and conversion operations. You can, if you prefer, do them separately, but this is less efficient. For example, you could use this approach:

```
in_str = input('Enter a number: ')
n = int(in_str)
```

These two statements work fine together, but there's no reason not to combine the operations.

```
n = int(input('Enter a number: '))
```

Here's an interactive session that uses a number entered at the keyboard and then multiplies it by 2:

```
>>>def main():
    n = int(input('Enter a number: '))
    print('Twice of that is:', n * 2)

>>>main()
Enter a number: 10
Twice of that is: 20
```

So, to get actual numeric input, as opposed to storing input in a text string, use the **int** and **float** conversions.

But what are **int** and **float**, exactly? Here I'm using them like functions, but they're actually the names of built-in data types, integer and floating point, respectively. In Python, there's a general rule that type names can be used in this fashion, to perform conversions (assuming the appropriate conversion exists).

Key Syntax

```
type_name(data)
```

Example 3.2.   *Quadratic Formula with I/O*

This next example takes the quadratic-formula example another step further, by placing all the statements in a `main` function and then relying on Python input and output statements to communicate with the end user.

```
>>>def main():
    a = float(input('Enter value for a: '))
    b = float(input('Enter value for b: '))
    c = float(input('Enter value for c: '))
    determ = (b * b - 4 * a * c) ** 0.5
    x1 = (-b + determ) / (2 * a)
    x2 = (-b - determ) / (2 * a)
    print('Answers are', x1, 'and', x2)

>>>main()
```

Here is a sample session that might follow after you type **main()**:

```
Enter value for a: 1
Enter value for b: -1
Enter value for c: -1
Answers are 1.618033988749895 and -0.6180339887498948
```

There are two different answers in this case, not equal to each other, because the golden ratio is either phi (the ratio of the large side to the small) or 1/phi (the ratio of the small side to the large), depending on how you look at it. The negative sign in the second answer is necessary for the math to come out right.

Nearly all the digits are identical in this case, except for a small difference due to rounding errors. The actual values of phi and 1/phi are irrational (which means you would need an infinite number of digits to represent them precisely).

Note ▶ Remember that the interactive environment supports cut-and-paste operations, as well as a "magic" technique for revising blocks of code.

So, if you enter a long function definition and realize you've made a mistake, you can save a great deal of time by doing the following:

1 Scroll up to the block of code.

2 Place your cursor on any line of code in this block.

3 Press Enter.

4 The block of code will appear in the window—at the new cursor position—ready for you to edit it.

Then go ahead and make your changes, scrolling up and down if you need. When done, type an extra blank line after the new block of code.

◀ Note

How It Works

In this chapter, we're still dealing with programs that are relatively short and translate into simple pseudocode.

Prompt the user for the values of a, b, and c.

Apply the quadratic formula to get x1 and x2.

Print the values of x1 and x2.

Because a, b, and c all need to refer to numeric data, the program applies a **float** conversion combined with the built-in **input** function. If these numbers are not converted to **float** format, you won't be able to do math with them.

```
a = float(input('Enter value for a: '))
b = float(input('Enter value for b: '))
c = float(input('Enter value for c: '))
```

Next, the quadratic formula is applied to get the two solutions for x. Remember that the operation ** 0.5 has the same effect as taking the square root.

```
determ = (b * b - 4 * a * c) ** 0.5
x1 = (-b + determ) / (2 * a)
x2 = (-b - determ) / (2 * a)
```

Finally, the program displays the output, featuring x1 and x2.

```
print('The answers are', x1, 'and', x2)
```

EXERCISES

Exercise 3.2.1.   In Example 3.2, instead of using the prompt messages "Enter the value of a," etc., prompt the user with the following messages:

> "Enter the value of the x-square coefficient."

> "Enter the value of the x coefficient."

> "Enter the value of the constant."

Do you have to change the variable names as a result? Note that the user never sees the names of variables inside the code, unless you deliberately print those names.

Exercise 3.2.2.   Modify Example 3.2 so that it restricts input to integer values.

Exercise 3.2.3.   Write a program to calculate the area of a right triangle, based on height and width inputs. Apply the triangle area formula: A = w * h * 0.5. Prompt for width and height separately and print a nice message on the display saying, "The area of the triangle is...."

Exercise 3.2.4.   Do the same for producing the volume of a sphere based on the radius of the sphere. I'll invite you to look up the formula for volume of a sphere. For the value pi, you can insert the following statement into your program:

```
pi = 3.14159265
```

Formatted Output String

In Example 3.2, typical output looked like this:

```
The answers are 3.0 and 4.0
```

(This is produced, incidentally, when the inputs to the quadratic formula are 1, –7, and 12.)

But we might like to place a period at the end, making the output read as a nice sentence. We'd like to get the following:

```
The answers are 3.0 and 4.0.
```

But the **print** function puts a space between each print field so that you end up getting the following, which has an unnecessary space before the last character.

```
The answers are 3.0 and 4.0 .
```

There are at least two solutions. One is to include the special **sep** (separator) argument to the **print** function. By default, print uses a single space as a separator. But we can use **sep=''** (this consists of two single quotes in a row) to indicate that **print** shouldn't put in any separator at all.

This is fine, because we just take on responsibility for putting in space separators ourselves. The output statement then becomes the following:

```
print('The answers are ', x1, ' and ', x2, '.', sep='')
```

And this works, although it's a fair amount of extra work. Not only do we have to add **sep=''**, but we have to add all those extra spaces.

But there's a better way. Python provides a way to create a formatted-output string. To use this approach, follow these steps:

1 Create a format specification string that includes print fields denoted with the characters {}. A print field is an indication of where output characters, produced by arguments, are to be inserted into the resulting string.

2 Apply the **format** method to this format-specification string, specifying the values to be printed as arguments.

3 Print the resulting output string.

For example, you can set up a format specification string (**fss**) as follows:

```
fss = 'The numbers are {} and {}.'
```

Then you apply the **format** method to this string. The result produces an output string.

```
output_str = fss.format(10, 20)
print(output_str)
```

And here's what the result looks like:

```
The numbers are 10 and 20.
```

Example 3.3. *Distance Formula in a Script*

Sooner or later, you'll want to write and permanently save your Python programs. The steps are as follows:

1 From within IDLE, choose the New File command from the File menu.

2 Enter a program (or copy text) into the window that appears, which serves as a text editor for your programs.

3 To save the program, choose Save or Save As from the File menu. The first time you save a program this way, the environment will prompt you to enter a name with a .py extension. (It will add this extension for you automatically.)

4 To run the program, make sure the program window has the focus. Then either press F5 or select Run Module from the Run menu.

5 After the program begins running, you may need to shift focus back to IDLE's main window (the *shell*). [An exception is that with tkinter (graphical) programs, you'll need to shift focus to the window *generated* by the program.]

Alternatively, you can write a program with any text editor you want, but be sure you save the file in plain-text format and give it a .py extension. Then you can load it into Python by using the Open command from IDLE's File menu.

Although the Python environment is still extremely useful for experimenting with, and getting help with, individual commands and features, the text-editor approach is usually better for writing and executing long programs.

This next example shows how to use the Pythagorean distance formula to calculate the distance between any two points on a Cartesian plane. Here's the formula:

$$distance = \textbf{square\_root}(horizontal\_dist^2 + vertical\_dist^2)$$

Here's the program listing:

```
dist.py
x1 = float(input('Enter x1: '))
y1 = float(input('Enter y1: '))
x2 = float(input('Enter x2: '))
y2 = float(input('Enter y2: '))
h_dist = x2 - x1
v_dist = y2 - y1
dist = (h_dist ** 2 + v_dist ** 2) ** 0.5
print('The distance is ', dist)
```

How It Works

The Pythagorean distance formula is derived from the Pythagorean theorem, which I'll have more to say about in Chapter 6. By applying this theorem, you can see that the distance between two points is equivalent to the hypotenuse of a right triangle, in which the vertical distance (v_dist) and horizontal distance (h_dist) are the two other sides.

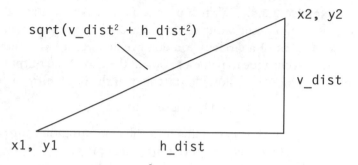

The square of the hypotenuse is equal to the sums of the squares of the other sides. Therefore, the hypotenuse itself is equal to the square root of this sum. (See the figure.)

Remember that the exponentiation operator in Python is **. Therefore, the following

```
amount ** 2
```

means to produce the square of `amount` (multiply itself by itself), whereas this next expression

```
b ** 0.5
```

is equivalent to taking the square root of b. Therefore, the distance formula is

```
dist = (h_dist ** 2 + v_dist ** 2) ** 0.5
```

EXERCISES

Exercise 3.3.1. As I just mentioned, the syntax x ** 2 translates as x to the second power, in other words, x squared. There is another, slightly more verbose, way of expressing the same operation. Revise Example 3.3 so that it uses this other means of calculating a square. Also, replace h_dist, v_dist, and dist in the program with h, v, and d. Then rerun and make sure everything works. For example, if you input the points 0, 0 and 3, 4, the program should say that the distance between the points is 5.0.

Exercise 3.3.2. Revise Example 3.3 so that it outputs the result and puts a period (.) at the end of the sentence, without any superfluous blank spaces. Use the format-specification-string technique I outlined in the previous section.

Exercise 3.3.3. Write a program that calculates the area of a triangle after prompting for the values of the triangle's height and width. Use the formula height * width * 0.5. Use the format-specification-string technique to print a period at the end of the output.

Exercise 3.3.4.   Write a program that calculates the area of a circle after prompting for the value of the radius. (I'll leave it to you to look up the formula for area of a circle if you don't remember it.) Use the format-specification-string technique to print a period at the end of the output. Also, to get the value of pi, place the following statement at the beginning of your program:

```
from math import pi
```

With this statement at the beginning of your program, you can use `pi` to refer to a good approximation of pi.

Chapter 3   *Summary*

Here are the main points of Chapter 3:

▶ A function definition lets you perform a series of calculations over and over, without having to reenter all the steps in number crunching. At least this is a simple way to understand the concept.

▶ The syntax of a function definition has this form:

```
def function_name(arguments):
    indented_statements
```

▶ The `arguments` may be blank, may have one argument name, or may be a series of argument names separated by commas.

▶ If you enter the function-definition heading correctly, the Python interactive environment automatically creates indentation. Remember that a correct function-definition heading ends with a colon (:).

▶ From within the Python interactive environment, you complete a function definition by typing an extra blank line after you've entered all the indented statements.

▶ To call a function, enter the name of the function followed by parentheses and argument values. These values are then passed to the function-definition code. Here's an example:

```
>>>convert(10)
```

▶ You can prompt the user for string input by using the **input** statement. The prompt message is a string printed on the console to prompt the user for input.

```
string_var = input(prompt_message)
```

▶ To get numeric input, use an **int** or **float** conversion, as appropriate.

```
var = int(input(prompt_message))
var = float(input(prompt_message))
```

▶ The built-in **print** function prints all its arguments in order. By default, arguments are printed with a single blank space separating them. You can use the optional **sep** argument to specify another separator character. **sep=''** specifies that no separator character should be used.

▶ You can use a format-specification string, in which {} indicates a print field. Here's an example:

```
fss = 'The square root of {} is {}.'
```

▶ You can then apply the format method to a format specification string to produce an output string.

```
format_spec_string.format(arguments)
```

▶ Here's an example:

```
fss.format(25, 5)
```

4 Decisions and Looping

To write any but the most elementary programs, you need to be able to make decisions. Programmers have a special term for decision-making abilities: *control structures*. A control structure determines whether a computer will turn left or turn right, in other words, whether it will continue to operate on a set of data or exit out of a loop.

This chapter explores some of the basics of decision-making and looping within Python.

▶ **if** and **elif**

▶ Looping with **while**

▶ Breaking from a loop

▶ A Python guessing game, illustrating these concepts

Decisions Inside a Computer Program

I once had a colleague named Myron who wrote that control structures give computers the ability to exercise "judgment." We never could agree on that.

A computer doesn't exercise judgment or discretion. It can only take actions based on simple comparisons. Here's an example:

```
n = int(input('Enter your age: '))
if n < 30:
    print('Don't trust anyone over 30.')
```

This example is simple. It compares n to the number 30. If n is less than 30, it executes the **print** statement. Otherwise, it skips that statement. The general syntax of **if** is as follows:

```
if condition :
    indented_statements
```

As with the **def** keyword, you must not forget the colon (:) at the end of the first line. Assuming you enter everything correctly, the Python interactive environment (if that's where you're writing the code) will automatically indent the statements that follow. Within the environment, you terminate the statement block by typing an extra blank line at the end.

Here's a sample interactive session:

```
>>>def is_even(n):
    remainder = n % 2
    if remainder == 0:
        print('n is even.')


>>>is_even(2)
n is even.
>>>is_even(15)
>>>is_even(202)
n is even.
```

The function is_even either prints the message n is even or it does nothing. Let's review the key parts. First, this code uses remainder division (%), also called *mod* division. It's used to divide by 2 in this case and produce the remainder. If that remainder is zero, n is even.

```
remainder = n % 2
```

The **if** statement, remember, uses double equal signs to compare the value to zero. This is an important rule in Python, as in the C family of languages. A single equal sign (=) specifies assignment. Double equal signs (==) specify test for equality and return either **True** or **False**.

```
if remainder == 0:
    print('n is even.')
```

What qualifies as a condition? In general, a condition is a comparison between two values (which also includes greater-than and less-than, etc.) or it's a combination of comparisons joined by the Boolean operators **and**, **or**, and **not**. Here's another example:

```
if age > 12 and age < 20:
    print('Wow!')
    print('You are a teenager.')
```

The *condition* after the **if** keyword is presumed to have a value that is **True** or **False**, so normally you'd use a condition such as n > 3.

However, you can use any valid expression, and Python will convert to a Boolean (**True**/**False**) as well as it can. For numeric values, zero is converted to **False**; other values are converted to **True**. (Also, the special value **None** is converted to **False**, while most non-numeric values are converted to **True**.)

```
do_more = True
if n > 3:
    do_more = False

if do_more:
    print('n is not greater than 3.')
```

See if you can determine for yourself precisely what these statements do. Then ask yourself if you can come up with a more direct way to write it. You can use the less-than-or-equal-to (<=) comparison operator if you want, or you can use the **not** operator.

Conditional and Boolean Operators

Python has a set of comparison operators as well as Boolean operators that enable you to combine conditions.

The Boolean operators (**and, or, not**) all have lower precedence than the comparison operators (==, >, <, etc.), so you can confidently write "if" conditions as follows:

```
>>>if n > 0 and n < 10:
    print('n is in range 1 to 10.')

>>>
```

Here are the operators:

OPERATOR	MEANING	EXAMPLE OF USE
==	Test for equality	n == 5
>	Greater than	x > y
<	Less than	x < 100.55
>=	Greater than or equal to	n >= 20
<=	Less than or equal to	age < 15
!=	Test for inequality	x != y
and	Boolean "and"	x > 12 and x < 20
or	Boolean "or"	a > b or a > 0
not	Boolean "not"	not (x > 12 and x < 20)

4

The if, elif, and else Keywords

But there's still more you can do with control structures involving the **if** keyword. Suppose you want to respond differently to a series of alternative conditions. You can create such structures with the help of **elif** and **else** clauses. The full syntax of **if** is actually as follows:

```
if condition :
    indented_statements
[ elif condition :
    indented_statements ]...
[ else:
    indented_statements ]
```

This syntax display does not use brackets literally. Instead, in this case, the brackets indicate an optional item. An **if** control structure must have one **if** clause. It can then have zero or more **elif** clauses (each with its own condition), and it can have at most one **else** clause.

Here's an example:

```
def check_range(n):
    if n < 1:
        print('n is below range 1 to 100.')
    elif n < 101:
        print('n is inside the range.')
        print('Thank you.')
    else:
        print('n is above the range 1 to 100.')
```

What the **elif** clause does—in this case there is exactly one—is to test for an alternative condition if the first condition (n < 1) fails. If all conditions fail and if there is an **else** clause, the statement or statements following **else** are executed.

An **elif** clause is essentially a test for an "else if" condition.

Interlude

Programs and Robots in *Westworld*

The 1973 film *Westworld*, written and directed by Michael Crichton, is about a futuristic adult theme park in which robots play the roles of cowboys, gunslingers, and saloon girls. By paying thousands of dollars a day, the human visitors to the park can shoot it out with the bad guys…all in perfect safety, because while the humans can shoot the robots, the robots can't shoot back, at least not with real bullets.

Interlude

▼ *continued*

Eventually, things go wrong, and one day the robots start shooting back with lethal ammunition. There's a computer breakdown or virus, and that's a problem, because the robots are in effect controlled by computer programs. So everything goes haywire.

The critically acclaimed HBO television series, also called *Westworld*, takes the same idea but raises it to an even more interesting level. The problem is not a bug in the programming of the robots but, on the contrary, the unforeseen *success* of the programming.

According to the premise, the programming of these robots (called *hosts*) is so sophisticated that they actually attain consciousness. Morally and ethically, they become no different from human beings. These "hosts" develop genuine emotions. And when they do, they start to resent being the playthings of humans.

And when that happens…when they decide it's wrong of humans to treat them as toys instead of conscious beings with real feelings…then they start shooting back.

This HBO series raises a fascinating question: is it possible for a computerized entity, given enough sophisticated programming, to attain consciousness? This means far more than being able to add numbers, predict the weather, or even play chess, which are things we all know that computers can do quite well. This is a deep philosophical question as to whether a computer or robot could ever feel genuine emotions, or even pain.

Having a robot experience just a moment of actual pain would be enough. But philosophically, this is a difficult bar to cross. You could program a robot, or an entity within a virtual environment, to avoid certain kinds of situations. You could simulate what happens when a living organism feels pain. You could, for example, program the robot to scream and say, "Ouch, that hurts!" if it should ever put its hand on a hot stove.

And if you ask the robot, "Are you feeling actual pain?" the robot will of course say "yes." But that begs the question…because it's programmed to say yes. So that proves nothing.

Maybe a robot would be genuinely conscious if it could somehow break its programming—an idea suggested in *Westworld*—but just how would it do that?

Philosophers have debated the question for centuries, but especially so in the last century, as the possibility of machine intelligence now seems like it might be a real thing. Some people feel that a sufficiently good simulation of pain is no different from the real thing. I happen to differ. Like most people, I feel that there is something mysterious that goes on inside the mind.

▼ *continued on next page*

Interlude

▼ *continued*

But in that case, what is this mysterious medium called "consciousness"? And what really is "mind"? What, really, is going on inside the cranium?

koya979. Shutterstock

Alan Turing, the great computer scientist who cracked the ENIGMA code in the 1940s, thought he had the answer: put a computer behind a curtain and have it communicate with a human interrogator through a console and keyboard. The interrogator has a finite amount of time to ask questions. If, after time is up, he or she is unable to determine whether he's been communicating with a human or computer, then the computer has attained consciousness.

This is one reason you'll increasingly hear references to Turing in science-fiction stories, movies, and television. You'll hear statements like, "Our robot has already passed the Turing test. What now?"

But as you read this chapter, consider what a robot or computer is doing when it's (apparently) making decisions and exercising "judgment." At the base level, you should know that it's not exercising judgment at all. A program can do nothing more than compare two numerical values and take different actions depending on whether the first value is less than, equal to, or greater than the other value.

Do you believe that consciousness and true judgment can be built up from such limited comparisons? Maybe a kind of judgment can result. Maybe a program making millions of these little decisions can put those decisions together to make a Really Big Decision, such as where to move the queen in a chess game or when to launch a missile strike. But whether this adds up to feeling even a nanosecond of pain or awareness is a deep philosophical question.

Example 4.1.   *Enter Your Age*

The following is about as simple a program as possible using an **if** statement. We'll quickly progress to more interesting programs after this.

Following the procedure outlined for Example 3.3, you can copy the following code to a file, save it, and then load it into the Python interactive environment.

```
age.py
age = int(input('Enter your age, please: '))
name_str = input('Enter your name, please: ')
print('Happy birthday, ', name_str, '.', sep='')
print('You are', age, 'years old.')
if age > 12 and age < 20:
    print('You are a teenager!')
else:
    print('You\'re NOT a teenager!')
```

Here's a sample session, illustrating input (in bold) and output (not in bold) that you might see when running the program:

```
Enter your age, please: 39
Enter your name, please: Brian
Happy birthday, Brian.
You are 39 years old.
You're NOT a teenager!
```

Alternatively, you can enter the entire program from within the interactive environment by placing all the statements inside a function called main and then executing main. Remember that if you mistype anything, you can copy and paste the code you entered earlier, make corrections, and then type an extra blank line after the end of the definition.

```
>>>def main():
    age = int(input('Enter your age, please: '))
    name_str = input('Enter your name, please: ')
    print('Happy birthday, ', name_str, '.', sep='')
    print('You are', age, 'years old.')
    if age > 12 and age < 20:
        print('You are a teenager!')
    else:
        print('You\'re NOT a teenager!')

>>>main()
```

How It Works

The interesting part of this little program is the last part. The program, which takes a value stored in age, which is input by the user, tests whether this value is in the range 13 to 19. To be considered in range, the value of age must be both greater than 12 and less than 20.

```
if age > 12 and age < 20:
    print('You are a teenager!')
else:
    print('You\'re NOT a teenager!')
```

There are other ways this same condition could have been written. Here's an example:

```
if not (age < 13 or age > 19):
    print('You are a teenager!')
else:
    print('You\'re NOT a teenager!')
```

These statements would have the same effect because they specify the same condition, although they express it in a different way.

EXERCISES

Exercise 4.1.1. Write a program similar to Example 4.1 that prompts the user for a number and tests to see if it is in the range 1 to 100. If it is, print a message verifying that it is in range; if not, print a message reporting that it is out of range.

Exercise 4.1.2. Modify the answer to Exercise 4.1.1, but use a different way of expressing the condition. The results should be precisely the same (given the same user input), but the condition should involve the use of the **not** and **or** keywords.

Exercise 4.1.3. Write a program that takes an integer n as input and then prints a message stating whether it is or is not a multiple of 7.

while: Looping the Loop

One of the most important concepts in computer programming is the loop, which simply means "After performing a set of tasks, go back to the beginning. Wash. Rinse. Repeat."

The simplest way to start writing loops is to use the **while** statement.

```
while condition :
    indented_statements
```

As with other Python control structures, a colon (:) has special meaning in the interactive environment. As soon as you correctly enter the first line of a **while** block, lines that follow are automatically indented. To end all statement blocks, type an extra blank line.

The following figure summarizes the basic operation of a loop created with the **while** keyword:

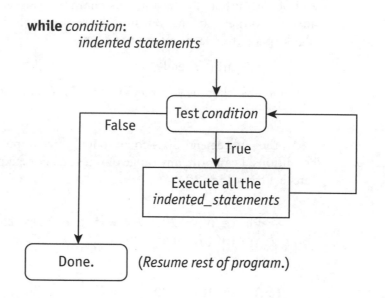

One of the issues with **while** is that there always needs to be a terminating condition, or at least some other way to break out of the loop, unless you want the loop to be infinite. In the following example, execution stops as soon as n equals or exceeds 10.

```
>>>n = 1
>>>while n <= 10:    # while n less than or eq. 10
    print(n, end=' ')
    n += 1           # This means n = n + 1

1 2 3 4 5 6 7 8 9 10
>>>
```

In this example, I added two comments. A comment is text put in to provide information to any human who might be reading the statements, but it is ignored by Python itself, starting with the comment symbol (#) and onward to the end of the physical line.

A comment has this general form:

```
# text
```

A comment can contain any message I want. Smart programmers add comments to give clues as to what a program is doing—at least if they want it to be readable.

I also used a variation on the **print** function by using the **end** keyword argument. This argument specifies what character, if any, is printed at the end of the output. By default, this character is a newline, causing output to advance to the next line. But in this example, I decided to just print a single blank space after each call to **print**.

```
print(n, end=' ')
```

Remember that the statement n += 1 is equivalent to this:

```
n = n + 1
```

All these statements do is count to ten. By manipulating starting and ending conditions, I can print any range of integers. For example, I could print all the integers from 15 to 20.

```
>>>n = 15
>>>while n <= 20:    # while n less than or eq. 20
    print(n, end=' ')
    n += 1

15 16 17 18 19 20
>>>
```

Once you start writing programs complex enough to have loops, pseudocode becomes especially useful; it helps you think of the steps of the program in something very close to human language. The count-to-ten program can be summarized this way:

Set n equal to 1
While n is less than or equal to 10,
    Print n followed by a space,
        Add 1 to n

You can envision operation of the program by looking at a simple flow chart. Counting to ten involves repeated actions.

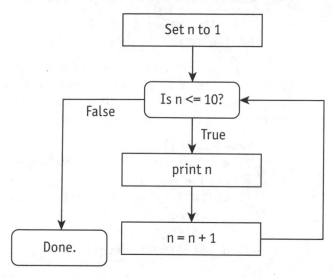

Example 4.2.   *Factorials*

Let's graduate to a more interesting example. A factorial for any positive whole number N is defined as follows:

```
Factorial(N) = 1 * 2 * 3... * N
```

In other words, multiply all the positive integers from 1 to N together. The factorial of 3 is 1 * 2 * 3, or 6. The factorial of 4 is 1 * 2 * 3 * 4, or 24, and so on. As you might imagine, factorials get very big very quickly. But Python, with its "infinite integer" capability, is perfectly suited to hold extremely large numbers.

fact.py

```
n = int(input('Enter value of n: '))
prod = i = 1
while i <= n:
    prod *= i
    i += 1
print('The factorial is:', prod)
```

Here's a sample session, which runs after you have saved this code as a text file, opened it from within the environment, and then selected the Run Module command, as mentioned near the end of Chapter 3.

```
Enter the value of n: 5
The factorial is 120
```

You can also enter the program from within the interactive environment itself, by creating a main function and executing it. Remember that you can correct mistakes by copying all the statements, pasting them in at the next cursor position, and then editing the statements.

```
>>>def main():
    n = int(input('Enter value of n: '))
    prod = i = 1
    while i <= n:    # While i less than or eq. to n,
        prod *= i
        i += 1
    print('The factorial is:', prod)

>>>main()
```

How It Works

This is not a very complex program to begin with, but we can still use pseudocode to clarify its operation.

> *Get value of n from user*
> *Set i and prod to 1*
> *While i is less than or equal to n,*
> > *Multiply prod by i*
> > *Add 1 to i*
> *Print value of prod*

Wow, that's pretty simple. All this program does, really, is to set both prod (short for "product") to 1 and then multiply by the numbers 1, 2, 3, and so on, until you've multiplied by n. At that point, stop. The variable i is used to hold the value of each factor in turn.

You can also visualize this action through a flow chart:

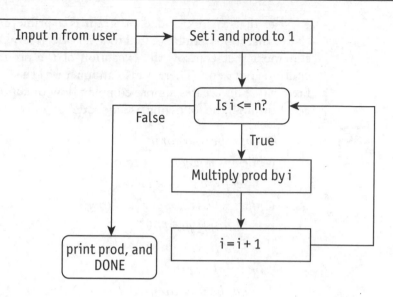

Optimizing the Code

In examining what this program does, you should be able to see that one of the operations—multiplying by 1—is always performed but is always unnecessary. A slight optimization, therefore, is simply to start i at the value 2, not 1:

```
i = 2
```

A more important optimization, from the standpoint of the user, is that a user might want to calculate several factorials rather than starting the program over and over. A superior program design, therefore, is to place everything inside a large **while** loop, in which the factorials are repeatedly calculated until the user enters 0. Here is one way to do that:

```
n = int(input('Enter n (0 to quit): '))
while n != 0:
    prod = 1
    i = 2
    while i <= n:
        prod *= i
        i += 1
    print('The factorial is:', prod)
    n = int(input('Enter n (0 to quit): '))
print('Bye now!')
```

Note that this expanded program is a prime example of a *nested loop*. (Note that loops can be nested to a very deep level.) There is an outer **while** statement that controls the execution of the program—that is, whether to continue or to end. There is also an inner **while** statement that calculates the factorial. This creates a more complex flow of control, which can be summarized through the following pseudocode:

Prompt the user for n
While n is not equal to zero
    Set prod to 1 and i to 2
While i is less than or equal to n,
    Multiply prod by i
    Add 1 to i
Print value of prod
Prompt the user for n

Here's a sample session of this expanded program. Note that the factorial of 10 is larger than you might have expected. As I pointed out earlier, factorials get very large very fast.

```
Enter n (0 to quit): 6
The factorial is: 720
Enter n (0 to quit): 10
The factorial is: 3628800
Enter n (0 to quit): 0
Bye now!
```

EXERCISES

Exercise 4.2.1.   Revise Example 4.2—in either the simple or expanded version—so that it prints a nicely formatted output statement ending in a period, as follows:

```
The factorial of 5 is 120.
```

(Hint: You can use the printing techniques from Chapter 3.)

Exercise 4.2.2.   Write a program to calculate and print the triangle number for any given input. Instead of using a variable named prod, call the variable sum. The triangle number for N is defined as follows:

```
1 + 2 + 3 + ... N
```

So, for example, the triangle number for 5 is $1 + 2 + 3 + 4 + 5 = 15$.

Exercise 4.2.3. Expand on the answer to Exercise 4.2.2 so that each time the program calculates a triangle number, it also tests the Triangle Number theorem and prints a message stating whether the theorem holds. This theorem states that for any given N,

```
1 + 2 + 3 + ... N  =  N * (N + 1) / 2
```

Example 4.3.   *Printing Fibonacci Numbers*

Now let's move on to an even more interesting use of a Python **while** loop: calculating Fibonacci numbers. Because of Python's "infinite integer" capability, first introduced in Chapter 2, you can easily use Python to calculate much bigger Fibonacci numbers than you can do in most any other language.

The Fibonacci series is the most famous series of numbers in mathematics—with the possible exception of the primes, which Python is also good at calculating.

The rules for producing this series are simple.

▶ The first number in the series is 1.

▶ The second number is likewise 1.

▶ The next number is determined by adding the two numbers immediately before it in the series. To get the third number, you add 1 + 1 to get 2. To get the fourth number, you add 1 + 2 to get 3. To get the fifth number, you add 2 + 3 to get 5.

In short, take the two most recent numbers in the series and add them together to get the next number. So, the first few numbers are as follows:

```
1   1   2   3   5   8   13
```

Remember that you add the last two numbers in the series to get the next. Therefore, the next Fibonacci number is 8 + 13, or 21.

```
1   1   2   3   5   8   13   21
```

You can imagine this process visually with the following figure, which shows how the next two figures in the sequence are calculated: adding 13 and 21 produces 34, and adding 21 and 34 produces 55. This process can be continued without limit.

Calculating the Fibonacci series is an ideal task for a computer, as long as the computer can hold sufficiently large numbers—because these numbers start to get large after a while. Fortunately, that's an easy task for Python.

To write the mini-program, we track two values, a and b, which represent the two most recent Fibonacci values. We start a and b off as 1 and 1, the first two numbers in the series.

```
>>>a = b = 1
```

Now, to calculate the next value, we add a and b together and assign this as the new value of a. In the meantime, b should "bring up the rear" by getting the old value of a. So, for example, if the most recent values of a and b are 2 and 3 (a always being larger), then:

▶ The new value of a should be the total of 2 and 3 (producing 5).

▶ The new value of b should be the old value of a (which is 3).

You should be amazed at how concise the Python code is. Assuming a and b have already been set to 1; all you need to do is write and execute the following **while** loop:

```
>>>while a < 200:
    a, b = a + b, a
    print(a)
```

The first statement inside the **while** loop is what makes this code so concise. Look at it again:

```
a, b = a + b, a
```

What this does is associate the name a with the sum of the old values, a + b. *Simultaneously*, it associates the name b with the old value of a.

More precisely, this operation creates a tuple. Assume a and b hold the values 5 and 13, respectively. The tuple a + b, a is evaluated as (21, 13). That tuple is then assigned to a, b so that a is now set to 21 and b is now set to 13.

Other languages would require a temporary variable so that the old value of a is preserved, to be assigned later to b. This is not necessary in Python, but you could do it that way if you wanted.

```
>>>while a < 200:
    temp = a
    a = a + b
    b = temp
    print(a)
```

But either the short approach or the long approach will work in Python. The result, in either case, is to print Fibonacci numbers up until the first value that is not less than 200.

```
2
3
5
8
13
21
34
55
89
144
233
```

To place these all on the same line, use the **end** argument of the **print** function.

```
print(a, end=" ")
```

With this change made to the **print** function, the loop produces the following:

```
2 3 5 8 13 21 34 55 89 144 233
```

Of course, by varying the **while** condition, you can print as many Fibonacci numbers as you like.

How It Works

In case it's not clear what this loop does, let's look at the pseudocode for this mini-program. In this case I'll use capital A and B just to make the algorithm clearer to read.

> *Set both A and B to 1.*
> *While A < 200,*
>> *Set A to the value A + B*
>> *Simultaneously, set B to the old value of A.*

Again, notice that with most other programming languages, you wouldn't be able to assign a value to A while simultaneously assigning B the old value of A. It wouldn't work, because the computer would lose track of the old value of A before B got assigned a value. You'd have no choice but to use a temporary variable (temp) as shown earlier.

But Python gets around this annoying problem beautifully by enabling you to assign multiple values simultaneously.

a, b = a + b, a

Note that before you rerun this loop, you need to first reset the A and B values to 1.

>>>a = b = 1

EXERCISES

Exercise 4.3.1. Write and test a program that prompts the user for the value n and then prints all the Fibonacci numbers up to but not exceeding n. You can either write a text file and run the program from the Run Module command or enter all the statements into a function called `main` and then execute `main()` from within the interactive environment.

Exercise 4.3.2. Instead of printing the Fibonacci numbers themselves, print the ratio of each two consecutive numbers and look for a pattern. In other words, print the ratio a/b each time through the loop and see what ratio this number converges to, if any.

You should find that this ratio converges to the number mathematicians call *phi*, which is equal to approximately 1.618. This is the same as the golden ratio that you earlier calculated in Chapters 2 and 3. (Maybe you can tell I'm fond of this number.)

"Give Me a break" Statement

How do you break out of the middle of a loop? The solution adopted in Example 4.2, in the section "Optimizing the Code," prompted the user for input in more than one place. While this works, it's not the best solution.

A more direct way is just to use the **break** keyword, which has the simplest possible syntax. This keyword does in Python exactly what it does in C, C++, Java, and other languages: it breaks out of the current loop.

break

Let's use it! The following statements cause numbers to be added until a 0 is detected. If 0 is detected, then the **break** keyword causes the loop to exit and the program to end after it prints results.

```
amt = 0
while True:
    n = int(input('Enter a number (0 to exit): '))
    if n == 0:
        break
    amt += n
print('The sum is ' amt)
```

As you can see, one virtue of this approach is that it involves only one use of the input statement rather than two.

Example 4.4. *A Number-Guessing Game*

You now know enough about Python to do some extensive programming, including the ability to write entertaining game programs.

In the following game, the computer picks a random number between 1 and 50 without revealing what the number is. Then, during each round of the game, the player—that is, the end user—makes a guess. The computer responds with one of three answers: "Too high," "Too low," or "Correct!"

guessing.py

```
import random
n = random.randint(1, 50)
while True:
    ans = int(input('Enter your guess: '))
    if ans == n:
        print('Success! You win!')
        break
    elif ans > n:
        print('Too high.')
    else:
        print('Too low.')
```

From the Python interactive environment (IDLE), you can enter these statements into a new file and save it as guessing.py. Then, from the Run menu, choose the Run Module command.

Here's a sample session. It assumes that Python randomly selected the number 40 as the secret number.

```
Enter guess:24
Too low.
Enter guess:37
Too low.
Enter guess:43
Too high.
Enter guess:40
Success!
```

How It Works

First, the program secretly picks a random number from 1 to 50 without telling the user. The following two statements get this random number:

```
import random
n = random.randint(1, 50)
```

The **import** statement doesn't do anything by itself, but it enables the program to use the functions in the Python randomization library.

The rest of program operation is described by the following pseudocode:

> *While True (do always),*
>> *Prompt for an answer and store result in ans*
>> *If ans equals n,*
>>> *Print Success message and exit*
>> *Else if ans > n,*
>>> *Print "Too high."*
>> *Else*
>>> *Print "Too low."*

Notice how **while True** seems to set up an infinite loop. What it actually does is to create a loop that does not end until **break** is executed. Each time through the loop, the program prompts for another guess and then reports whether it is too high, too low, or just right.

Like Goldilocks.

After picking the secret number, the program prompts the end user for a guess. Note that because this guess has to be in numeric form—so that you can use it in numeric comparisons—the input must be converted to an integer using the **int** function. Python enables you to combine this in one smooth operation.

```
ans = int(input('Enter your guess: '))
```

The following figure illustrates the action of this program:

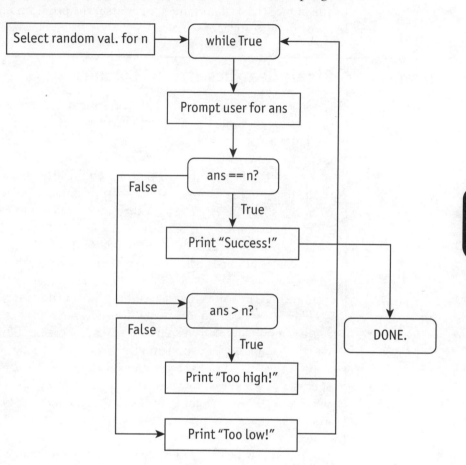

EXERCISES

Exercise 4.3.1. Instead of having the program pick a secret number from 1 to 50, revise it to pick a number from 1 to 100. This should be easy, as you have to change only one line.

Exercise 4.3.2. Revise the program so that it gives some instructions up front, advising the end user that it will be guessing a secret number in a certain range.

Exercise 4.3.3. Revise the loop so that it repeats the game until the end user wants to stop. The user indicates this by entering 0 at any time. To make this work, the "success" alternative will need to choose a new random number and then continue the game. You'll also need to add an **elif** alternative that tests whether ans is equal to 0, at which point it should break.

Exercise 4.3.4.   Let the end user pick a range from 1 to N before the program begins. Once this is determined, of course, the program must still pick a number within this range, in secret.

Interlude

Binary Searches and "O" Complexity

If you play this game a few times, you should quickly realize what the best strategy is, if you don't already know: you should pick a number close to the halfway point in the range of legal values. If you're successful, that's great. Otherwise, the answer you get (too high or too low) should enable you to reduce the possible answers to (roughly) the upper half or lower half of the range. After each guess, the possible range of values should either get a "Success!" or enable you to cut the range roughly in half…again.

The important thing is: each time you should be able to cut down the range of possible values by roughly one-half.

By doing this repeatedly, you should be able to get the answer much faster than a simple *linear search*. A linear search starts at the beginning and then examines one item after another, getting the simple answer "right" or "wrong."

The faster technique teaches the essence of what's called a *binary search*. As the number of steps increases, the size of how many values can be covered increases exponentially. You could find one number out of a trillion in just 40 steps if you played optimally! A linear search, which starts at one end and moves forward, examining just one item at a time, would on the average take *centuries* to find one number out of a trillion, assuming that each question and response used up only one second and you played 24 hours a day!

Computer scientists and programmers use something called Big-O notation to signify how fast the number of steps increases with the size of the data set to be covered. The binary search technique is the inverse of exponential growth—because *exponential* describes the converse relationship—which is logarithmic growth.

So, for example, assume it requires N seconds to search 1,000 items. It would take N * 2 seconds to search 1,000,000 items. And it would take only N * 3 seconds to search 1,000,000,000 items. This is what's meant by logarithmic growth. The time taken grows much more slowly than the amount of data to search.

Computer scientists have a notation for this. **O(log n)** says that the number of steps covered to solve the problem is proportional to the logarithm of n. In plain English, this means that the growth in the number of steps slows down as n increases without limit. In other words, the procedure becomes more and more efficient for very large n.

Interlude

▼ *continued*

This is not trivial. It helps explain why computers, communication systems, and databases are useful servants. If most procedures were **O(n)**, meaning that the time required is directly proportional to the size of the data set, large databases would be useless.

The slower growth relationship, **O(log n)**, makes databases remarkably efficient in the modern world because it really doesn't take that long to search a database with hundreds of millions of records. If database access were *not* **O(log n)**, then both the Internet and credit-checking systems, to name just two, would be impractical.

Chapter 4 *Summary*

Here are the main points of Chapter 4:

▶ The **if** statement has the following syntax. The condition should be a Boolean value, that is, a value that is either **True** or **False**. If this condition is true, then the indented statements are all executed; otherwise, they are skipped.

```
if condition:
    indented_statements
```

▶ You can optionally have an else clause that is executed if the condition is false.

```
if condition:
    indented_statements
else:
    indented_statements
```

▶ You can also include any number of (that is, zero or more) **elif** clauses. The **elif** keyword in Python means "else if," and each tests a separate condition. Only if the **if** condition and all **elif** conditions are false is the **else** clause executed. The complete syntax is therefore as follows:

```
if condition:
    indented_statements
[ elif condition:
    indented_statements ]...
[ else:
    indented_statements ]
```

▶ The **while** keyword sets up a loop. A loop is executed as long as the condition is true. Here's the syntax:

```
while condition:
    indented_statements
```

▶ More specifically, the condition after **while** is tested first. If it is true, all the indented statements are executed. Control of the program then returns to the top of the loop, and the **while** condition is tested again. Rinse and repeat. Normally, the loop ends only when this condition is tested and is false. At that point, all the indented statements are skipped.

▶ This creates a problem if you want to exit from the middle of the loop. The easy way to do that is to use the **break** keyword.

```
break
```

▶ The words while True: set up an infinite loop that continues forever unless you break out.

```
while True:
    # Do some stuff
    if (n < 0):
        break
    # Do some more stuff
```

▶ List assignment—or rather, tuple assignment—enables you to perform multiple assignments simultaneously. For example, the following statement assigns the value of a + b to a, and the value of a to b; and it does these operations simultaneously so you don't have to worry about how one such assignment would affect the other:

```
a, b = a + b, a
```

Python Lists

Until you understand lists, you don't know Python.

Along with text strings, lists are the most important example of an *iterable* in Python: a source of data you can always get "the next value" from (until you can't). The biggest key to writing efficient, high-quality Python code is to understand the Python concept of lists.

This chapter explains how to do the following:

▶ Use lists to sort information

▶ Get selected subranges of data, called *slices*

▶ Work efficiently with the Python **for** statement

The Python Way: The World Is Made of Collections

A Python list is like a set of ordered boxes into which you place data. A simple example stores the high temperatures for each day of a one-week period.

```
temp_list = [79, 79, 80, 68, 79, 68, 80]
```

For the Pacific Northwest—specifically, the Seattle area—this might describe the daily highs of a typical week in June. Pleasantly warm but not hot. (Unless you live in Canada and these are Celsius temperatures, in which case these temperatures are lethal to human life; remember that 100 is actually the boiling point of water.)

The result of this assignment is to make the name `temp_list` refer to a list. After a list has been created, the most efficient way to extend it is to use the **append** method.

```
temp_list.append(85)
```

This statement preserves the existing data but modifies it. The name `temps` refers to the same list that it did before, just altered. However, consider this:

```
temp_list = temp_list + [85]
```

This statement joins two lists and creates a new list altogether and then reassigns the variable `temp_list` to it. The effect is usually the same, but it's less efficient. (But note that, as we'll see later, assignments like that can have large consequences because they break the old data association. This will matter when we return to passing variables to functions.)

Yet the following isn't even legal, because you can't join a list to a nonlist:

```
temp_list = temp_list + 85
```

List specification has the following syntax:

[*items* **]**

In this syntax, *items* is zero or more items, separated by commas if there are more than one. Yes, you can have an empty list if you choose. Python lists have some important features.

▶ A list can contain any number of duplicate values. For example, I might have a week in which the high temperature is 82 for five days in a row.

▶ The order of values is significant. In this example, the first temperature (Sunday) is 79, and the last (Saturday) is 80. These can't be reversed without altering the meaning of the data.

▶ Python lists are *mutable*, meaning you can change contents without having to create a whole new list.

So, for example, [77, 80, 99] might record weekend temperatures. [77, 80, 99] is not the same as [99, 80, 77], which would reverse Friday and Sunday. You can test this.

```
>>>[77, 80, 99] == [99, 80, 77]
False
>>>[77, 80, 85] == [77, 80, 80 + 5]
True
```

Lists can contain any type of data, including other lists—but numbers and strings are common. The following example contains four strings.

```
beat_list = ['John', 'Paul', 'George', 'Pete']
```

The order might be meaningful or it might not be. It might, for example, represent the order the members joined the band. But if you sort a list of strings, Python imposes alphabetical order. Consider these statements:

```
>>>beat_list2 = beats[:]
>>>beat_list.sort()
>>>beat_list == beat_list2
False
```

These statements demonstrate several fine points of Python lists.

The first of these statements introduces a new syntax, which I'll cover in detail later. It uses *slicing* to force Python to create beat_list2 as a separate list and then do a member-by-member copy of all the values.

```
>>>beat_list2 = beat_list[:]  # Copy elements.
```

In contrast, the following statements make beat_list2 an alias for the same list referred to by beat_list. Remember that all Python variables are aliases; that is, they are really references to data. Creating an alias does not make any new copies of the underlying data. It guarantees that the two lists refer to the same data, even if that data changes.

```
>>>beat_list2 = beat_list       # Make an alias.
>>>beat_list.append('Brian')
>>>best_list2 == beat_list      # Equal?
True
```

Do you see what happened? The last statement entered by the user was not an assignment (=) but a test for equality. And because beat_list2 was made an alias for beat_list, the **append** method did not change the relationship between the two variables; they still refer to the same data.

But assume we do things the first way: we use syntax that indicates the list data is to be *copied*, one element at a time. The variable beat_list2 then refers to a *separate copy of the data*, so there are now two separate lists that start out equal. Now let's sort beat_list.

```
>>>beat_list.sort()
```

This statement tells Python to reorder beat_list, but not beat_list2, alphabetically:

```
['John', 'Paul', 'George', 'Pete'] # beat_list2
['George', 'John', 'Paul', 'Pete'] # beat_list
```

Remember that in this case, we're assuming that one list was originally created by doing a member-by-member *copy*, rather than making one name an alias for the other. If, instead, one name is an alias for another, then changes to one will be reflected by both.

As you can see, the order of the members has changed, making the lists different. So in this case, if you compare these lists for equality (==), Python returns **False**.

Python provides many ways to manipulate the contents of a list. You can add and remove individual members using **append** and **remove**.

```
beat_list.remove('Pete')
beat_list.append('Ringo')
```

I always feel sorry for Pete, don't you?

Another useful feature is the **in** keyword, which determines whether an item is in the list. This is useful because if an item is not included in a list to begin with, then trying to remove it causes an error. Here's an example:

```
if 'Pete' in beat_list:
    beat_list.remove('Pete')
```

Processing Lists with for

One of the most common things to do with a list is to perform the same operation on all the elements, one at a time. Python provides the **for** keyword to do just that.

```
for var in collection:
    indented_statements
```

This is essentially a "for each" control structure. It sets *var* to each element in *collection* in turn and executes all the *indented_statements*. Here's an example:

```
beat_list = ['John', 'Paul', 'George', 'Ringo']
for b_str in beat_list:
    print(b_str)
```

These statements carry out the following actions:

▶ The variable b_str gets the value of the first element of beat_list, which happens to be the string "John."

▶ The indented statement is then executed, with b_str set to this value ("John"). So in this case, "John" gets printed.

▶ The loop then advances to the next element. The text string "Paul" is assigned to the variable b_str and now it gets printed. Then, "George" is printed, and finally "Ringo."

▶ This continues until all the elements of beat_list have been processed this way.

So in this case, the **for** statement loop says, "For each element of beat_list, print the element."

```
John
Paul
George
Ringo
```

This next figure summarizes the process visually:

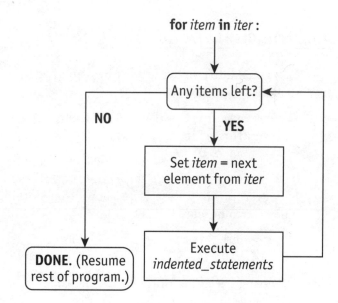

Let's take another example. The following statements operate on a list of numbers, printing ten times the number in each case:

```
num_list = [1, 13, 7, 9]
for i in num_list:
    j = i * 10
    print(j, end=' ') # Print m followed by a space.
```

The output of this example is

```
10 130 70 90
```

You can even process lists by initializing them inside the **for** statement header. Here's an example:

```
for i in [10, 30, 50]:
    print(i)
```

This prints the following:

```
10
30
50
```

It's easy to use the **for** statement. It basically says for each element in the collection, execute the *indented_statements*, passing the value of each element in turn.

Modifying Elements with for (You Can't!)

Can you modify values in a list by using **for**? Yes and no. Try to predict what the following does:

```
>>>num_list = [4, 10, 7, 90]
>>>for n in num_list:
    n = 0
```

It probably looks like this should set all the elements of num_list to 0. However, printing num_list shows that nothing happened to its contents. They were not set to 0.

```
>>>num_list
[4, 10, 7, 90]
```

During execution of the loop, the values 4, 10, 7, and 90 are all passed in turn to the variable n. Then n is set to 0, over and over. But that has no effect on the list.

To modify the collection itself, we need to index into it. But there's a more direct way to build a list. Suppose we have a series of Celsius temperatures that we want to convert to corresponding Fahrenheit temperatures. Here are the Celsius temperatures:

```
>>>cels_list = [15, 20, 25, 30]
```

We can build a new list containing Fahrenheit temperatures this way:

```
>>>fahr_list = []
>>>for c in cels_list:
    x = c * 1.8 + 32.0
    fahr_list.append(x)

>>>fahr_list
[59.0, 68.0, 77.0, 86.0]
```

Another important feature of lists is that it's easy to sort them; you just call the **sort** method, as was done earlier in the chapter. Example 5.1 is going to use it again.

list.**sort()**

A call to this method does not return a value, but it modifies the contents of the list, as does the **append** method. To see an example, read on.

Example 5.1.   *A Sorting Application*

I once used an application like this to help me to compile index entries in a book, so it is not at all trivial.

You can enter this text into a blank file after selecting the New File command from within IDLE. Or you can enter it into a text file named sort.py, using any plain-text editor you choose, and then load that file into IDLE using the Open command. Both these commands are available on the File menu.

sort.py

```
a_list = []
while True:
    str1 = input('Enter a name: ')
    if str1 == '':    # If string is empty,
        break
    a_list.append(str1)
a_list.sort()
print('Here is the alpha sorted list...')
for str1 in a_list:
    print(str1)
```

Here's a sample session:

```
Enter a name: John
Enter a name: George
Enter a name: Paul
Enter a name: Ringo
Enter a name: Brian
Enter a name:
Here is the alpha sorted list...
Brian
George
John
Paul
Ringo
```

In response to the sixth and last "Enter a name," the end user in this session entered an empty string, by just pressing Enter without entering any text.

How It Works

This program is amazingly short. But the main thing it has to do is prompt for strings and add them to a list.

First, however, the program must create an empty list. This is critical. Unlike a C programmer, you don't "declare" an empty list and then operate on it. You must have a list variable before you call the **append** method. And that means you must assign some variable the empty list value, [ ].

```
a_list = []
```

Given this assignment, all the program has to do now is: 1) get a string from the end user, 2) append the string to the list, and 3) repeat, until the user enters an empty string, which is notated by quotation marks with no text between them.

```
while True:
    str1 = input('Enter a name:')
    if str1 == '':   # If string is empty,
        break
    a_list.append(str1)
```

The **sort** function then does most of the work. This is usually the part of a sort program that is most difficult to write because you have to figure out some sophisticated algorithm for sorting the different elements. But you don't have to do that with Python, because the sorting ability is built into lists.

```
a_list.sort()
```

The final lines print the list. The loop variable in this case is str1, but we could've used any word that was not a keyword. This code just cycles through every element in a_list, printing each one in turn.

```
for str1 in a_list:
    print(str1)
```

Optimizing the Code

As I explained in the previous chapter, certain values equate to **False** when evaluated as conditions. In particular, empty strings are considered **False**. Therefore, consider the following code:

```
if s == '':
```

You can save a little space by rewriting this as:

```
if not s:
```

If s is empty, then `not s` has the effect of **True** within an **if** condition.

EXERCISES

Exercise 5.1.1.   As the program takes input from the end user, have it count the number of names entered. Then before the sort names are output, print a message stating how many names were input.

Exercise 5.1.2.   Instead of printing the sorted names one to a line, print all the names on the same line.

Exercise 5.1.3.   Input a series of numbers and then sort them numerically, not alphabetically. (Hint: a list of numbers stored as integers or floating point, not strings, will be sorted numerically if you use the **sort** method on the list.)

Indexing and Slicing

If you've programmed in another language, such as C++, you're used to manipulating a list by accessing one member at a time, through indexing. You can index lists as well when you need to do so.

You can use brackets to index individual elements in the list, just as you can in other programming languages that have arrays. Index numbers for a list of length N run from 0 to N-1. For example, consider this list of three members:

```
ls = ['Peter', 'Paul', 'Mary', 'Simon' ]
```

This is a list with four elements, which therefore uses indexes running from 0 to 3. You can think of it this way:

'Peter'	'Paul'	'Mary'	'Simon'
ls[0]	**ls[1]**	**ls[2]**	**ls[3]**

The following statements print out the individual members of this list, along with the length:

```
print('ls[0] =', ls[0])
print('ls[1] =', ls[1])
print('ls[2] =', ls[2])
print('ls[3] =', ls[3])
print("The length is", len(ls))
```

These statements print out the following output:

```
ls[0] = Peter
ls[1] = Paul
ls[2] = Mary
ls[3] = Simon
The length is 4
```

Negative numbers have a specialized usage in Python lists. An index of –1 accesses the last element in the list. An index of –2 accesses the next-to-last element in the list. And so on. In the previous example, ls[-1] refers to the last element, Simon.

Negative indexes run backward from –1 to –N, where N is the length of the list.

'Peter'	'Paul'	'Mary'	'Simon'
ls[-4]	ls[-3]	ls[-2]	ls[-1]

Here's an example using negative indexes:

```
print('Last element in list is', ls[-1])
```

When executed, this prints the following:

```
Last element in list is Simon
```

Accessing one element at a time is the obvious way to use an index. But Python also supports a technique called *slicing*, which enables you to access a subrange of list elements. The result is to produce a new, possibly smaller, list. But it's still a list.

INDEXING SYNTAX	MEANING
[*begin*: *end*]	Include all elements from the index named *begin*, up to but not including *end*.
[*begin*:]	Include all elements from the index named *begin* forward to the end of the list.
[: *end*]	Include all elements up to but not including *end*.
[:]	Include all elements of the list. When this appears on the right side of an assignment, it forces copies to be made of all elements.
[*begin*: *end*: *step*]	The *step* argument, if included, indicates which elements of the list to include. For example, a step value of 2 indicates that every other item is to be included. A negative argument (such as –1) causes the direction to be reversed.

Here's an example using lists of numbers. The slicing in this example says, "Include all elements beginning with the second element (index 1) *up to but not including* the fifth element (index 4).

```
>>>a_list = [10, 200, 300, 44, 55, 999]
>>>a_list[1:4]
[200, 300, 44]
```

Note that when two positive indexes are used this way, you can always predict the length of the resulting list by subtracting the two numbers. For example, the following figure shows how the expression **[1:4]** works:

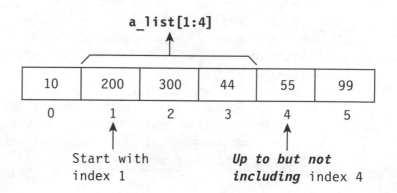

With slicing, it's easy to say "Get the first N elements" or "Get the last N elements." To get the first N elements, just use **[:N]**.

```
>>>a_list[:3]
>>>[10, 200, 300]
```

Likewise, you can use negative indexes to get the last N elements, using **[-N:]**.

```
>>>a_list[-3:]
[44, 55, 99]
```

You can also "mix and match" positive and negative indexes. Here's an example that gets the elements starting with the third element (index 2) up to but not including the last:

```
>>>a_list[2:-1]
[300, 44, 55]
```

When indexing and slicing, you can use integer variables as well as constants.

Finally, notice that a third argument can be used: *step*. If included, it specifies how quickly to step through the list; it can even specify direction. For example, the following use of slicing creates a complete reversal of the original string. It starts out at with the last element (indicated by –1) and moves backward through the string, because the step argument is also –1:

```
>>>a_list = [1, 2, 3, 4]
>>>reversed_list = a_list[-1::-1]
>>>print(reversed_list)
[4, 3, 2, 1]
```

The middle argument, *end*, is omitted in the expression a_list[-1::-1]. When *end* is omitted, the slicing simply goes as far as it can, in this case, all the way to the beginning of the string.

Note ▶ Indexing and slicing look similar, but there are important differences. Indexing returns a specific element, not a list. When you use indexing to get an element, you must use an index in range or the result is a runtime error.

Slicing (for example, [2:–1]) produces a list, not an element, even though it may be a list of length 1 or even length 0 (an empty list). Out-of-range indexes, used in slicing, do not produce runtime errors. For example, list[10:] gets a list starting with the 11th element. If there are fewer than 11 elements, list[10:] just produces an empty list. **◀Note**

Copying Data to Slices

Because Python lists are *mutable* (changeable), you can use slicing to specify a target, as well as the source, of an assignment. For example, assume the following list:

```
>>>x_list = [1, 2, 5]
```

The slice notation [:2] selects the first two elements in a list. Therefore, the following statement replaces the first two elements, 1 and 2, with the values 10, 20, and 30:

```
>>>x_list[:2] = [10, 20, 30]
```

The result is that most of the list values change, making it four elements long. Three elements (10, 20, and 30) have replaced two elements (1 and 2).

```
>>>x_list
[10, 20, 30, 5]
```

If you try to replace an element without using the slicing notation, you put a list inside a list. Here's an example:

```
>>>x_list[0] = [1, 2]
>>>x_list
[[1, 2], 20, 30, 5]
```

If this is not what you want—if instead you want to replace a single element with a series of other elements but not create a two-dimensional list—then remember to use slicing. Assume that the previous operation was not performed. Instead, the following notation is used to select a slice with just one member, consisting of the first element:

```
>>>x_list[:1] = [11, 22]
>>>x_list
[11, 22, 20, 30, 5]
```

This technique can even be used to insert elements into the indicated position. The following statement inserts the values –2, –2 before the first element (index 0):

```
>>>x_list[0:0] = [-2, -2]
>>>x_list
[-2, -2, 11, 22, 20, 30, 5]
```

Ranges

If you want to actually change list elements from inside a loop, use indexing.

Let's return to a problem that we didn't completely solve earlier. Take an array of three values, all of them specifying a Celsius temperature. Suppose we want to change all these values to Fahrenheit temperatures. Indexing provides a way to do this.

```
temp_list = [0.01, 250.5, 22.77]
for i in [0, 1, 2]:
    temp_list[i] = temp_list[i] * 1.8 + 32.0
```

Or, suppose that the list has five elements.

```
temp_list = [0.01, 67.003, 21.2, 15.9, 10.7]
for i in [0, 1, 2, 3, 4]:
    temp_list[i] = temp_list[i] * 1.8 + 32.0
```

Do you see the pattern? To operate on a list of size N, you need to generate a list of integers that range from 0 to N-1, where N-1 is the length of the first list.

Fortunately, Python provides an easy way to generate just such a set of numbers automatically, by using the built-in **range** function. This function can be used in three ways.

```
range(end)
range(start, end)
range(start, end, step)
```

Each of these does something a little different. The basic action is to generate a series of numbers beginning with *start* and continuing up to but not including *end*. If *start* is omitted, it is 0 by default.

When working with index numbers, it's often most efficient to specify the length of a list as the *end* argument and leave *start* set to 0 (the default). Here's an example:

```
for i in range(len(temp_list)):
    temp_list[i] = temp_list[i] * 1.8 + 32.0
```

If you specify a third argument, it's interpreted as the *step* argument, which specifies how much the index (i in this case) should increase during iteration. For example, the following statement operates only on items with an even number, starting with index number 0.

```
for i in range(0, len(temp_list), 2):
    temp_list[i] = temp_list[i] * 1.8 + 32.0
```

Remember that the range of numbers generated includes integers *up to but not including* the *end* argument. This is called the *excluded end point*.

The following table shows examples of how uses of **range** translate into a series of numbers:

EXAMPLE RANGE	RESULTING LIST
range(3)	[0, 1, 2]
range(4)	[0, 1, 2, 3]
range(1, 4)	[1, 2, 3]
range(1, 5)	[1, 2, 3, 4]
range(1, 6)	[1, 2, 3, 4, 5]
range(10, 16)	[10, 11, 12, 13, 14, 15]
range(10, 16, 2)	[10, 12, 14]
range(0, 10, 3)	[0, 3, 6, 9]

It's common to combine the **range** function with the **len** function, as shown earlier. The latter has the following syntax:

```
len(collection)
```

Here's a simple example of the **len** function in use, to determine the length of a list:

```
>>>my_list = [3, 2, 1]
>>>len(my_list)
3
```

Example 5.2. *Revised Factorial Program*

Let's revisit the factorial example from the previous chapter. This section introduces a shorter version, using the **for** keyword instead of **while**.

```
fact2.py

n = int(input('Calculate factorial for which n? '))
prod = 1
for i in range(1, n + 1):     # For 1 to n, inclusive
    prod = prod * i
print('The result is: ', prod)
```

This is a short program, but it does a lot. An important thing to remember is that range(1, n + 1) generates the numbers 1 through n…because of the excluded end point.

Here's a sample session:

```
Calculate factorial for which n? 5
The result is 120
```

How It Works

This program works the same way as the factorial program in Chapter 3, except that it replaces the following version that uses **while**:

```
i = prod = 1
while i <= n:
    prod = prod * i
    n = n + 1
```

The program replaces these statements with the following block of code, which is both shorter and easier to read:

```
prod = 1
for i in range(1, n + 1):
    prod = prod * i
```

Again, the *end* specification in the **for** statement is n+1, not n, because of the excluded end point. Remember that range generates numbers *up to but not including*, its "end" argument.

The pseudocode for this version is also shorter.

Prompt the user for the value of n.
Set prod to 1.
For each element i in the range 1 to n inclusive,
    Multiply prod by i
Print the value of prod.

So if, for example, n were set equal to 5, i would be multiplied in turn by 1, 2, 3, 4, and 5, causing the same effect as the following calculation:

```
prod = 1 * 2 * 3 * 4 * 5
```

Optimizing the Code

Recall that when multiplying one number by another, you can often use the *= (multiplication assignment) operator as a shortcut.

```
prod *= i    # Multiply prod by i, store result in prod
```

This is a slight "optimization" in that it reduces a few keystrokes.

An alternative approach, but not necessarily more efficient, would be to use range(n), producing 0, 1, 2, ... n-1. But to translate this into 1, 2, 3, ... n, it's then necessary to add 1 to the index number. The following code shows the result:

```
fact3.py

n = int(input('Calculate factorial for which n?'))
prod = 1
for i in range(n):
    prod = prod * (i + 1)
print('The result is:', prod)
```

EXERCISES

Exercise 5.2.1. Write a **while** statement around the rest of the program that quits whenever the user enters 0 as the input but otherwise continues and repeats. In other words, make the program repeat operation until the end user quits by entering 0 at any time. This way, the end user can calculate many factorials without having to reload the program over and over.

Exercise 5.2.2. Verify that the program works for small numbers. Then, before working on larger numbers, think about the factorial of 50, and try to make an educated guess as to how many trailing zeroes there are in the result. Then run the program to see if you're right.

Example 5.3. *Sieve of Eratosthenes*

One of the classic examples in computer programming is the "sieve of Eratosthenes," which is used to generate prime numbers. The sieve is frequently used as a benchmark to demonstrate how fast a computer program is.

A prime number is a whole number divisible only by itself and 1. Prime numbers include 2, 3, 5, 7, 11, 13, 17, and so on. They do not include 9, for example, because 9 is divisible by 3; yet 3 itself is prime because it's divisible by no number smaller than itself except for 1. A number divisible by some number other than itself, and 1 is called a composite number.

For the purpose of this example, we're going to use a Boolean list, which is a list in which every element is either **True** or **False**. Remember that Python does not declare types of variables or collections, but we can create a list and initialize it with Boolean values.

```
bool_list = [True] * 100
```

This statement uses a special syntax—which we'll revisit in Chapter 13—that uses the multiplication operator (*) to repeat an element over and over. Multiplying an array by N, an integer, says, "Create a longer array that repeats the element, or elements, N times."

The value **True** indicates the corresponding index number is prime; the value **False** indicates it is not prime. We start by assuming all the numbers are primes.

The sieve recognizes a prime number and then eliminates all multiples of that number from the rest of the list, by assigning the value **False** to higher index numbers. For example, suppose you have a list representing the numbers from 1 to 20. We ignore the first two numbers, 0 and 1. Then, 2 is recognized as a prime number, and all multiples of 2 are eliminated by assigning **False** to the appropriate index positions.

We assign the value **False** to bool_list[4], bool_list[6], bool_list[8], bool_list[10], bool_list[12], and so on, because all those indexes correspond to numbers that are multiples of 2.

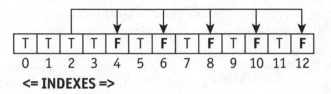

<= INDEXES =>

Then, we do this for the next prime number, which is 3. Eliminating multiples is done the same way, by increasing each index by 3. We assign the value **False** to `bool_list[6]`, `bool_list[9]`, `bool_list[12]`, `bool_list[15]`, `bool_list[18]`, and so on.

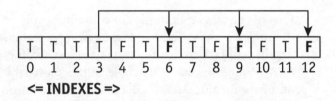

<= INDEXES =>

After that, we get to the number 4, but it has earlier been eliminated when its value was marked as **False**. So, the number 4 is ignored because it's not prime. The procedure continues this way until the end of the list is reached. All those elements that have *not* been marked **False** are prime.

Here's the program listing. It is quite short for what it does.

prime.py

```
bool_list = [True] * 100
for prime in range(2, 100):
    if bool_list[prime]:
        print(prime, end=' ')
        for i in range(prime * 2, 100, prime):
            bool_list[i] = False
```

Here's the output you can expect this program to print, assuming it is properly entered and run in Python. Remember, these are all the numbers, up to but not including 100, which are divisible only by themselves and 1.

```
2 3 5 7 11 13 17 19 23 29 31 37 41 43 47 53 59 61 67 71
73 79 83 89 97
```

How It Works

Although this program is short, it is slightly complex because of its use of a **for** statement that is nested two levels down, as reflected by the following pseudocode:

Initialize the list named "bool_list" to contain 100 values of True.
For each number 'prime' in the range 2 to 99
    If bool_list[prime] contains True,
        Print prime
        for each i in the range 2*prime to 99, step by prime,
            Set bool_list[i] to False

In case it's not immediately clear what this does, I'll step through this program a line or two at a time. The first line creates a Boolean list with 100 members, each member set to the value **True**, and then associates this list with the name bool_list.

```
bool_list = [True] * 100
```

The appearance of [True] by itself creates a list with just one member, and this member is given the value **True**, which is Boolean. When the multiplication operator is (*) used, it creates a much longer list, in which all 100 members are set to **True**. Finally, the resulting list of 100 elements is associated with the name bool_list.

For example, you could create a list this way:

```
bool_list = [True] * 4
```

It would be equivalent to

```
bool_list = [True, True, True, True ]
```

For ease of reading, I created a variable called prime as a loop variable to keep track of where we are in the list. Be careful, though: this may look like a keyword, but it's not. I'm using it as a suggestive name to make the program more readable.

The next two lines in the program scan the list, one at a time, looking for a value that is equal to the Boolean value **True**.

```
for prime in range(2, 100):
    if bool_list[prime]:
```

This **for** loop starts with index value 2 and goes up to but not including 100, so this creates a range from 2 to 99 inclusive. For ease of writing the program, we include the first two elements, bool_list[0] and bool_list[1], in the data structure itself but otherwise ignore them. Such an approach is slightly inefficient—the first two elements are never used—but this approach makes it easier to write the program by making all the indexing obvious.

If the next element contains **True**, that means we've found a prime number; it hasn't been eliminated yet. The first thing to do when a prime is found is print it.

```
print(prime, end=' ')
```

Next, all multiples of prime, starting with prime*2, are composite numbers and therefore should be flagged as such by having the corresponding elements set to **False**.

The inner loop marks composite numbers as false—that is, not prime. For example, since 2 is prime, every multiple of 2, starting with 4, should be flagged as **False**. So, all the elements bool_list[4], bool_list [6], bool_list[8], etc., get set to **False**, because 4, 6, 8, and so on, are multiples of 2 and therefore not prime.

Python's **range** statement supports an optional "step" parameter, which tells how much to increase the loop variable each time. The loop variable in this inner loop is i, and we want to increase it by prime places at a time, where prime is the number that's been identified.

```
for i in range(prime * 2, 100, prime):
    bool_list[i] = False
```

This says, starting with 2 times the value of prime (the prime number that was found), mark every multiple of 2 with the value **False**.

The first element so marked is bool_list[4]; the index is then increased by the amount prime—in this case, that's 2. Therefore, this loop marks every even element, starting with index 4.

Optimizing the Code

One of the most important principles you'll ever learn about optimizing Python programs is this: **print** statements are very expensive in terms of time taken to execute the program. If you can replace repeated calls to **print**, sprinkled throughout the program, with a single output operation, it improves performance. The string **join** method comes to our aid here by creating one string out of a series of strings.

In this case, we can do that by building a new list, call it primes_found, and then printing that list at the end. That list is first created as an empty list, and then we call the **append** function repeatedly.

```
prime2.py
bool_list = [True] * 100
primes_found_list = []
for prime in range(2, 100):
    if bool_list[prime]:
        primes_found_list.append(str(prime))
        for i in range(prime * prime, 100, prime):
            bool_list[i] = False
out_str = ' '.join(primes_found_list)
print(out_str)
```

Also, if you think about it, it's more efficient for the sieve to start eliminating composite numbers at `prime * prime` (the square of the latest prime found) rather than `prime * 2`, because composite numbers smaller than `prime * prime` have already been eliminated. If you doubt this, try doing the sieve manually for a few cycles.

The **join** method is one of the most useful string methods. Chapter 7, "Python Strings," covers this subject in greater detail. For now, you should just accept that **join** works as shown here.

EXERCISES

Exercise 5.3.1.   Instead of finding all the prime numbers between 2 and 100, allow the user to specify the upper limit on prime numbers to report. Ask for a number N at the beginning of the program and then use this number instead of 100.

Exercise 5.3.2.   Calculate the number of primes that you found. There is a way to cheat this result: build a list called `primes_found` (as shown in the previous section) and then just take the length of this list by using the **len** function. The other way, which takes a little more work, is to increment a variable inside one of the loops. For extra credit, use both ways of getting this value.

Exercise 5.3.3.   Just as an exercise, rewrite the innermost **for** loop as a **while** statement.

List Functions and the in Keyword

Python provides so many powerful ways to manipulate lists, it's difficult for one chapter to mention them all. But there are several functions that are especially important for dealing with lists; they also apply to other collections, such as strings.

▶ **len**, which returns the length of a collection

▶ **min**, which returns the value of the lowest element

▶ **max**, which returns the value of the highest element

The **len** function has appeared in this chapter before. It's one of the most useful tools for dealing with collections. Python returns the correct value for the length of any list; however, this value counts the elements in *the top layer* of a Python list. Here's an example:

```
>>>my_list = [[0, 1, 2], 30, ['John', 'Paul']]
>>>len(my_list)
3
```

The **min** and **max** functions do just what you'd expect. But they can only be used with lists in which every element can be meaningfully compared to every other element in the list. In the following example, some elements are integers and some are floating point, but all can be compared:

```
>>>nums = [10, 3.1415, -9, 10.5]
>>>min(nums)
-9
>>>max(nums)
10.5
```

The **sort** method of lists is similar to **min** and **max**, in that sorting works only when all the elements are close enough in type to be compared. Otherwise, you get an "incompatible types" error.

The **in** and **not in** keywords are also very useful, and we'll use them in upcoming chapters.

```
>>>my_list = [300, 400, 50]
>>>300 in my_list
True
>>>50 not in my_list
False
```

Interlude

Who Was Eratosthenes?

Eratosthenes was one of the greatest minds who ever lived. He was, among other things, the chief librarian of the great Library of Alexandria, more than 2,000 years ago.

Alexandria is located in Egypt and is still considered one of the great cities of that country. But after the conquests of Alexander the Great, many Greek intellectuals settled there and made it, in ancient times at least, more Greek than Egyptian. Some of the greatest Greek scientists were residents of Alexandria.

Eratosthenes' greatest achievement may be the measurement of the earth, which he performed by noticing that on a certain day, a pole in southern Egypt cast no shadow at noon, but on the same day, a pole in Alexandria cast a shadow of several feet. He used primitive trigonometry to determine the circumference of the earth, based on the curvature of the earth inferred from the angle between the poles.

Based on these calculations, he was able to estimate the circumference of the earth with 98 percent accuracy. The irony is that almost 2,000 years later, Columbus ignored this estimate in favor of smaller, less accurate guesses. Had Columbus used Eratosthenes' more accurate figure, he would've

Interlude

▼ *continued*

known the ocean was more than half the circumference of the earth and therefore impossible to cross with the resources he had. It turned out, though, there were entire continents in the middle of this mega-ocean.

Eratosthenes could not have known about digital computers, but his method for finding prime numbers—one of the most famous methods in mathematics for more than 2,000 years—turned out to be a perfect test to run on computers to demonstrate their speed and efficiency.

Chapter 5   *Summary*

Here are the major points of Chapter 5:

▶ In Python, a list is an ordered collection, similar to an array in C++ or Java, but with far more built-in capabilities. This is the notation for specifying a list:

```
[item, item,…]
```

▶ You can also specify lists with only a single item or with no items at all.

```
my_list = [ ]
```

▶ In a list, order is meaningful, as are duplicate values.

```
[25, 25, 30, 27, 20, 20, 20]
```

▶ By "order is meaningful," I mean that [3, 2, 1] does not equal [1, 2, 3].

▶ You can use the **for** keyword to loop through a list. In this syntax, `thing` is a variable that represents each element in turn, but you can use any variable name you like.

```
for thing in my_list:
    print(thing)
```

▶ For a list of length N, index numbers run from 0 to N-1.

▶ You can also access elements through negative indexes, in which the last element is indexed as –1, and then indexes run backward to –N, indicating the first element.

▶ The **range** keyword can be combined with the **for** keyword to process a list by its index numbers. Here's an example:

```
for i in range(len(my_list))
    my_list[i] = 0   # Reset each elem to 0.
```

▶ The expression **range(***N***)** generates a series of integers starting with 0, up to but not including *N*.

▶ The expression **range(***start, end***)** generates a series of integers beginning with start, up to but not including *end*.

▶ The expression **range(***start, end, step***)** is similar, but *step* specifies how much to increment the index each time.

▶ The **len** function returns the length of a list or any other Python collection. It is often combined with range.

▶ You can use the splicing syntax both to produce a subrange of data from a list and to assign to it. **[***start : end***]** selects all elements beginning with start, up to but not including *end*, in which *start* and *end* are index numbers.

▶ **[***start***:]** selects all elements beginning with start, continuing to the end of the string.

▶ **[:***end***]** selects all elements from the beginning of the string, up to but not including end.

▶ **[:]** selects the entire string for copying purposes.

▶ The **in** and **not in** keywords return **True** or **False**, depending on whether a specified element can be found in the specified container.

List Comprehension and Enumeration

Python version 2.0 introduced some exciting new features that, while not mandatory, can make your Python code more compact, error-free, and streamlined. The current version of Python (Python 3.0) inherits these powerful features.

This chapter explores these features:

▶ The built-in **enumerate** function, which automatically supplies a loop counter.

▶ Enhanced use of the **format** function, to format output.

▶ *List comprehension*, a technique that collapses an entire **for** loop into a single line. Although the result may at first look cryptic, you'll eventually wonder how you ever programmed without it.

Indexes and the enumerate Function

Standard Python style encourages iteration directly on a list—or other *iterable*. An *iterable* is most often a collection. But technically, it is anything that returns a steady stream of data, one item at a time; you can always ask for "the next item" until there are no more. This book has so far featured lists and strings as two common kinds of iterables in Python.

When iterating through a collection, you may be tempted to use the approach used in C++ and many other languages, relying on index numbers.

```python
for i in range(len(my_list)):
    print(my_list[i], end=' ')
```

But Python style strongly prefers **for** loops that iterate directly through the list, without the use of the **range** function, whenever possible. This is "thinking Pythonically."

101

```
for item in my_list:
    print(item, end=' ')
```

It should be clear why this form is better. It's shorter and expresses the action more directly: for each element in my_list, print out the element. Also, you don't have to worry about the indexes going out of range because Python handles that for you

But sometimes it's convenient to have access to an index number. For example, suppose you want to print a numbered list.

1. 10
2. 20
3. 30

If you don't want to revert to using the **range** function, you can introduce an extra variable to keep track of how many iterations have been performed.

```
i = 1
for item in my_list:
    print(i, '. ', item, sep='')
    i += 1
```

This produces the desired result, but it introduces an extra variable, separate from the **for** statement. It also adds two lines of code. It works, but it's ugly.

Python 2.0 introduced a better solution. The **enumerate** function lets you iterate directly over the data while getting an index number "for free." Assume you have the following list:

```
beat_list = ['John', 'Paul', 'George', 'Ringo' ]
```

By using **enumerate**, you get an index number brought to you free of charge by Python! These numbers start with 1 in this case, because 1 is explicitly specified here.

```
for i, b_str in enumerate(beat_list, 1):
    print(i, '. ', b_str, sep='')
```

This prints the following:

1. John
2. Paul
3. George
4. Ringo

The **enumerate** function is a built-in function that generates a series of value pairs (*tuples*) of the form *index, item*, in which *index* is a running count, and *item* refers to an element. The function has this syntax:

enumerate(*iterable, start*=0**)**

The *iterable* is a set of data, such as a list, tuple, or string, that you can always get the "next" element of, until the end is reached; an iterable is usually a collection but may also be a generator (a topic we'll return to in Chapter 18). The second parameter, which sets the starting value of the "index number," is optional; if omitted, its value is 0.

The **enumerate** function is most often used within **for** statements. Remember that each call to this function produces an *index, item* pair.

for *index, item* **in enumerate(***iterable, num*=0**):**
    indented_statements

A common use is to print the *index* and *item* for each element of *iterable*, side by side, as in the upcoming example. This example also uses formatted output.

The Format String Method Revisited

Chapter 3, "Your First Programs," introduced the **format** string method, which formats one or more fields of output in an output string. That chapter gave a simple example of use, shown again here:

```
format_spec_str = '{} results in {}.'
print(format_spec_str.format(x, y))
```

Remember that the basic syntax includes a format-specification string, followed by the word **format**, followed by arguments in parentheses.

format_spec_str.**format(***args***)**

The result of this syntax is to produce a new string, which includes the arguments arranged and printed according to the *format_spec_str*, a string that combines print fields with other text.

The *format_spec_str* itself contains curly braces, {}, to define a print field corresponding to one of the arguments, or *args*. Other text that appears is considered "template" or "boilerplate" and is printed unconditionally.

In this chapter we'll use a further refinement. You can modify fields by specifying left or right justification. Left justification is usually best for words and other kinds of text; right justification is usually best for displaying columns of numbers.

SPECIFICATION	MEANING
{:>n}	Right-justified field *n* spaces wide. This field is usually best for columns of numbers; it is also the default for numbers, so that {:n} is equivalent to {:>n} for numeric fields.
{:<n}	Left-justified field n spaces wide. This field is usually best for ordinary text; it is also the default for non-numeric fields, so that {:n} is equivalent to {:<n} for non-numeric fields.
{:^n}	Center-justified field *n* spaces wide.

So, for example, to print a column of even numbers from 2 to 100, right-justified, you might print them each in a field three characters wide.

```
for i in range(2, 100, 2):
    print('{:>3}'.format(i))
```

"Justification" tells how to position text within the field. If the size of the text exceeds the size of the field, some text will overflow to the right. But you should try to ensure that the size of a print field is large enough to print the corresponding argument. Right justification is the default for numeric fields so that the previous statements have the same effect as these:

```
for i in range(2, 100, 2):
    print('{:3}'.format(i))
```

Example 6.1.   *Printing a Table*

Save the following code in a file called `table.py`, open that module from within the Python interactive environment, and choose Run Module:

```
table.py

fib_list = [1, 2, 4, 5, 8, 13, 21, 34, 55, 89, 144]
format_str = '{:>2}. {:>4}'
for i, item in enumerate(fib_list, 1):
    print(format_str.format(i, item))
```

Amazingly, this is only a four-line program, and yet it illustrates the use of both the **enumerate** function and the **format** method. Here is the output of the program:

```
 1.    1
 2.    2
 3.    4
 4.    5
 5.    8
 6.   13
 7.   21
 8.   34
 9.   55
10.   89
11.  144
```

You can also enter this program from the interactive environment, as follows:

```
>>>def main():
    fib_list = [1, 2, 4, 5, 8, 13, 21, 34, 55, 89, 144]
    for i, item in enumerate(fib_list, 1):
        print('{:>2}. {:>4}'.format(i, item))

>>>main()
```

How It Works

This example, Example 6.1, features the **enumerate** function, as well as making expanded use of the **format** method.

The following line creates the format-specification string, called `format_str` in this example.

```
format_str = '{:>2}. {:>4}'
```

This creates two print fields, one of which is a field two spaces wide, in which the data is right-justified. The second creates a print field four spaces wide, in which the data is also right-justified. That's usually the correct approach for printing numbers.

Alternatively, you could left-justify the data within these two print fields by using left arrows rather than left.

```
format_str = '{:<2}. {:<4}'
```

To create the output string for any given line, apply the **format** method.

```
format_str.format(i, item)
```

Remember that i and item together form a *tuple* (a group) output by the **enumerate** function within the **for** statement. That function produces a series of *index, item* pairs—which in this example are then printed together on each line.

```
for i, item in enumerate(fib_list, 1):
    print('{:>2}. {:>4}'.format(i, item))
```

You should also remember that because the starting index number used in this case is 1, not 0, the number 1 must be specified as the second argument to **enumerate**. The first argument is just the name of the list to be iterated through.

EXERCISES

Exercise 6.1.1.   Revise Example 6.1 so that it produces precisely the same output but without using the built-in **enumerate** function. (Hint: Use the **range** function instead.) Again, make sure the output is precisely the same.

Exercise 6.1.2.   Instead of initializing fib_list, use a loop that produces the first 11 Fibonacci numbers. (Hint: Look at Chapter 3 if you need to.) Then make sure the whole program still works correctly.

Exercise 6.1.3.   Revise the example so that it has three print fields. The third should be printed only if the current index is 1 or greater. It should be the current element minus the previous element. Make the print fields 3, 5, and 5 in size, respectively.

Exercise 6.1.4.   Do you see any pattern in the final column (assuming you've done Exercise 6.1.3)? How would you describe this difference?

Simple List Comprehension

List comprehension is another technique that, while not strictly necessary, can be a very nice addition to your Python skills.

One of the most common uses of a **for** statement is to append items, one at a time, to a list. For example, to create a list consisting of all even numbers, you can write the following:

```
my_list = []
for i in range(1, 51):
    my_list.append(i * 2)
```

It turns out there used to be a great deal of Python code that looked like this. We can say such coding techniques have this general form:

```
list_name = []
for_statement_header :
    list_name.append(expression)
```

Now here comes the magic. The designers of Python realized how common such code was and created a shortcut for it. The shortcut looks like this:

```
list_name = [expression  for_statement_header]
```

More generally, this syntax can be used to create an iterable series of values, for which the most common use (though not the only) is to create a list.

```
expression  for_statement_header
```

To make sense of this technique, you need to look at several concrete examples. First, look at one of the simplest uses possible: creating a list from 0 to 9.

```
a_list = []
for i in range(10):
    a_list.append(i)
```

Using list comprehension, you can replace these three statements with one.

```
a_list = [i for i in range(10)]
```

This syntax inside the brackets includes the following:

▶ The expression i, which is the value to be appended during each iteration

▶ The **for** statement header, for i in range(10)

You can think of this visually.

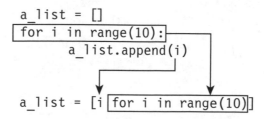

The next example creates a list from 0 to 18, including even numbers only. It is the same as the previous example, except that it appends the value i * 2 instead of i.

```
a_list = []
for i in range(10):
    a_list.append(i * 2)
```

And here is the list-comprehension version:

```
a_list = [i * 2 for i in range(10)]
```

The conceptual diagram for this example is the same, except that the value to be appended, i * 2, now appears at the front; it is then followed by the same **for** statement header, up to but not including the colon.

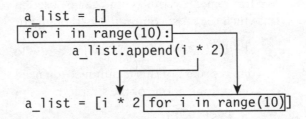

Here's an even simpler example, which doesn't use the **range** function at all but just copies from one list to another:

```
new_list = []
for i in old_list:
    new_list.append(i)
```

Using list comprehension produces a shorter, more compact version of this code. It begins with i, the value to be appended, followed by the **for** statement header, for i in old_list.

```
new_list = [i for i in old_list]
```

Again, you can understand this conceptually by remembering that it includes the value to be appended in each case, i, followed by the **for** statement up to but not including the colon.

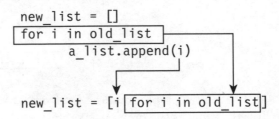

The effect, in either case, is just to copy each element of old_list onto new_list. Incidentally, for a simple copy, you can use either of the following alternative techniques to achieve the same result:

```
new_list = list(old_list)
new_list = old_list[:]
```

If i * 2 is used instead of the initial i, then new_list becomes a list containing the double of each element in old_list. For example, if old_list contained [5, 7, 9], then new list would contain [10, 14, 18].

```
new_list = [i * 2 for i in old_list]
```

Likewise, the use of the expression i * 3 at the front would create a new list containing a triple of each element in old_list; this would result in [15, 21, 27].

```
tri_list = [i * 3 for i in old_list]
```

Example 6.2. *Difference Between Squares*

Difference between squares is another succinct program that does something interesting. This program uses list comprehension to create a list of the squares of the first six integers, and then it calculates the differences between one square and the previous square.

squares.py

```
sqr_list = [i * i for i in range(1, 7)]
format_str = '{:>3}  {:>3}  {:>3}'
old_val = 0
for i, item in enumerate(sqr_list, 1):
    print(format_str.format(i, item, item - old_val))
    old_val = item
```

Here are the results printed by the program:

```
1    1    1
2    4    3
3    9    5
4   16    7
5   25    9
6   36   11
```

Do you notice anything interesting happening in the third column? What these results suggest is that the difference between any two successive square numbers is an odd number that gets 2 bigger each time. In other words, these results predict the following relationship:

```
N*N = 1 + 3 + 5 + ... 2N - 1
```

If you compare all three columns, you'll see that the difference between any square number and the preceding square is an odd number but not just any odd number: it is the odd number 2N – 1, where N is the number in the first column.

I'll discuss this mathematical pattern more in the upcoming interlude.

How It Works

The first statement in this program is the interesting one. This is the most efficient way to create a list of square numbers.

```
sqr_list = [i * i for i in range(1, 7)]
```

This statement produces squares of the numbers 1 to 6 inclusive because the built-in **range** function generates elements beginning with the first number, up to but not including the second.

The first part of this expression is i * i—calculate the squares. The second part is for i in range(1, 7), which means "get all the numbers from 1 to 6, inclusive.

The next statement sets up the output format. The following format-specification string indicates that a row of the table will have three print fields—each of which is three characters wide and is right-justified.

```
format_str = '{:>3}   {:>3}   {:>3}'
```

The rest of the program has to print each successive integer and its corresponding square, which is easy. The program also prints the difference between each square and the one before it, which is a little more challenging.

```
old_val = 0
for i, item in enumerate(sqr_list, 1):
    format_str.format(i, item, item - old_val)
    old_val = item
```

Usually, you don't want to rely too much on variables created outside the **for** loop, but this is the most convenient way to attack this particular problem. The variable named old_val starts off at 0, but each time through the loop its value is reset, so it always refers to the *previous* square number in the series rather than the current one.

The statement `old_val = item` sets up `old_val` so that during the *next* iteration, `old_val` will refer to the previous value of the item—which, remember, will hold N², or rather $(N-1)^2$.

EXERCISES

Exercise 6.2.1.   Revise Example 6.2 so that it gets a number n from the user; this should be the number of squares and differences to print. Also, alter the format string so that each print field is four characters wide, not three. This will help accommodate larger numbers.

Exercise 6.2.2.   After making the changes specified in Exercise 6.2.1, add another change: print out cube numbers (`n * n * n`) along with their differences. Does any pattern emerge in the third column? Are these differences all odd? All even? Or a mix?

Exercise 6.2.3.   Can you rewrite the **for** loop in Example 6.2 so that it does not use the "dangling variable," `old_val`? (Hint: Printing the first row without a runtime error may be difficult, so you may have to skip it. You may also need to resort to the built-in **range** function and to explicit indexing.)

Interlude

Proving the Equation

Proving the difference-of-squares equation is one of the basic tasks in elementary algebra, so forgive me if this section seems familiar. The geometric proof, which I include, is a good deal more interesting.

Here's the exact equation to be proved:

```
N*N = 1 + 3 + 5 + ... 2N - 1
```

In proof by induction, we start by observing that it works for the first case, N = 1:

```
1 * 1 = 2 (1) - 1
    1 = 1
```

Both sides simplify to 1. Therefore we can conclude that this equation works for the case that N equals 1. This is trivial: 1^2 is equal to all the odd numbers *up to* 1 (which is simply 1 itself).

▼ *continued on next page*

Interlude

▼ *continued*

Now it remains to show that each time N increases...as the left side goes from (N)**2 to (N+1)**2, the difference will be an odd number—more precisely, it will be the next odd number in the series. For N + 1, corresponding odd number is as follows:

```
2(N + 1) − 1 = 2N + 1
```

Therefore, we just need to show that the difference between N^2 and $(N + 1)^2$ is 2N + 1. This is easy, given basic algebra.

```
(N + 1) * (N + 1) = N *(N + 1) + 1 * (N + 1)
                  = (N*N + N) + (N + 1)
                  = N*N + 2N + 1
```

Now, subtract N^2. What's left is

```
                  = 2N + 1
```

Voilà! We've demonstrated that the difference between $(N + 1)^2$ and N^2 is indeed 2N + 1, which is exactly what we needed to show.

That's a simple algebraic proof. The "geometric proof," which is visual and intuitive, is more fun. In the following figure, by comparing 4^2 to 5^2, you can see that the difference must be an odd number, specifically, 2(4) + 1, or 9. And it should be intuitively obvious that this pattern will hold for any value of N.

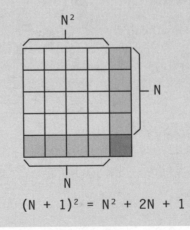

$$(N + 1)^2 = N^2 + 2N + 1$$

"Two-Dimensional" List Comprehension

When you've been programming for a while, you'll likely have occasion to use nested **for** loops. For example, suppose you want to create a multiplication table. One way to do this is to create a one-dimensional list and then print it, a subgroup at a time, creating a two-dimensional table.

A more natural solution might be to create a two-dimensional list, but I'll introduce that technique in Chapter 13. Two-dimensional lists raise special issues in Python.

Here's what the one-dimensional list would look for a small table:

```
[1, 2, 3, 2, 4, 6, 3, 6, 9]
```

Printing three to a line produces a table.

```
1  2  3
2  4  6
3  6  9
```

Generating this list of values is the interesting part. It's a good example of what you might use a nested **for** loop to do. Here's the code:

```
nums = []
for i in range(1, 4):
    for j in range(1, 4):
        nums.append(i * j)
```

This looks just like a candidate for list comprehension, aside from the fact that there are two **for** loops, one nested inside another. But it turns out you can use list comprehension for any number of nested loops. This gives us the following:

```
nums = [i * j for i in range(1,4) for j in range(1,4)]
```

Conceptually, you can visualize the list comprehension as follows. The expression to be added, i * j, appears at the beginning, followed by the two **for** statement headers, one after the other—not including the colons.

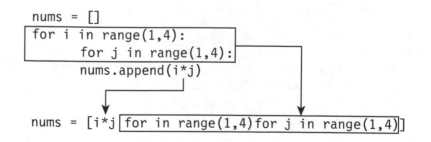

Printing three numbers to a line is then easy enough. The following pseudocode shows a way to print three numbers to a line.

For each element of nums,
   Print the element
If index number MOD 3 is zero,
   Print a blank line

And here are actual Python statements to implement this pseudocode. The **enumerate** function, introduced earlier in this chapter, is helpful because it provides an index number (in this case, set to start at 1) for free.

```
for i, item in enumerate(nums):
    print(item, end='')
    if i % 3 == 0:     # After every 3rd element,
        print()        # Print blank line
```

List Comprehension with Conditional

What if, instead of printing a symmetrical multiplication table, you want to print an asymmetrical table, which does not duplicate any values? In the case of our simple 3 × 3 multiplication table, the asymmetrical would look this way:

```
1
2  4
3  6  9
```

How do you produce this table? First, start with the nested for loops shown earlier. Then, add the conditional i >= j... adding that conditional prevents inclusion of values in which j, the column number, is bigger than i, the row number.

```
nums = []
for i in range(1, 4):
    for j in range(1, 4):
        if i >= j:
            nums.append(i * j)
```

List comprehension, amazingly, has another piece of syntax that accommodates this **if** conditional, while making it possible to reduce these five lines of code to a single virtual line, although this virtual line may carry over into more than one physical line.

```
num_list = [i * j for i in range(1,4)
                  for j in range(1,4) if i >= j]
```

Wow! That's concise! Five lines of code replaced by one "virtual" line.

The resulting syntax may look complex, but all we've done is add one part, if i >= j, at the end of the expression. In general, here is the full syntax for list comprehension:

```
list = [ value  for_stmt_header  conditional_expr ]
```

Or, more generally, we can say that the following syntax produces an iterable—a series of values that can be read one at a time:

```
value  for_stmt_header  conditional_expr
```

But to this, we have to add these qualifiers:

▶ The *for_stmt_header* appears one or more times, as it can include any number of nested **for** statement headers.

▶ The *conditional_expr* is optional and appears at most one time.

Example 6.3. ___*Sieve of Eratosthenes 2*___

Using the principles of list comprehension introduced so far, we can write a much more succinct version of the sieve of Eratosthenes. This is the program from Chapter 4, which listed all the prime numbers up to a specified number, N, by first determining the composite numbers—numbers divisible by some other number (other than itself and 1). Numbers that are not composite numbers are primes.

```
sieve2.py

n = 20     # Print primes from 2 up to 20.
comp_list =  [j for i in range(2, n)
                for j in range(i * i, n, i)]
prime_list = [i for i in range(2, n)
                if i not in comp_list]
print(prime_list)
```

This program prints all the primes from 2 to 20, in a list. By changing the value of n in the first line, you can print as many prime numbers as you like.
Here is the output of the program:

```
[2, 3, 5, 7, 11, 13, 17, 19]
```

How It Works

This program features two uses of list comprehension. The first usage replaces a nested **for** loop.

```
comp_list = [j for i in range(2, n)
                for j in range(i * i, n, i)]
```

As before, the easy way to think about this is to remember that the initial appearance of j is the value expression; it's the value produced. The rest of the code between the brackets consists of the two **for** statement headers. This statement is equivalent to the following:

```
comp_list = []
for i in range(2, n):
    for j in range(i * i, n, i):
        comp_list.append(j)
```

The effect of these statements, in pseudocode form, is as follows:

For all the numbers i from 2 up to N,

   *For every j, where j ranges from i*i to N, increasing i at a time,*

      Append j to comps.

In even plainer language, for each number i, do the following: take all the multiples of i, starting with i*i, and append them to the list named comps. So, for example, if i is set equal to 2, then comps (composite numbers) will include 4, 6, 8, 10, etc.—that is, all the multiples of 2. Then all the multiples of 3 are appended to the list starting with 9, and so on.

This means that some numbers—such as 12—might be appended to list named comps more than once. That may be inefficient, but it doesn't produce any wrong results.

The second use of list comprehension uses a conditional.

```
prime_list = [i for i in range(2, n)
                if i not in comp_list]
```

This statement says, "For all the numbers from 2 to N, select that number if it is *not* in comps; add selected numbers to the list named primes." You could write it out as follows:

```
prime_list = []
for i in range(2, n):
    if i not in comp_list:
        prime_list.append(i)
```

In other words, if a number 2 or greater is *not* a composite, it's a prime. It's that simple. The list named `primes` will include a number from the range 2 to 20, if and only if that number is not in `comps`.

Optimizing the Code: Sets

In the preceding discussion, you may have noticed that the list named `comps` will end up with multiple copies of the same number. Subsequently, when the program detects to see if a number is in this list, it does some redundant work. As you deal with larger and larger ranges, this becomes a greater efficiency issue.

Ideally, you'd use a data structure for `comps` that stores a given value at most once. Python does provide such a structure; it's called the *set*. You create a set in almost the same way you create a list.

To use a "set" data structure for the comps, use curly braces instead of brackets.

```
comps = {j for i in range(2, n) for j in range(2*i, n, i)}
```

If you type this statement into the interactive environment, after assigning a number of your choice for n, you'll find that none of the values are repeated. For example, if n equals 20, you get the following set, in which each value is unique:

```
{4, 6, 8, 9, 10, 12, 14, 15, 16, 18}
```

If instead you had created this data structure as a *list*, it would be longer and have some duplicate values.

Sets and lists have some important differences.

▸ An element of a set must be unique within the set. It can appear at most one time. In contrast, a list may repeat any number of duplicate values.

▸ Order does not matter in a set, although it definitely matters in lists. For example, the sets {1, 2, 3} and {3, 2, 1} are considered to be equal. But [1, 2, 3] defines a different list from [3, 2, 1], because in lists, order is significant.

▸ Sets are usually displayed in sorted order, if possible, for the sake of presentation. But a list is not displayed in sorted order unless the values have been kept sorted—either they were appended in that order or the **sort** method has been used. There is usually no need to use a **sort** method on a set because that would serve no useful purpose; in fact, sets do not even support that method.

EXERCISES

Exercise 6.3.1.   Revise Example 6.3 so it prompts the number n from the user and then uses that number to decide how many prime numbers to print.

Exercise 6.3.2.   Revise Example 6.3 so that it prints the results by iterating over the list named primes. Use a **for** statement to iterate through this list directly.

Exercise 6.3.3.   Write a short program to print the first ten triangle numbers, using list comprehension to produce this list. A "triangle number" is a number of the form 1 + 2 + 3... + n = number. For example, 1 + 2 = 3, 1 + 2 + 3 = 6, and 1 + 2 + 3 + 4 = 10, so the first four triangle numbers are 1, 3, 4, and 10. (Hint: the Nth triangle number is equal to N * (N + 1) /2. This will give you a floating-point result. If you want to convert it to an integer, use int(N).)

Exercise 6.3.4.   Take the program you wrote for Exercise 6.3.3 and revise it so that the results only include triangle numbers that are even.

Exercise 6.3.5.   Using list comprehension, create two lists, evens and odds. If a number between 1 and 20 is a multiple of two, include it in evens. Then, using the clause if i not in evens, build a list containing odd numbers only.

Example 6.4. *Pythagorean Triples*

The final example in this chapter showcases another famous group of numbers in mathematics: Pythagorean triples. These are integers that fulfill the Pythagorean theorem for right triangles.

```
a² + b² = c²
```

Do such numbers exist? Yes, infinitely many of them. An obvious case is (1, 0, 1).

```
1*1 + 0*0 = 1*1
```

But this is a trivial and uninteresting case. We can limit ourselves to values of a, b, and c that are all greater than zero. The smallest and best known case is (3, 4, 5).

```
3*3 + 4*4 = 5*5
    9 + 16 = 25
```

Assume we'd like to find all such Pythagorean triples, in which each value of a, b, or c ranges between 1 and 20. Here is the code, using list comprehension, that produces these triples; each such triple is stored in a tuple of the form (a, b, c).

```
pythag.py

nums = range(1, 21)
trips = [(a, b, c) for a in nums for b in nums for
    c in nums if a*a + b*b == c*c]
print(trips)
```

How It Works

The compactness of this program is, once again, remarkable. The second statement is shorthand for the following:

```
trips = []
for a in nums:
    for b in nums:
        for c in nums:
            if a*a + b*b == c*c:
                trips.append((a, b, c))
```

This doubly nested for loop may look intimidating, but all it says is this:

For every combination of a, b, and c within nums (which is 1 to 20),
    If the relationship $a^2 + b^2 == c^2$ holds,
        Add the tuple (a, b, c) to the list called "trips."

So, the program begins by establishing a general range, 1 to 20 inclusive; you can, of course, specify a much wider range if you want.

Then the program uses a triply nested **for** loop to consider all possible combinations of a, b, and c, in which a, b, and c are all in range. Each combination that fulfills the required condition is appended to the master list, named trips, in this format:

```
(a, b, c)
```

This is a tuple. It would have been just as easy to add a list:

```
[a, b, c]
```

In that case, the result would have been a series of three-member lists within a much larger list, in other words, a two-dimensional list. That's a topic I'll return to in Chapter 12.

> **Note** ▶ A tuple is similar to a list, except that it is immutable and does not provide all the same functionality. However, its use is more efficient at the machine-code level, so if you need a list-like data structure that doesn't need to be manipulated, tuples are often the right choice.
> But don't confuse "tuple" with Pythagorean "triple."

◀ Note

EXERCISES

Exercise 6.4.1. Revise Example 6.4 so that it prints each tuple, one to a line, in the format a = {:>3}, b = {:>3}, c = {:>3}, where the items in curly braces each describe a three-character, right-justified print field. (Hint: Review the section titled "The Format String Method Revisited," earlier in this chapter, if needed.) Remember to iterate over the list named trips directly. Also revise the example so it gets a number n from the user and then uses that to establish a range for a, b, and c.

Exercise 6.4.2. Using list comprehension, write a program that finds every combination of integers a and b, in which a and b are numbers ranging from 1 to 10 inclusive, and a*a + b*b is less than 100. For each such combination of a and b, print a*a, b*b, and their total.

Exercise 6.4.3. Using list comprehension, write a program that finds all *Pythagorean quadruples* in which the numbers a, b, c, and d are all in the range 1 to 10, inclusive, and in which $a^2 + b^2 + c^2 = d^2$. Such numbers do exist, for example, (1, 2, 2, 3).

Exercise 6.4.4. Is it possible to find "Pythagorean triples" for positive integer values of a, b, and c, but raised to a power higher than 2? For example, can you find a, b, and c such that a^3 plus b^3 equals c^3? (Warning: Do not spend too much time on this. Either you know the answer or you don't. If you don't, I recommend doing an Internet search on *Fermat*.)

Interlude

The Importance of Pythagoras

It's not known with certainty whether the ancient Greek philosopher Pythagoras invented the theorem that bears his name, although many historians would not begrudge him the credit.

What is known is that there was a Pythagorean cult. This was a mysterious group of Greek intellectuals who met in secret, for whom numbers were their religion.

Interlude

▼ *continued*

When I say that numbers had religious significance, I'm not exaggerating. The members of this cult considered numbers to be supernatural entities, almost like gods. Amounts that could be expressed as perfect fractions—a ratio between two whole numbers—were called *rational*; the word *rational* itself came to signify that there was order in the world.

Every number, they thought, was rational. And therefore the universe itself was rational.

Can you imagine the horror that members of this cult felt when they realized that there were infinitely many *irrational* numbers? The square root of two, for example, which is the length of the diagonal of a square and therefore important, is not expressible as the ratio of any two whole numbers, and this led members of the cult to the suspicion that the universe was essentially "irrational"—and therefore was a realm of Chaos and Disorder.

For that reason, the discovery that the square root of two was irrational, if mentioned to anyone outside the cult, was grounds for excommunication. To reveal that secret was to betray the truth: that maybe the universe itself was not so reasonable after all.

But for whatever reason, one of the most important equations in all of mathematics—some might say *the* most important equation, certainly in geometry—was named after Pythagoras.

$$a^2 + b^2 = c^2$$

And this is true whenever a, b, and c represent the measures of three sides of a right triangle—a triangle having a 90-degree angle. Side c, which is opposed to the right angle, is necessarily the longest side:

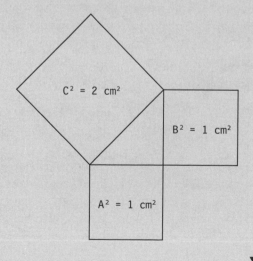

▼ *continued on next page*

▼ *continued*

Interlude

It's difficult to think of any equation in the history of mankind, even E=mc², having so much impact. The field of trigonometry, as well as the entire profession of surveying, rests firmly upon this equation. The most important identity in trigonometry is derived from it.

```
(sin x)² + (cos x)² = 1
```

Even Einstein appealed to the Pythagorean theorem to work out the mathematics of special relativity.

It's possible that what we call the Pythagorean theorem was anticipated by earlier cultures. But the crowning achievement fell to the Greek mathematician Euclid, who is known to have published the first proof of the theorem, which meant that for the first time in history, people could really *know* that this equation was true, not merely suspect it.

Euclid's proof is too long to show here, but here I give a short and simple geometric proof:

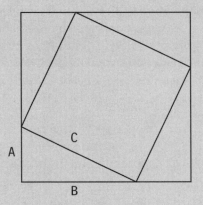

Each of the four "wedges" around the side of the square is equal to (1/2) times A times B, according to the equation for area of a triangle. The total area of these wedges is 2AB:

```
4 * ((1/2) * A * B) = (4/2) * A * B = 2AB
```

Therefore, you can see that the figure demonstrates the following true statement for any right triangle:

```
(A + B)² = C² + 2AB
```

From this you can easily derive the following:

```
A² + 2AB + B² = C² + 2AB
```

▼ *continued*

Interlude

Now subtract 2AB from both sides, and we get a pleasing final result.

$$A^2 + B^2 = C^2$$

Voilà! We produce the Pythagorean theorem, one of the foundational pieces of knowledge of the human race.

Chapter 6   *Summary*

Here are the main points of Chapter 6:

▶ The built-in **enumerate** function, applied to an iterable data set, produces an iterable series of *index, item* pairs. The function takes two arguments: an iterable set of data (such as a string or list) and an optional argument setting the first index number produced. By default, the number is zero.

```
enumerate(iterable, start=0)
```

▶ You usually would use the **enumerate** function as part of a **for** statement.

```
for index, item in enumerate(iterable, start=0):
    indented_statements
```

▶ The format-specification string used with the **format** string method can include left- and right-justified print fields, such as {:>3} and {:<4}. The arrow indicates right or left justification; the number indicates the size of the print field. Here's an example of a format-specification string with three print fields:

```
format_spec_str = '{:>2} plus {:>2} yields {:>3}.'
```

▶ Here is an example of how such a string could be used to print output. The **format** method, which takes arguments corresponding to the print fields, applies to the print-specification string. There are three print fields in this case, so there need to be three arguments.

```
print(format_spec_str.format(12, 13, 25))
```

▶ List comprehension provides a way to collapse a complex **for** statement into a single expression. The general syntax is as follows:

```
list = [expression  for_statement_header]
```

▶ This statement corresponds to the following statements:

```
list = []
for_statement_header :
    list.append(expression)
```

▶ Here is an example that creates a list of square numbers, each number being the square of a number from 1 to 10 inclusive (up to but not including 11).

```
a_list = [i * i for i in range(1, 11)]
```

▶ List comprehension can also include an optional **if** clause, which determines whether the *expression* will be appended during any particular iteration of the **for** statement.

▶ For example, here is a use of conditional list comprehension to create a list of the square of even numbers. Squares of odd numbers, in this case, are not included.

```
a_list = [i * i for i in range(1, 11) if i % 2 == 0]
```

Python Strings

Computer programs do more than crunch numbers. They communicate with the end user. This is what text strings are for: they contain human-readable information made up of printable characters. One of the most important tasks of programs is *tokenization*—breaking down a line of input into individual words.

In this chapter, we're going to get inside of strings and show how to efficiently pull them apart and put them together.

▶ Counting characters

▶ Stripping trailing and leading spaces

▶ Splitting lines of input (tokenization)

▶ Building strings efficiently with **join**

Creating a String with Quote Marks

In many other programming languages, it's common to specify strings by enclosing text in double quotation marks. You can do this in Python, too.

```
a_string = "To be or not to be."
```

But in Python you can also use single quotation marks.

```
a_string = 'To be or not to be.'
```

There's no difference between these two statements. The effect is the same. Although quotation marks are used to delineate the string, they are not part of the string itself. The actual text is

```
To be or not to be.
```

which is what gets printed if you use the **print** function.

```
>>>s = 'To be or not to be.'
>>>print(s)
To be or not to be.
```

But single and double quotation marks are not interchangeable. The beginning and ending marks must match. For example, the following assignments are both valid:

```
name1 = 'Brian'
name2 = "Sam"
```

The following are not valid, because they use quotation marks that don't match:

```
name1 = 'Brian"    # Syntax error!
name2 = "Sam'      # Syntax error!
```

Which, then, should you use? It's more common for Python programmers to use single quotation marks when given a choice, but that's not an absolute rule.

Sometimes you may want to embed a quotation mark. Suppose you want to create the following string:

```
That's odd, said Alice.
```

In this case, use double quotation marks, because doing that allows you to embed the single quote mark.

```
s1 = "That's odd, said Alice."
```

Conversely, suppose you want to embed double quotation marks.

```
She sighed. "That is odd," said Alice.
```

In this case, it makes sense to use single quotation marks to delineate the string, because that enables you to embed the double quotation marks (") without errors.

```
s2 = 'She sighed. "That is odd," said Alice.'
```

What if I want to embed *both* kinds of quotation marks? One solution is to use triple quote marks, consisting of three single quotation mark characters ('). This creates a *literal quotation*, which reads all characters between the triple quotes (''') as they are. Here's an example:

```
s3 = '''She sighed. "That's odd," said Alice.'''
```

If you then print s3 using the **print** function, you'll get the exact text between the first and second occurrences of the triple quote marks (''').

```
>>>s3 = '''She sighed. "That's odd," said Alice.'''
>>>print(s3)
She sighed. "That's odd," said Alice.
```

Triple quote marks have another special feature. You can place any characters between them, including newline (end-of-line) characters. Here's an example:

```
>>>s4 = '''Now sit back and hear the tale
of "Gilgamesh's Island"!'''
```

Now, printing this string causes Python to output all the characters between the triple quotation marks (''') exactly as shown, including newlines.

```
>>>print(s4)
Now sit back and hear the tale
of "Gilgamesh's Island"!
```

There's another technique for handling embedded quotation marks—as well as other kinds of special characters. You can use the backslash (\) as an escape character.

```
>>>s5 = 'Gilgamesh\'s Island'
>>>print(s5)
Gilgamesh's Island.
```

The backslash has other uses, the most important of which is to embed newlines (\n) and tab characters (\t). But if you put a backslash before a quotation mark, that mark is considered part of the string.

Indexing and "Slicing"

Python supports many of the same indexing and slicing abilities for strings that it does for lists. All indexes in Python run from 0 to N-1, where N is the length of the thing being accessed. So, for example, the string "Hello" would be indexed as follows:

H	e	l	l	o
0	1	2	3	4

<= INDEXES =>

The substring-accessing syntax in Python echoes the list-member accessing closely. Here is the syntax:

```
string_name[index]
string_name[begin : end]
string_name[begin :]
string_name[: end]
string_name[:]
string_name[begin : end : step]
```

All of these are correct. When the first form is used, the expression generates a character at the specified *index*, in which the indexes run from 0 to N-1.

With the other forms—which use *slicing*—the expression generates a substring starting with the character indexed by *begin*, up to but not including the character indexed by *end*. Again, indexes run from 0 to N-1.

The third argument, if it appears, is the *step* argument. It specifies how quickly to move through the string. A step value of 2 means include every other character. A step value of –1 means to move backward through the string. The following statement—which deliberately omits the middle argument—reverses a string, because it begins with the last character and then moves to the *left*:

```
rev_str = a_str[-1::-1]
```

Note that the "double colons" (::) are not double colons at all, but an omitted second argument. When the second argument is omitted, that means to process the string as far as possible in the direction specified…in this case, all the way to the *beginning*!

Here are examples of both the first and second kinds of string syntax, using the interactive development environment, so you can follow along:

```
>>>s = 'Hello'
>>>print(s[0])
H
>>>print(s[1])
e
>>>print(s[1:3])
el
```

Take a closer look at these examples. The first index, 0, refers to the first character, since indexes in Python run from 0 to N-1. The value 1 indexes the second character, and 2 indexes the third character.

The meaning of [1:3] is "Get all characters beginning with the second character, *up to but not including* the fourth character." Therefore, s[1:3] produces a substring containing the second and third characters, el.

As with lists, Python supports the use of negative index numbers for strings. The last character can be indexed as –1, the next-to-last character can be indexed as –2, and so on. You can index characters in the string "Hello" as follows:

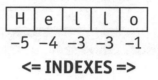

H	e	l	l	o
–5	–4	–3	–3	–1

<= INDEXES =>

So, for example, you can use –1 to get the last character in the string.

```
>>>print(s[-1])
o
```

By the way, it isn't always necessary to use the **print** function from within the interactive environment. I've been using it to demonstrate that the quotation marks are not part of the string. But if you type the name of a string, the environment prints it with quotation marks (giving preference to single quotation marks) to show that the item is string data.

```
>>>s[-1]
'o'
```

Here's another example. This example creates a string, "DragonFly," and then uses slicing to get all the characters except the last three.

```
>>>s2 = "DragonFly"
>>>s2[:-3]
'Dragon'
```

This last example of slicing tells Python to get all the characters starting with the first character in s2, *up to but not including* the third-to-last character, F.

Conceptually, you can think of it this way:

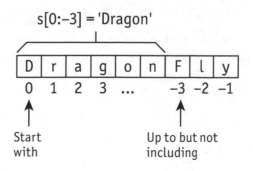

The next list of examples in this section, assume that the variable s is assigned the string data DragonFly.

```
s = 'DragonFly'
```

Here is a table that shows a list of examples and what they produce:

EXAMPLE	DESCRIPTION	OUTPUT
s[0]	First character.	D
s[1]	Second character.	r
s[2]	Third character.	a
s[-1]	Last character.	y
s[-2]	Next to last ("second to last") character.	l
s[-3]	Third to last character.	F
s[0:6]	Gets characters starting with the first, up to but not including the 7th. Means the same as **s[:6]**.	Dragon
s[1:6]	Gets characters starting with the second, up to but not including the 7th.	ragon
s[:6]	Gets the first six characters; more specifically, it gets all characters from the beginning of the string up to but not including the seventh character (index number 6).	Dragon
s[-3:]	Gets the last three characters; more specifically, it gets characters starting with the third-to-last character, F, and onward to the end of the string.	Fly

String/Number Conversions

Chapter 3, "Your First Programs," described how strings can be converted to numeric form. This is important, because if a user enters a string such as **'33'**, you can use it for display purposes, but you can't perform arithmetic on it.

```
>>>3 + '33'        # ERROR! Type mismatch error!
```

An apparent exception is multiplication. You can (apparently) multiply a string by an integer; but this does not mean what you might think. Instead, it means to extend the string through repetition—a special operation enabled in Python.

```
>>>3 * '33'
'333333'
>>>4 * '1 1'
'1 11 11 11 1'
```

Remember that the **input** function returns a string, and conversion is necessary if you want to use the data to perform arithmetic. If so, convert to numeric by using **int** or **float**.

```
n = int(input('Enter a number: '))
print('Three times your number is', n * 3)
```

But there's a flip side. Suppose you have a number, and you want to analyze it as a text string. For example, you might want to count the occurrences of a certain digit. The solution is to use a **str** conversion, which converts to string format. Here's an example:

```
n = 800555
s = str(n)
print('This string is', len(s), 'characters long.')
```

The effect of **str** in this case is to take the numeric value 800555 as input and produce "800555", a digit string consisting of six characters.

You can then apply string-handling functions and operations, such as getting the length of the string with the **len** function. You can also access individual digit characters.

```
print('The first two characters are', s[:2])
print('The last three characters are', s[-3:])
```

These statements print the following:

```
The first two characters are 80
The last three characters are 555
```

Example 7.1. *Count Trailing Zeros*

In Chapter 2, "A Python Safari: Numbers," I showed how Python, with its "infinite integer" capability, can calculate factorials that are immense. A fun game to play with factorials is to deduce, mathematically, how many trailing zeros such a number has.

But when you get to very large factorials (100 factorial has 24 trailing zeros) it becomes tedious to count trailing zeros by hand. Instead, let's have Python do it.

Note ▶ This example shows how to count trailing zeros one at a time. Example 7.2 shows a faster way of doing the same thing by using the **strip** method. Example 7.1 is useful, however, for demonstrating how to index individual characters.

◀ Note

This example converts a large number into a string and then counts occurrences of the digit character 0 at the end of the string.

```
Zeros.py

prod = 1
for i in range(1, 51):  # For 1 to 50 inclusive,
    prod = prod * i
s = str(prod)    # Convert factorial to string s
n = len(s)       # n = length of string s
z = 0
while n > 0 and s[n - 1] == '0':
    z = z + 1
    n = n - 1
print('50! is', s)
print('The number of trailing zeros is', z)
```

Enter these statements into a plain-text file and save it as `zeros.py`. Then open it from within the interactive environment and choose the Run Module command. If you correctly entered the program, you should get this output:

```
50! is 30414093201713378043612608166064768844377641568960
512000000000000
The number of trailing zeros is 12
```

Note that 50! is mathematical notation that means the factorial of the number 50, a rather large number by human standards.

How It Works

The first thing the program does is calculate factorials as we did in an earlier chapter. Remember that the meaning of 50 factorial is as follows:

```
50! = 1 * 2 * 3 *...* 50
```

You should also remember that the **range** keyword generates a list of values, starting with the *start* argument, up to but not including the *end* argument.

Therefore, **range(1, 51)** generates the following:

```
[1, 2, 3, 4,...50]
```

All the loop has to do, then, is to multiply these numbers together. The variable `prod` accumulates the product.

The next few lines do some much-needed initialization, including setting the initial count of zeros, which I call z, to 0.

```
s = str(prod)    # Convert factorial to string s
n = len(s)       # n = length of string s
z = 0
```

Now, what the second loop does is, in effect, to say, "Check to see if the number of remaining characters (n) is greater than 0, *and* if the character currently indexed by n-1 is a 0 character."

If both those conditions are true, first reduce n by 1 and then increase the count of zeros by 1. The effect is to start by accessing index number N-1, referring to the last character in the string. If this character exists and is 0, then up the count of zeros and move N one position to the left.

```
while n > 0 and s[n - 1] == '0':
    z = z + 1
    n = n - 1
```

I've engaged in some defensive programming here. If there isn't at least one character remaining, then s[n - 1] results in an out-of-range error—a possibility you want to avoid. The **while** condition tests the length of the string first.

Python uses "short circuit" logic. The first half of an **and** condition is tested, and if it's false, the second condition is never evaluated. The following figure illustrates how the two subconditions in this **and** condition are evaluated, one after the other:

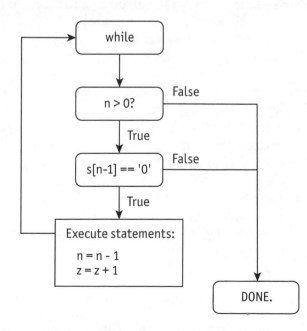

The point of this program is to use s[n-1] to access the last character. If this character is a zero numeral, that is, 0, then the loop continues. Each time through the loop, n is decreased by one, effectively moving s[n-1] one position to the left.

The purpose of the variable z is to count the number of successful times through the loop—the number of zeros at the end of the string. In the case of the string 3628800, you can see that z is increased two times before the loop exits, leaving z equal to 2.

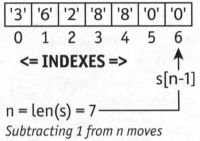

'3' '6' '2' '8' '8' '0' '0'
 0   1   2   3   4   5   6

<= INDEXES =>

s[n-1]

n = len(s) = 7

Subtracting 1 from n moves index to the left.

EXERCISES

Exercise 7.1.1. Rewrite all the number crunching to use combined assignment operations where possible. These include the operators +=, *=, and −=.

Exercise 7.1.2. Instead of calculating the factorial of 50 (notated as 50!), have it calculate the N factorial, where N is any integer greater than 0. Prompt the user for this value. Report both the result and the number of trailing zeros.

Exercise 7.1.3. Instead of using positive indexes to access the "last character" from within the loop, rewrite the loop so it uses negative indexes, such as −1, −2, etc. You can start with −1 and just subtract one number from it each time (for example, moving from −1 to −2), or you can calculate the index based on the value of z, which increases each time through the loop.

Exercise 7.1.4. Set up a loop around the whole program so that the computer keeps repeating the operation—asking for N and calculating the results—until the user enters 0. (Hint: The **break** keyword is helpful for breaking out of loops in these situations.)

Interlude

Python Characters vs. Python Strings

If you've programmed in C or C++, you're used to thinking of character and strings as different kinds of entities. You'd use double quotation marks to create a string and single quotation marks to refer to an individual character.

```
char my_str [] = "i am a string.";
my_str [0] = 'I';
```

For the C programmer, one of the obstacles to learning Python is that Python accepts both double and single quotation marks as meaning the same thing. The difference is mostly a matter of convenience.

But—and the importance of this principle can't be overstated—single characters are accessed in Python as strings of length equal to 1. For example, the following are valid statements in Python:

```
if my_str[1] == "A":
    print('Second char. is an "A".')
```

Does this equivalence—single characters are strings of length 1—cause confusion? Generally no. Python operators and functions consistently follow this principle. They all work on strings, not individual characters, although those strings may be of length 1.

Efficiency is another matter. The C family of languages treats individual characters not as strings but as numeric codes. In Chapter 8, you'll learn how to get the numeric code corresponding to any character, but in general, Python treats characters as substrings.

Because character access is a little less direct in Python, you do pay a small penalty in terms of execution speed. But with today's modern computers, this difference is small. Nonetheless, the need for super-efficiency is a reason that commercial software is typically written in C or C++.

Stripping for Fun and Profit

In addition to the indexing and splicing operations shown earlier, this chapter introduces three important methods unique to strings.

▶ **strip**, which applies to a string and returns another string that is stripped of trailing and leading characters (which are typically zeros or spaces)

▶ **split**, which applies to a string and returns a list of smaller strings

▶ **join**, which applies to a separator string, takes a list of strings as an argument, and returns one large string

This chapter also highlights the use of the **len** function, which returns the length of a string, list, or other collection.

Let's look at **strip** first. This method can be used to strip any trailing or leading character, but it's most commonly used on spaces. Suppose you have the following string:

```
king_str = '   Henry V   '
```

This has both leading and trailing spaces. To produce a stripped string, apply the **strip** method.

```
king_str = king_str.strip()
```

And here's what happens:

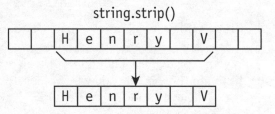

string.strip()

There is an internal space that is untouched; only trailing and leading spaces are stripped away. Here's the formal syntax:

new_string = *string*.**strip**(*chars*)

The *chars* is a string specifying which characters to strip. If *chars* is not specified, the default value is a "whitespace," which matches both blank spaces and tab characters ('\t').

Note that if *chars* is specified, the action of **strip** is to remove each and every instance of *any* character in *chars* that are trailing or following the rest of the text, regardless of what order they are found in. They don't necessarily have to appear together. Here's an example:

```
s = '***+++Hello**there+++*+**!'
s = s.strip('*+!')
```

Printing s now produces this:

```
Hello**there
```

Example 7.2.   *Count Zeros, Version 2*

This next example demonstrates how a use of the **strip** method can be used to make the previous example, Example 7.1, substantially shorter. The front end of the program is similar; it takes a number, calculates a factorial, and converts the result into a string.

But the second half of the program—counting the trailing zeros—comes down to one simple line of code, thanks to the **len** function and the **strip** method.

```
Zeros2.py

n = int(input('Enter number to calc. factorial for:'))
prod = 1
for i in range(1, n + 1):  # For 1 to n inclusive,
    prod = prod * i
s = str(prod)              # Convert fact. to string
z = len(s) - len(s.strip('0'))
print(n, 'factorial is', s)
print('The number of trailing zeros is', z)
```

How It Works

The main work of this program is done by a single statement, which shows how incredibly succinct and powerful Python can be.

```
z = len(s) - len(s.strip('0'))
```

Let's take the example of 10 factorial. Converted to a string, it looks like this:

```
'3628800'
```

This string, stripped of trailing 0 numerals, looks like this:

```
'36288'
```

Now it's only necessary to subtract the length of the second string from the first. This yields the correct answer, which is 2. Isn't that amazing?

EXERCISES

Exercise 7.2.1.   Put a **while** loop in the program that causes it to operate repeatedly until the user enters 0. Also, replace any assignment statements (=) with combined-op statements (*=, etc.) wherever possible.

Exercise 7.2.2. Can you use a similar technique to calculate the number of digits of precision in the default Python floating-point format? Try calculating 1/3 and getting the length of the resulting string. Finally, use a technique similar to that in Example 7.2 to determine the number of trailing 3 digits.

Let's Split: The split Method

The **split** method for strings is one of the most powerful weapons in the Python arsenal, especially when getting a line of input. Consider a typical task, such as getting three names.

```
line_str = input('Enter names of the members:')
```

Let's suppose the session goes as follows, with user input (as usual) highlighted in bold.

Enter names of the members: Tom Bob Joe

Now you have a single text string containing "Tom Bob Joe"—what can you do with it? The easiest way to evaluate it is to use the **split** method.

```
list_of_guys = line_str.split()
```

The result of this statement is to create list_of_guys as a list containing three strings.

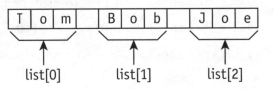

Now you have a list of strings, each of which contains one of the three names, while spaces (by default) are thrown out. More formally, here is the split syntax:

list = source_string.**split(***delims***)**

The **split** method generates a list. The *delims* is a string containing one or more delimiter characters, which are used to separate one substring from another. Only one delimiter may be specified, but it may be multiple characters long. By default, the delimiter is a whitespace, which matches any combination of blank spaces and/or tab characters.

Here's an example:

```
>>>s = 'A man, a plan, a canal, Panama!'
>>>a_list = s.split(',')
>>>for str1 in a_list:
    print(str1)
```

```
A man
 a plan
 a canal
 Panama!
```

These string operations interpret a comma as the separator between substrings, because the *delims* string contains a comma. The example may still seem incomplete, because three of these four substrings contain a leading space.

However, thanks to previous sections in this chapter, we know how to get rid of leading spaces: just strip each string before printing it.

```
>>>for str1 in a_list:
    print(str1.strip())
```

```
A man
a plan
a canal
Panama!
```

And now the display is perfect. (Another solution, which would work in this particular case, would be to specify a space and a comma [,] as the delimiter. This would require *both* a space and a comma between each item.)

Building Strings with Concatenation (+)

Python strings are immutable, as are certain other data types such as tuples. This has important practical implications. You cannot change part of a string. Suppose you have a string referred to by the variable named s.

```
s = 'hello'
```

We might like to change just the first character, capitalizing it. It would be convenient to do the following:

```
s[0] = 'H'   # Error! Not a legal assignment target
```

The problem is that you can't modify the contents of string. But the following is valid:

```
s = 'Hello'  # This is completely fine.
```

What's going on here? This may seem an inconsistency. But strings are immutable in Python.

The solution is to *assign a new string altogether*, which does the following: 1) it breaks the old association the variable had, if any, and 2) it associates the variable with completely new string data. The old string data itself is untouched, but now it's ignored! Here's an example:

```
s = 'Hello'
```

So, how do you build up completely new strings out of old? Concatenation, although not always the most efficient solution, comes to our aid. Here's an example:

```
s1 = 'Dragon'
s2 = 'Fly'
s3 = s1 + s2
print(s3)
```

This produces the following:

```
DragonFly
```

When you use concatenation, Python does not automatically insert a blank space. If you want to place two or more words into one string, you need to account for blank spaces yourself.

```
>>>s3 = s1 + ' ' + s2
>>>s3
'Dragon Fly'
```

What happens here is that s1, a blank space, and s2 are all used to create a new string. That string is then associated with the name s3.

You can also use a combined assignment-concatenation operator (+=).

```
s1 = 'live'
s1 += ' and let live'
```

This last line does the same as the following statements, which work because assignment, remember, builds a new string, breaks the old association that s1 had, and associates s1 with the new string.

```
s1 = 'live'
s1 = s1 + ' and let live'
```

This looks just like the **append** method for lists, but although the effect may be similar, the implementation is different.

Later in this chapter, I'll show how you can achieve more efficient results by using the **join** method. For now, however, remember that you can build up strings through concatenation.

```
my_string = ''
for i in range(5)
    my_string += 'hello '
```

In this example, it's necessary to start with an empty string so that it can appear on the right side of an assignment:

```
my_string = mystring + 'hello '
```

Example 7.3.   *Sort Words on a Line*

The following program is a variation on the sort program from Chapter 5. The difference is that in this case all the words are entered on a single line, which is then split into a list.

```
sort2.py
in_str = input('Enter items:')
a_list = in_str.split()
a_list.sort()
print('Here is the sorted list...')
for s in a_list:
    print(s)
```

This is an incredibly short program, thanks to Python's programming power. All it does is get a line of string input, split it into a list, sort the list, and print. That's it. Done. Amazing. Don't you wish everything in life were this easy?

Here's a sample session:

```
Enter items: John Paul George Ringo Brian
Here is the sorted list...
Brian
George
John
Paul
Ringo
```

How It Works

This example program is so incredibly simple, there's almost nothing to say about it. The interesting lines are the ones using the **split** and **sort** methods. The following uses **split**:

```
a_list = in_str.split()
```

The call to **split** creates a list consisting of the individual names John, Paul, and so on. Because the separator argument is omitted, the default value of a whitespace is used as a separator—that is, to interpret input. Here's how Python displays this list:

```
['John', 'Paul', 'George', 'Ringo', 'Brian']
```

Now the list needs to be sorted. This is a piece of cake, because all we have to do is call the **sort** method.

```
a_list.sort()
```

EXERCISES

Exercise 7.3.1.   Revise Example 7.3 so that instead of accepting a list of names separated by spaces, it accepts a list of names separated by commas. Note that applying the **split** method may result in strings that contain a leading space or two, so use the **strip** method on each element so that there are no leading spaces.

Exercise 7.3.2.   Revise Example 7.3 so that instead of printing the sorted results one to a line, it prints out all the results on a single line, items separated by a single space.

Exercise 7.3.3.   Revise the result of the previous exercise so that instead of printing the elements one at a time, it builds a single string. (Hint: Consult the previous section, "Building Strings with Concatenation (+).") Then print the entire line of output by using one **print** statement. Do you find runtime performance noticeably improves?

Exercise 7.3.4.   Instead of printing a list of items separated by spaces, as in the previous examples, use a comma-separated list. But do not print a comma after the last item. (Hint: use [:-1] or [:-2] to select everything but the final space or two. However, you should test the length of the string before applying such an operation, because an out-of-range index for an empty string will cause a runtime error.)

The join Method

Some of the statements in the previous section involved building strings, one substring or group of characters at a time. But Python provides the **join** method for much more efficiently joining groups of characters together to form a single string.

Assume that a_list is a list containing four strings.

```
>>>a_list = ['John', 'Paul', 'George', 'Ringo']
```

The **join** method can be used to generate a string that combines the elements of this list, separated by commas.

```
>>>', '.join(a_list)
'John, Paul, George, Ringo
```

The same method can also be used to generate a string that combines elements of this list, but this time separated by hyphens (-).

```
>>>'-'.join(a_list)
'John-Paul-George-Ringo
```

Here's an illustration of how the **join** method works:

'-'.join(a_list)

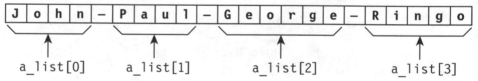

Here's a syntax summary for **join**. The following produces a new string, containing all the strings in the list:

separator_string.**join**(*list_of_strings*)

Remember that the **join** method is a method of strings, not lists, and it's applied to the separator string, which is usually no more than a character or two.

Here's another example:

```
>>>sep_string = ', '
>>>print(sep_string.join(a_list))
John, Paul, George, Ringo
```

Using a different set of separator characters, of course, changes the resulting string that's produced by the **join** method.

```
>>>sep_string = '---'
>>>print(sep_string.join(a_list))
John---Paul---George---Ringo
```

One of the conveniences of the **join** method is that it automatically avoids printing the separator characters at the end of the list. It knows enough to only print the separator characters *between* items, not at the end.

To print the results shown earlier, you'd need to do the following if you didn't have **join**...in particular, you'd need to trim off the last two characters from the result so that an extra comma and space do not get included.

```
s = ''
for thing in a_list:
    s = s + thing + ', '
if len(s) > 1:
    s = s[:-2]
```

But it's clearly much more efficient to use the **join** method, don't you think? Not only does it require fewer lines of code, but it's more efficient in terms of runtime performance.

```
s = ', '.join(a_list)
```

Isn't that far more convenient?

If we print the string, we get the following:

```
John, Paul, George, Ringo
```

Chapter 7   *Summary*

Here are the main points of Chapter 7:

▶ You can use either single quotation marks or double quotation marks to delineate a text string, but the quotation marks must match.

```
s1 = 'To be or not to be'
s2 = "That is the question"
```

▶ You can embed a single quotation mark in string delineated by double quotation marks, and vice versa.

```
s1 = 'My name is "Money." '
s2 = "They call me 'Mr. Bill.' "
```

▶ Remember that the quotation marks used for delineation are not part of the actual string. The previous examples, when printed, result in the following text being output:

```
My name is "Money."
They call me 'Mr. Bill.'
```

▶ Strings can be indexed just as lists can, and the index numbers run from 0 to N-1, where N is the length of the string. You cannot assign to parts of a string, however, because strings are immutable, which means they cannot be modified.

```
a_str [0] = 'H'       # Error! Assignment not allowed.
```

▶ But that last rule doesn't stop you from assigning directly to the string variable itself, which has the effect of associating the name with an entirely new string. Therefore, no string is being modified; rather, the variable is reassigned to refer to new data.

```
a_str = 'This is an utterly new string.'
```

▶ You can use *slicing* to produce parts of a string, just with lists. **[*start*: *end*]** produces a string beginning with the *start* index, up to but not including the *end* index.

▶ **[:*end*]** produces a slice up to but not including the *end* index.

▶ **[*start*:]** produces a slice beginning with the *start* index and including the remainder of the string.

▶ Strings can also be indexed with negative numbers. −1 refers to the last character, and −2 refers to the next-to-last character, and so on.

▶ Slicing also supports a third argument, *step*, which lets you specify how many characters at a time to move through the string. Use of this argument enables you to reverse a string as follows:

```
reversed_s = s[-1: :-1]
```

▶ The **strip** method produces a string without leading or trailing instances of a character, such as a blank space (which is the default character to strip).

```
king_str = '    Henry V    '
print(king_str.strip())
```

▶ The **split** method takes a long input string and returns each substring, as delineated by the specified characters (and again, a blank space is the default character).

```
s = input('Enter a list of names:')
a_list = s.split()
```

▶ The **join** method applies to a separator string, such as a comma (,) or hyphen (-). This separator is used to join the elements in a list.

```
s = '-'.join(a_list)
print(s)
```

This might produce output such as the following:

```
John-Paul-George-Ringo
```

Single-Character Ops

The previous chapter showed how easy it is to input, build, and pull apart strings in Python. This chapter is about manipulating individual characters.

Normally, you don't need to do this. The virtue of Python strings is how easy they are to operate on at a high level. But certain applications need to test and evaluate single characters. This chapter applies those techniques in specialized applications.

▶ "Case-free" comparisons

▶ A palindrome tester, with which you can test strings like "Madam, I'm Adam"

▶ Encryption and decryption of secret messages

Naming Conventions in This Chapter

As I mentioned in Chapter 2, Python lets you use any variable name (subject to very few limitations, such as having to start with a letter or underscore) with any data. Unfortunately, because there are no declarations, there's no way to look up the data type for any variable except by using the **type** function. (One good place to use it is when you are in IDLE, the interactive environment.)

That's why all through this book, I've tried to stick to consistent naming conventions to help make the code more readable. The following are conventions especially relevant to this chapter:

NAMING PATTERN	DATA TYPE
*xxx*_str; also or variations on s such as s, s1, s2, etc.	A Python string.

▼ *continued on next page*

147

NAMING PATTERN	DATA TYPE
*xxx*_ch	A single-character Python string. There is no difference between such strings and longer ones, except length. But the difference is important in this chapter, because some functions are designed to work on strings of length 1.
*xxx*_list	A Python list. The lists in this chapter are all lists of strings.

Other variables, not covered by the previous conventions, are almost always used with integers.

Accessing Individual Characters (A Review)

First, let's review a basic principle from Chapter 6. There is no separate character type in Python; characters are simply one-length strings. For example, you can test a string, such as dog, as follows:

```
>>>s = 'dog'      # Assign a string value.
>>>s == 'dog'     # Test it.
True
```

Given that s contains the string 'dog', you can meaningfully test the first character by using indexing.

```
>>>s[0] == 'd'    # Test first character.
True
```

A character in Python is treated as a string of one length in size. This approach keeps things simple in Python. Indexing a string in Python does not produce a different data type (such as char in C or C++). A single character is represented in a string—it's just a string one character in length.

There are, however, cases in which you might want to translate an individual character into its ASCII character code (a numeric equivalent). Encryption of coded messages—as you'll see in the latter half of the chapter—is such a case.

Getting Help with String Methods

Python has so many functions and methods that apply to strings that it's hard to remember them all. Fortunately, the interactive environment provides a useful help system. To get a printout of all the functions and methods supported for Python strings, type the following at the prompt:

```
>>>help(str)
```

The resulting printout is a syntax summary, not a tutorial. You may want to try to look up these functions and methods in this book. You can get similar help for list functions and methods by typing the following:

```
>>>help(list)
```

In both cases, the help printouts will probably be much too long to display on one screen. But you can scroll the window up and down to view all the output.

Testing Uppercase vs. Lowercase

One of the most useful things you can do with a character is test its case. Is a character uppercase (for example, H) or lowercase (for example, h)? The following four methods are all Boolean, meaning they return either **True** or **False**. But although they are often used on single-character strings, they can be used on longer strings as well.

METHOD	BEHAVIOR
string.**isupper()**	Returns **True** if all letters in the string are uppercase letters and if there is at least one such letter. With a one-character string, this method just tests whether or not it is an uppercase letter.
string.**islower()**	Returns **True** if all letters in the string are lowercase letters and if there is at least one such letter. With a one-character string, this method just tests whether or not it is a lowercase letter.
string.**istitle()**	Returns **True** if the beginning of each word begins with a capital letter and if there is at least one such letter. With a one-character string, this method just tests whether or not it is an uppercase letter.
string.**isalpha()**	Returns **True** if every character in the string is alphabetical—that is, a letter. For a one-length string, obviously, this just tests the one character.

For example, the following statements test whether the fourth character in a string is an uppercase letter:

```
>>>s = 'TheBeatles'
>>>if s[3].isupper():
    print('Fourth char. is uppercase letter.')
```

```
Fourth char. is uppercase letter.
```

But the **istitle()** method, if applied to the whole string, TheBeatles, returns **False** because one of the uppercase letters (B) immediately follows a lowercase letter (e).

```
>>>s.istitle()
False
```

Both **isupper** and **islower** return **False** in this case, because the string TheBeatles does not consists of all uppercase or all lowercase letters.

```
>>>s.isupper()
False
>>>s.islower()
False
```

But testing the first character, of course, reveals that it is uppercase, as expected. Remember that indexing a string produces another string—but a shorter string of only character in this case.

```
>>>s[0].isupper()
True
```

Finally, here's an example of the **isalpha** method, which will become useful in an upcoming exercise. Calling **isalpha** returns **True** if all the characters in the string are alphabetic.

```
>>>s = 'Car'
>>>s.isalpha()
True
```

Converting Case of Letters

It's frequently useful to convert between uppercase and lowercase letters. These operations are more useful than you'd think. For example, what do you do if you want to perform a case-insensitive comparison? Remember that tests for equality use the double equal signs (==).

```
s1 = 'dog'          # Assignment (=)
s2 = 'Dog'
s1 == s2            # Test for equality (==)
False
```

The problem is, I wanted the comparison of s1 and s2 to match, because the letters were in fact the same—they just had a different case.

The solution is to convert both strings to all uppercase and *then* compare them. Here's an example:

```
s1.upper() == s2.upper()
True
```

Alternatively, you could convert both to lowercase and then compare.

```
s1.lower() == s2.lower()
True
```

Note, however, that the first technique (convert to upper) is strongly recommended because it works much more correctly with international character sets.

Here's a summary of what these two methods do:

METHOD	BEHAVIOR
string.**upper()**	Produces a new string formed by converting every character in the target *string* to uppercase if it's a letter. Nonletter characters are left as is.
string.**lower()**	Produces a new string formed by converting every character in the target *string* to lowercase if it's a letter. Nonletter characters are left as is.

Note that, as with the other methods, you can use it on a single-character string (that is, a string of length 1) or on larger strings.

8

Testing for Palindromes

Now we get to the fun part of the chapter. In the previous chapter, I featured a famous palindrome.

```
A man, a plan, a canal, Panama!
```

Here's another famous palindrome. It consists of the very first words that Adam said upon seeing Eve for the first time.

```
Madam, I'm Adam.
```

Do you see what's special about these sentences? They contain the same letters whether read backward and forward. If you ignore punctuation, capitalization, and internal spacing, a Palindromic string is equal to the reverse of itself.

A good test for string-handling functions is to prompt the user for a line of input and report whether or not a palindrome was entered.

You can do this with a simple two-step process:

1 Convert the input string into an intermediate string that is stripped of spaces and punctuation and in which all the letters are converted to all uppercase.

2 Write a test that compares the first half of the string to the last; if the string is equal to its own reversal, it is a Palindrome.

For example, take Adam's famous words to Eve ("Madam, I'm Adam") and then convert to uppercase.

```
MADAM, I'M ADAM
```

Then remove all nonletters. This produces the following:

```
MADAMIMADAM
```

It's then easy to test this string for being a palindrome.

Example 8.1.   *Convert Strings to All Caps*

In this example, we'll convert a string to all-uppercase form, with nonletters removed.

```
convert.py

input_str = input('Enter input string: ')
output_str = input_str.upper()
s = ''
for ch in output_str:
    if ch.isalpha():
        s = s + ch
print(s)
```

Here's a sample session. The output is a converted string. That string is one that we can test directly for being a palindrome, as I'll show in the next section.

```
Enter input string: Madam, I'm Adam
MADAMIMADAM
```

How It Works

This is a short program, with two tasks. The first is to convert all letters to uppercase.

```
output_str = input_str.upper()
```

The other task is the more challenging one because it's not directly supported by Python: we need to delete all nonletters from the string. You can't delete or insert characters directly because strings are immutable; they can't be changed.

But you can build an entirely new string by inspecting the contents of an old string and then either including that character or not.

When building a new string like this, it's usually necessary to start with an empty string:

```
s = ''
```

From within the loop, the string data referred to by the variable s is built up, one character at a time. Or, more accurately, a new string is created over and over, and each time the variable s is assigned to refer to this ever-growing amount of string data.

```
for ch in output_str:
    if ch.isalpha():
        s = s + ch
```

The following pseudocode summarizes what the loop does:

For each letter in output_str,

    If that letter is alphabetic,

        Place that letter onto the end of string s

If you examine the code, you'll see why s had to be initialized to an empty string. Consider the following statement, placed at the deepest level of this simple program:

```
s = s + ch
```

Do you see why s had to be initialized to an empty string? Because otherwise, in this innermost statement, s would appear on the right of the assignment without previously being set, and that would produce an error the first time Python attempted to execute this statement.

From now on I'll assume you understand this principle. Lists and strings (as well as other complex data types) have to be initialized to some value—even if it is an empty list or empty string—before they appear on the right of an assignment or are used in any other operation, such as the **append** method for lists.

Optimizing the Code

In the preceding section, the use of string concatenation (+) works perfectly well. But in general, it's better to use the **join** method to bring a series of strings together. In applications that build a string out of a great many small strings, it's possible to see a performance difference.

So, you'll want to get into the habit of preparing for a **join** operation by appending each string into a list and then calling the **join** method.

```
a_list = []
for ch in output_str:
    if ch.isalpha():
        a_list.append(ch)
s = ''.join(a_list)
```

This version is a line longer, so you might not think it worth the effort. But there are ways of making it more compact. The following two lines take advantage of list comprehension, the technique explained at length in Chapter 6. This works because strings, just like any collections, are iterables.

```
a_list = [ch for ch in output_str if ch.isalpha()]
s = ''.join(a_list)
```

That's the most compact version yet!

EXERCISES

Exercise 8.1.1.   This is a review question, to which you should already know the answer: strings are immutable. How, therefore, can we assign new values to s, which refers to string data?

Exercise 8.1.2.   Revise Example 8.1 to use combined assignment operators (+=, *=, etc.) wherever possible. Better yet, implement and test the "list comprehension" version described in the section "Optimizing the Code."

Example 8.2.   *Completing the Palindrome Test*

Utilizing the Python code in Example 8.1 as a starting point, it's now an easy matter to complete a program that tests an input string and returns **True** or **False** depending on whether or not it's a palindrome.

The strategy, remember, is to take an input string, convert the letters to all uppercase, and omit all the nonalphabetic characters. So this input string

```
Madam, I'm Adam.
```

...produces the following string after conversion:

```
MADAMIMADAM
```

Now, the final trick is to see if the string is equal to the reverse of itself. There are several ways to do this. I'm going to show you how Python makes this incredibly easy. But first, let's do it the obvious way: the way that a C or C++ programmer would solve the problem. Then I'll show the Python way.

The straightforward way is to compare the first and last characters, one at a time, and then move inward, comparing the second and second-to-last characters. Continue until you reach the middle.

With the string `"MADAMIMADAM"`, here's how the algorithm would proceed.

1 Compare the first letter to the last. Both are `"M"`.

2 Compare the second letter to the next-to-the-last letter. Both are `"A"`.

3 Compare the third letter to the third-to-the-last letter. Both are `"D"`.

Finally, when we reach the middle of the string, we stop. Also, if a mismatch is found, then the code can stop the comparisons immediately. But if all the comparisons check out, the string is a palindrome.

The following figure illustrates the first three comparisons out of the five needed:

Where is the correct stopping point? A little reflection suggests that the number of comparisons is exactly half the length, rounded down, because if the length is odd and there is an extra character in the middle of the string, that character is simply ignored.

Chapter 2 explained how double forward slashes (//) indicate integer division, which automatically rounds down. The number of comparisons we need to do is

```
len(string) // 2
```

Here's another example. The string RACECAR is a palindrome, which can be established by performing comparisons between letters at the two ends. Because the length of the string is 7, the number of comparisons needed is 7//2, equal to 3.

We can now write the code for the Palindrome-testing program.

```
palin.py

    # From Example 8.1: converts to all upper.

    input_str = input('Enter input string: ')
    my_str = input_str.upper()
    a_list = [ch for ch in my_str if ch.isalpha()]
    s = ''.join(a_list)

    # This part is NEW. Tests for matching letters.

    is_palin = True    # Assume True until proven false.
    for i in range(len(s)//2):
        if s[i] != s[-i-1]:  # If mismatch,
            is_palin = False

    if is_palin:
        print('String is a palindrome.')
    else:
        print('String is NOT a palindrome.')
```

How It Works

The heart of the program is the loop that tests for a mismatch between a character near the front and a character near the end. If there is a mismatch, it breaks and sets the Boolean condition (is_palin) to **False**.

```
    if s[i] != s[-i-1]:  # If mismatch,
```

The starting position, s, is 0. The effect of this loop is therefore as follows:

1 Compare s[0] to s[-1].

2 Compare s[1] to s[-2].

3 Compare s[2] to s[-3].

4 And so on.

The following figure shows how this works with the palindromic string RACECAR:

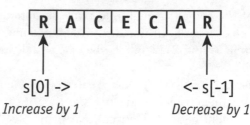

s[0] ->   <- s[-1]

Increase by 1   *Decrease by 1*

Optimizing the Code

Now I'm going to explain the more efficient way of testing a palindromic string, the Python way! You can use the slicing syntax to specify the exact reversal of a string. This use of slicing syntax deliberately omits the second argument.

```
rev_str = a_str[-1::-1]
```

You might recall from Chapter 7, "Python Strings," that there are up to three arguments to the slicing syntax.

▶ The first argument specifies the starting point. A starting point of –1 means to start with the last character of the string.

▶ The second argument is omitted in this case, which means to continue as long as possible (that is, there is no stopping point except running out of characters).

▶ The third argument is the *step* argument, which determines which character to get next. A step value of –1 means to move backward through the string.

Some testing of this syntax should convince you that it works.

```
>>>'dog'[-1::-1]
'god'
>>>'Dog backwards is goD'[-1::-1]
'Dog si sdrawkcab goD'
>>>'ABC'[-1::-1]
'CBA'
```

So, to test whether a string is its own reversal, all you need is the following statement, which replaces the **for** loop:

```
is_palin = (s == s[-1::-1])
```

EXERCISES

Exercise 8.2.1. A general rule of good programming is to never execute more statements than you need to. Once a mismatch is found—that is to say, one of the comparisons found two characters not equal to each other—the loop can quit early. Utilize this principle to make the program more efficient at run time. (Hint: Remember what the **break** statement does.)

Exercise 8.2.2.   Python was created with the assumption that small increases in runtime efficiency are not significant, but it's not a bad idea to write more efficient code just on general principle. If you look at the second loop, it appears to calculate the limit of the range, `len(s)//2`, over and over. Revise the program so as to guarantee that this number is never calculated more than once.

Exercise 8.2.3.   Revise the program so that it runs any number of times, quitting execution only when the user enters an empty string—that is, presses Enter without typing any input.

Interlude

Famous Palindromes

It's fun to develop new palindromes, although it takes a lot of trial and error. The programs presented in this chapter can help, by enabling you to quickly test strings. This chapter has featured several of the better known palindromes.

The first one describes the presidency of Teddy Roosevelt, while the second one may be a quote from the Garden of Eden.

```
A man, a plan, a canal, Panama!
Madam, I'm Adam.
Racecar.
```

The word *racecar* is one of a number of one-word palindromes. This, in turn, led me to create a silly one of my own.

```
I'm a racecar, Ami!
```

Here are some other palindromes, starting with one of the most famous of all. Suggestive of what Napoleon might have said, it may be the most famous one in English (although Napoleon was French).

```
Able was I ere I saw Elba.
Amore, Roma.
A Toyota's a Toyota.
Are we not drawn onward to new era?
A slut nixes sex in Tulsa.
Wow, Bob, wow!
```

Converting to ASCII Code

Now we're going to switch to an exciting subject: techniques for encrypting (*encoding*) and decrypting (*decoding*) a string.

The simple techniques presented here would be easy for the CIA and NSA to crack. But no matter which technique you use to encrypt messages, your programming language needs to examine the mathematical value of individual characters.

You've probably read somewhere that a computer can store only numbers. More specifically, it can only store 1s and 0s. This is true, but the binary number system enables a computer to use patterns of 1s and 0s to represent much larger numbers. Decimal numbers (such as 27 or 99) are typically used for input and output.

Note ▶ It's easy to write programs that convert back and forth between binary and decimal representation. So don't worry about the difference.

◀ Note

How are letters, punctuation, and numerals represented inside a computer? Computers use a special coding system for this purpose called ASCII. Python actually uses Unicode, which is an extended coding system used for internationalization. But it's a superset of ASCII, and the principles are roughly the same.

The system translates back and forth between Unicode, which is numeric, and printable characters, which can actually be displayed on the screen. To get a code for a character, use the Python **ord** function.

ord(_one_char_string_**)**

This function takes one argument, _one_char_string_, which must be a string, but it must have a length of exactly one character. The function produces an integer value.

For example, this function can be used to produce the numeric codes for the first five letters. Consider the following loop:

```
for ch in 'abcde':
    n = ord(ch)
    print(ch, n)
```

This loop applies the **ord** function to each of the letters *abcde* and then prints the resulting value next to the letter itself. Here are the results:

```
a 97
b 98
```

```
c  99
d  100
e  101
```

If you look closely at this list, you should see an obvious pattern. If you don't see it right away, then you're thinking too hard. The pattern is just that these numbers are all in sequence.

When, later, we devise an encryption system, that fact is going to be important.

You can use almost identical code to list the values of the first few capital letters. Use a loop identical to the one just shown, except instead of using *abcde*, use *ABCDE*. The results are as follows:

```
A  65
B  66
C  67
D  68
E  69
```

There are several things you can count on with regard to character code:

▶ The codes for lowercase letters are in a sequence, from *a* to *z*.

▶ The codes for uppercase letters are in a sequence, from *A* to *Z*.

▶ Other characters, such as punctuation, are not part of either sequence.

Converting ASCII to Character

Python supports an equally simple function for converting ASCII numeric codes back to character form.

chr(*numeric_code* **)**

This function produces a string of length 1, containing the character corresponding to *numeric_code*.

For example, in the previous section, we learned that the ASCII character code for the letter *A* is 65. Therefore, applying the chr function to the number 65 should produce an *A*.

From within the interactive environment, enter **char(65)**:

```
>>>chr(65)
'A'
```

It's clear what this does. You can see, therefore, that it's easy to go back and forth between a character and the numeric value that represents it inside the computer.

You should be able to see the usefulness of that in the next section. By the way, **ord** and **chr** are *inverses* of each other, so you should be able to guess what the following does, even before looking at the results:

```
>>>chr(ord('B'))
'B'
```

Example 8.3. *Encode Strings*

One of the simplest encoding schemes is to move each letter one position to the right, replace all *A*s with *B*s, all *B*s with *C*s, and so on. Finally, *Z* is replaced with *A*...in the case of *Z*, we go "off the edge" and return to the beginning of the alphabet.

You can think of this process conceptually as follows:

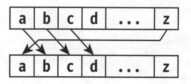

What about spaces and punctuation? Let's leave those unchanged. That gives us exactly 52 cases to worry about, specifically, the 26 uppercase letters and the 26 lowercase letters, each of which has its own unique code.

Because Python strings are immutable, the encrypted string must be built up one character at a time.

Handling 52 separate cases is theoretically possible, but it makes for incredibly tedious programming. You could, if you wanted, use **if** and **elif** to examine these 52 cases.

```
if old_str[i] == 'a':
    s += 'b'
elif old_str[i] == 'b':
    s += 'c'
...
```

Clearly, this is going to be too much work. But instead of considering 52 separate cases, we have to consider only three: the character is an uppercase letter, a lowercase letter, or neither. Each such case requires a separate action involving the ord and chr functions.

The following program shows how:

```code.py
input_str = input('Enter string to encode: ')
a_list = []
for ch in input_str:
    n = ord(ch) + 1
    if ch.isupper() and n > ord('Z'):
        n -= 26
    elif ch.islower() and n > ord('z'):
        n -= 26
    if ch.isalpha():
        a_list.append(chr(n))
    else:
        a_list.append(ch)
s = ''.join(a_list)
print('Coded string is', s)
```

As usual, you can implement the program by saving in a text file called code.py. Then, from within the interactive environment, load the file and then choose the Run Module command. Here is a sample session.

```
Enter string to encode: I am HAL.
J bn IBM.
```

How It Works

The basic operation of this program is very simple, but it has to handle some exceptions. Here's the basic idea:

> *For each letter in the input string:*
>   *Convert character to numeric form.*
>   *Add 1 to this number.*
>   *Convert the resulting number back to a character.*

Because—as I noted earlier—all the uppercase letters are in numeric sequence and all the lowercase letters are in numeric sequence, the most basic operation of this program is just to translate each letter to the next in the sequence.

But there are some exceptions.

First, the encryption technique leaves spaces and other nonletter characters alone: they are simply transferred into the output string "as is." Not all
encryption techniques do that, by the way. But it makes for more readable
output.

Another exception is what to do with letters z and Z. These letters are transformed into a and A, respectively. An easy way to do that is to subtract 26, so
that when 1 is added to the ASCII code of z or Z, it yields a number one past
the normal sequence of uppercase and lowercase letters. Subtracting 26 pushes
the number back to the beginning, so to speak.

I could have handled numbers greater than z and Z as unique cases, but
as you'll see when doing some of the exercises, subtracting 26 creates a more
general solution. It solves the problem even when letters are shifted by more
than one position.

EXERCISES

Exercise 8.3.1. Example 8.3 uses the combined assignment-action operators, and
that will be the standard practice for the rest of the book. Purely as an exercise, revise these statements so they just use standard addition and subtraction
operators (+, −, and =).

Exercise 8.3.2. Revise the example so that the user can enter any shift number
they choose, not just the number 1. The way the code is written now ought to
make this very easy to do. For example, if the user enters 2, each letter should
be transformed two positions in the alphabet, not one.

Exercise 8.3.3. Implement Exercise 8.3.2, but do it in a way such that integers
larger than 25 are converted to the range 0 to 24. The easiest way to do this
is to use remainder, or modular division, carried about the modular division
operator, %.

Exercise 8.3.4. Revise the example so that inside the loop, the first thing the
code does is to test whether a character is alphabetic or not. If it isn't, then
simply add the character onto the end of the output string and go to the next
letter in the input string. This should achieve precisely the same results, but
simply do things in a slightly different order. Is this order more efficient or
less? Do you expect to see any difference in execution speed?

Interlude

The Art of Cryptography

The encryption scheme presented in this chapter is about as simple a "code," or cypher, as exists. Even with the aid of a computer or other tools, an expert from the CIA or NSA could probably crack this code fairly easily. Consider the following coded message:

    `J bn pof xip mpwfe upp xfmm, opu xjtfmz.`

A cryptography expert would start by supposing that *J* is actually *I*, since among one-letter words, *I* is the most common, especially as it appears at the beginning of a sentence. Next, an expert would observe that *upp* stands for a three-letter word in which one letter is followed by two copies of some other letter. Among such words, *too* is probably the most common. Finally, and this is a little more of a stretch, *f* is the most common of the remaining letters and therefore a good candidate for representing *e*.

Making all these substitutions, which are reasonable guesses, gets us this far:

    I bn **ooe** xi**o** m**o**wee **too** xemm, **oo**t xi**te**mz.

This still reads cryptically to most people (pun intended), but at this point an expert is likely to seize on an important observation. These substitutions, which look promising, all have one thing in common: the coded letters differ from their substitutions by the same distance, specifically, just one position in the alphabet. Filling in the rest of the letters according to this pattern produces the entirely decoded string.

    I am one who loved too well, not wisely.

Most forms of cryptography used professionally are much more sophisticated. For example, the ENIGMA machine developed by the Germans in World War II used a series of gears that associated each character in the message with a different "delta" so that there was no obvious connection between the way one letter was transformed and the next. At first the British thought this created the uncrackable code. But Alan Turing, and his associates at Bletchley Park, eventually found a way.

Example 8.4.   *Decode Strings*

This next program just reverses the encryption process that was used in Example 8.3.

```
decode.py
input_str = input('Enter string to decode: ')
a_list = []
for ch in input_str:
    n = ord(ch) - 1
    if ch.isupper() and n < ord('A'):
        n += 26
    if ch.isalpha():
        a_list.append(chr(n))
    else:
        a_list.append(ch)
s = ''.join(a_list)
print('Coded string is', s)
```

Here is a sample session, using the output from Example 8.3. If all goes well, this should produce the original input string.

```
Enter string to decode: J bn IBM.
I am HAL.
```

How It Works

This example essentially does everything that Example 8.3 does, but does it in reverse. Instead of adding 1 to the ASCII code of a letter—thereby advancing *a* to *b*, for example—this program subtracts 1 from the ASCII code, and then if the resulting ASCII code is less than the code for *a* or *A*, as appropriate, it adjusts the code number upward by 26 rather than downward.

It's worth asking yourself if Examples 8.3 and 8.4 really need to be separate programs. If you revise these examples so that the "delta," or change factor, can be any number between 1 and 25, then ask yourself what the difference is between subtracting 1 (replacing *b* with *a*) and adding 25. The latter operation would add 25 but then subtract 26 and so ends up having the same effect.

EXERCISES

Exercise 8.4.1. Revise Example 8.4 so that it takes any "delta" between 1 and 25. You can either restrict user input, reprompt until the user enters a valid number, or use modular division to get a number in the correct range.

Exercise 8.4.2. Assume that you accept the argument that subtracting 1 produces the same result as adding by 25. In that case, revise Example 8.3 (the previous example) so that it can either "encode" or "decode" depending on the user's command.

Exercise 8.4.3. After doing the previous exercise, alter the program so that it operates over and over (each time either coding or encoding) until the user indicates that the program should exit by entering an empty string.

Chapter 8   *Summary*

Here are the main points of Chapter 8:

▶ The **ord()** function converts a one-length string, containing a single character, into its corresponding ASCII code, an integer.

```
n = ord('A')
```

▶ The **chr()** function is the inverse of **ord()**. It takes a numeric code and produces a one-character string containing the character corresponding to that code.

```
print(n, 'corresponds to', chr(n))
```

▶ The **upper** and **lower** methods convert an entire string to uppercase and lowercase letters, respectively. When **upper** is used on a string with multiple characters, alphabetic characters are converted to uppercase, while non-alphabetical characters are left alone. The **lower** method works in a similar way, except that it converts letter characters to lowercase. In either case, a new string is produced from the old one.

▶ The **isalpha** function returns **True** if every character in a string is an alphabetic character.

▶ The **isupper** function returns **True** if every letter in a string is uppercase and there is at least one letter.

▶ The **islower** function returns **True** if every letter in a string is lowercase and there is at least one letter.

▶ Although it is permissible to use repeated string concatenation to build new strings, it's usually better to build up a list of substrings—even if they are only one character in length each—and then apply the **join** method.

▶ Remember that a great deal can be done with Python slicing syntax, both for lists and for strings. In particular, use of the third argument—the **step** argument—can be used to completely reverse a string.

```
reversed_str = a_str[-1::-1]
```

Advanced Function Techniques

The concept of functions is fundamental and was first introduced in Chapter 3, "Your First Programs." But Python provides a number of advanced features used with functions. They make for simpler, easier, and more efficient programs.

By the end of this chapter, we'll have explored how to use Python to play one of the most popular casino games in the world (without taking your money, however).

This chapter includes the following functional features:

▶ Multiple arguments

▶ Named arguments

▶ Default arguments

▶ Imported functions

Multiple Arguments

Chapter 3 introduced the concept of passing multiple arguments, so if you're comfortable with the concept, you can skip to the next section.

The ability to pass more than one argument is universal among programming languages. You can have as many arguments as you want—the only basic rule being that the number of arguments in a function definition must (as a general rule) match the number of argument values during a call.

```
function_name(argument, argument,...):
    indented_statements
```

The *arguments* are separated by commas if there is more than one.

A simple example is a function that returns the average of two numbers that are input and returns the result in floating-point format.

```
>>>def avg(a, b):
    return (a + b) / 2
>>>
```

Having entered this function definition, you can then call it any number of times.

```
>>>avg(1, 9)
5.0
>>>avg(100, 201)
150.5
```

You can even include a call to the function as part of a larger expression, although you can do this only because it returns a numeric value. (Functions that do not explicitly return a value return the special value **None** by default.)

```
>>>100 + avg(4, 5)
104.5
```

Because there are two arguments, a and b, each call to the avg function must include two argument values. By default, the values are passed to a and b in that order, as shown in the following figure:

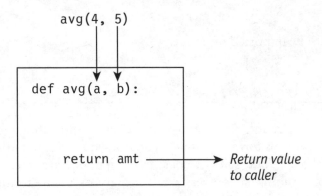

Returning More Than One Value

A more difficult question is this: what if I want to give the function the ability to permanently change the value of a variable passed to it?

The short answer is you can't. You can accomplish the same objective, however, even by returning a series of values separated by a comma.

There is no "pass by reference" in the sense of BASIC, Fortran, C++, or any number of other languages. Here's a simple example:

```
def double_it(n):
    n = n * 2


n = 5
double_it(n)
print('The value of n=5 after "doubling":', n)
```

These statements should show the value n as now containing 10, but they don't. Instead, n still has the value 5, which is the same value it had to begin with.

```
The value of n=5 after "doubling": 5
```

What happened? When n was passed to the function, the function got a reference to 5, so in a sense, n is a reference variable. But as with all Python assignments, when you assign new data to a variable, the association with old data is broken, so the local copy of n no longer affects the variable n outside the function.

```
n = n * 2
```

Python doesn't enable you to create a simple "output" parameter. Fortunately, such output parameters are not necessary; you can always return multiple values.

To pass back multiple return values, just place a series of comma-separated values after a **return** statement.

return *value, value, ...*

There's no limit to the number of values you can return, but the caller of the function must expect all these values. For example, we can define a function that returns three values.

```
def func(n):
    return n, n+10, n+20
```

Because the function, func, returns three values, you need to assign its return value to a series of comma-separated variables. Alternatively, you can assign these values to a tuple of size 3.

```
a, b, c = func(2)
print(a, b, c)
```

The result of these statements is

```
2 12 22
```

6

In this case, the variables a, b, and c all become, in effect, output parameters. In effect, then, you can have a Python function take as many inputs as needed and pass back as many outputs as needed. You can think of it this way:

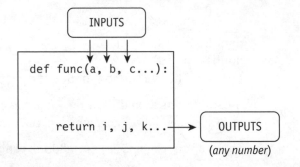

Passing and Modifying Lists

Interlude

If you've programmed in another language such as C++, the lack of a true in/out parameter (reference argument) may strike you as a frustrating limitation. There are several ways around this, however—one of them being the ability to return multiple values.

Another solution is to put your in/out parameters in a list. Here's an example:

```
def double_it(list_arg):
    list_arg[0] *= 2

a = [5]
print('Value before is:', a[0])
double_it(a)
print('Value after is:', a[0])
```

These statements, when executed, produce the following output:

```
Value before is 5
Value after is 10
```

Doing things this way—placing a value in a one-element list and then passing the list—is slightly more work, but it does make the argument into a true in/out parameter. This example works because, first, Python lists are *mutable* (changeable) and because, second, there's no reassignment of the list variable itself.

You also get all the flexibility that comes with Python lists. You can use a list to specify as many "outputs" as you want, even adding to the size of the list that was passed. Here's an example:

```
def double_it(list_arg):
    list_arg.append(1)
    list_arg.append(2)
```

▼ continued

Interlude

This function, when it returns, will append 1 and 2 onto the end of whatever list you passed to it. But note that the following does not work—assuming what you want to do is to enable the function to effectively pass new values back to the caller.

```
def double_it(list_arg):
    list_arg = list_arg + [1, 2]   # Does not work!
```

What is wrong with this function? The problem is that it uses direct assignment to the list variable itself. And when such an assignment occurs in Python, what happens is that 1) a new list is created from the expression on the right, and 2) the argument name—list_arg in this case—is associated with a completely new list. And that means it no longer has a connection to the list that was passed to the function.

You can, however, assign to any list element, as shown earlier, and the change will be recognized. Just make sure the index is not out of range.

```
if len(list_arg) > 2:
    list_arg[2] = 555
```

And you can change any *or all* the values in a list if you want, by using slicing. This is where the notation **[:]** comes in handy; use it to represent the "slice" that contains the entire list. The following statement succeeds in copying new information to the existing list. This statement does not re-assign the variable name list_arg to a whole new list; instead, it changes the individual values "in place" but continues to refer to the same list.

```
list_arg[:] = [1, 2, 3]    # Replace entire list
                           # by copying new values
```

This is a subtle but important distinction. The previous statement manages to permanently alter data from within a function, where the following does not:

```
list_arg = [1, 2, 3]       # list_arg no longer refers
                           # the original list!
```

But remember this caveat: Python does not check the type of an argument when you define or call a function. If you use incompatible types, Python raises an error during execution. Simply put, if the function expects a list argument, you better pass a list argument.

Remember, also, that Python raises an error whenever you use out-of-range indexes, so be careful how you index. Again, testing a list with the **len** function is helpful as a way of ensuring that your indexes won't be out of range, if you're in any doubt.

6

Example 9.1.   *Difference and Sum of Two Points*

The following program highlights a function that takes several inputs and passes back two outputs: the first output being the distance between two points and the second being the sum. It also features an output function, `get_point`, that gets two inputs (from the end user) and returns two outputs.

```
def main():
    x1, y1 = get_point()
    x2, y2 = get_point()
    dist, sum = calc_pts(x1, y1, x2, y2)
    print('The distance between points is:', dist)
    print('The sum of the points is:', sum)

def get_point():
    s = input('Enter point in "x, y" format:')
    a_list = s.split(',')
    a = int(a_list[0].strip())
    b = int(a_list[1].strip())
    return a, b

def calc_pts(x1, y1, x2, y2):
    dist1 = y2 - y1
    dist2 = x2 - x1
    dist = (dist1 ** 2 + dist2 ** 2) ** 0.5
    sum = [x1 + x2, y1 + y2]
    return dist, sum

main()
```

Here is a sample session:

```
Enter point in "x, y" format: 1, 1
Enter point in "x, y" format: 4, 5
The distance between points is 5.0
The sum of the points is [5, 6]
```

How It Works

The main function makes two calls to `get_points`. Each call prompts the user to enter a point in the form "x, y." The `get_points` function uses a combination of the **split** method, which divides the string input into two strings;

and **strip,** which strips away leading and trailing spaces. Chapter 7, "Python Strings," introduced these methods.

The result is that get_points returns two coordinates as a series of values.

```
a_list = s.split(',')
a = int(a_list[0].strip())
b = int(a_list[1].strip())
return a, b
```

Therefore, calling this function twice produces a total of four coordinates: x1, x2, y1, and y2. All four are passed to the calc_pts function to calculate these two answers:

▶ Distance, specifically, the linear distance between the points, calculated by the Pythagorean distance formula

▶ The sum of the two points, which is a third point that contains x1 + x2 as its x coordinate and y1 + y2 as its y coordinate

The main function then prints the results.

Note that the calc_pt function returns two values, each being a different kind of data: a simple number (the distance) and a list of two numbers. No problem arises as long as the caller of the function handles each of the return values (a number and a list) correctly.

EXERCISES

Exercise 9.1.1. Revise Example 9.1 so that it accepts point input in the format "(x, y)" as well as "x, y." Also modify the main function so that it outputs the sum as a point in the form "(x, y)."

Exercise 9.1.2. Write a program that prompts for four numbers and then calls a function to determine both the sum and the average. Finally, print the sum and average.

Exercise 9.1.3. Write a function that takes a list of numbers of any size and then returns the sum as well as the average and returns these two values. Then write a main function that prompts for a series of values, puts them in the list, and calls the function.

Arguments by Name

Python supports a couple of argument-passing techniques used widely in Python built-in functions. You can also use them in your own functions.

The first technique is named arguments, in other words, arguments specified by name. You've seen this used with the **print** function.

```
print(10, 20, 30, 40, sep='-', end='!\n')
```

This prints

```
10-20-30-40!
```

The **sep** and **end** arguments are special because they're named during the function call. Such named arguments should be specified at the end of the argument list.

Calls to your own Python functions can use the same technique. Consider the following function definition:

```
def expo(a, b, e):
    return a * (b**e)
```

You can call this function normally, with "positional arguments"—that is, the ordinary way, without naming the arguments during the call.

```
expo(1, 2, 5)
```

This prints 2 raised to the 5th power.

```
32
```

But you can also name arguments. Remember that such named arguments must appear after any other arguments appear. Arguments passed the usual way are considered *positional arguments*.

```
expo(1, e=3, b=2)
```

Because the first argument is not named during this call, it is assigned by position. Therefore, the value 1 gets passed as the "a" argument. The values e and b are assigned out of order, and that isn't a problem, because they are named. This function call returns the value 8.

You can pass every argument by name, if you choose. In that case, you can pass all the arguments in any order at all.

```
expo(b = 2, e = 3, a = 1)
```

The complete procedure, by the way, is this: named assignments are performed first. Remaining argument values are then paired with remaining function arguments in the order they appear.

Default Arguments

The second advanced technique for passing arguments requires changes to the function definition. Instead of listing an argument by just using a name, you can give an argument in the form *arg* = *default_value*. Here's a simple example:

```
def repeat_s(a_str, n = 1):
    for i in range(n):
        print(a_str)
```

This function prints the string argument n times. Within the interactive environment, you might use it this way:

```
>>>repeat_s('Hello', 3)
Hello
Hello
Hello
```

But the second argument, n, has a default value, 1, specified in the function definition itself. That argument may be omitted in a function call. If it is, it takes on the default value. For example, you could enter the following in the interactive environment:

```
>>>repeat_s('Hello')
Hello
```

Default arguments must be placed at the end of the list of arguments in the definition.

These two techniques are often used together but are distinct. It's easy to get them confused. To keep them separate, remember that

▸ During a function call, an argument may be omitted if the argument has a default value in the function definition, using the form *arg* = *default_value*.

```
def func(x = 0, y = 0):
        # Definition follows

func()  # Use default values for both x and y.
```

▸ During a function call, "call by name" passes an argument by naming it, using *arg* = *value*. The *value* is assigned to the named argument rather than by position.

```
func(y = 10.5)  # x gets default val, y gets 10.5.
```

The **print** function has arguments that are referred to by name as well as having default values. For example, **print** has default values you've already seen, of **sep=' '** and **end='\ n'**. These default values are a blank space and a newline, respectively.

Example 9.2. *Adding Machine*

One of the simplest applications just adds a series of numbers. The only tricky part is how does the end user indicate that he or she wants to terminate the series of inputs?

An obvious approach is to let the user press Enter, with no input, to terminate entries. So far, so good, but if input is handled by a "get number" function, then it really needs to pass back two pieces of information: 1) the number entered by the user, and 2) whether the user has entered the end-the-series indicator.

```
adding.py
def main():
    amt = 0
    while True:
        b, n = get_num()
        if not b:
            break
        amt += n
    print('The total is', amt)

def get_num(num = 0.0):
    s = input('Input number (ENTER to quit): ')
    if not s:
        return False, num
    else:
        return True, float(s)
main()
```

How It Works

This example really does nothing special except for having a function passing back two pieces of information, which it does through its **return** statement.

```
if not s:
    return False, 0.0
else:
    return True, float(s)
```

The first value passed back is Boolean; it is **True** if and only if a non-zero-length string was entered by the user. If this value is **False** (meaning the user entered a zero-length string), the caller stores **False** in the variable name b, which in turn causes the function to exit.

```
b, n = get_num()
if not b:
    break
```

Alternatively, if the user *does* enter a number, the number entered is stored in the variable named n.

Note that the get_num function takes an argument, num, which has a default value of 0.0. Because the argument is omitted, 0.0 is assumed. This is the number passed back if the user enters an empty string. (However, that value is never actually used in this program.)

Here's a sample session:

```
Input number (ENTER to quit): -1.5
Input number (ENTER to quit): 2.5
Input number (ENTER to quit): 100
Input number (ENTER to quit):
The total is 101.0
```

Optimizing the Code

Although it's useful to be able to pass back multiple values (which was the point of this example), a Python function can always pass back the special value **None** if you choose. This value can then be used as the exit code rather than have to pass that code back in a separate value. Using this approach, you could revise the example as follows:

```
def main():
    amt = 0.0
    while True:
        x = get_num()
        if x is None:
            break
        amt += x
    print('The total is', amt)

def get_num():
    s = input('Input number (ENTER to quit): ')
    if not s:
        return None
    else:
        return float(s)
main()
```

Note ▶ This chapter uses the optimization `if not s`, introduced in the previous chapter. In each of these lines of code, I could have used

```
if s == '':
```

This line of code tests the string `s` and returns **True** if and only if `s` is an empty string. The following line of code does precisely the same thing (assuming `s` is a string) but is shorter and easier to read. An empty string equates to the value **None** when tested. **None** is equivalent to **False**, but the **not** operator reverses the logical value to **True**. Therefore, `not s` is a test for whether the string is empty.

```
if not s:
```

◀ Note

EXERCISES

Exercise 9.2.1.   Instead of applying the **float** conversion within the get_num function, could you apply an **int** conversion instead? What would be gained or lost?

Exercise 9.2.2.   Revise the get_num function so that it takes one default argument: a value to return for n if the user enters a zero-length string. If the function is called with no argument value, this argument should default to 0. Does any other statement need to change as a result?

Importing Functions from Modules

Although Python provides many powerful built-in functions, still more are available from Python modules, which are extended libraries that provide even more functionality. Some of these come standard with Python. These include the math and random libraries.

There are three different techniques for importing functions from modules.

```
import module_name
from module_name import function_name
from module_name import *
```

With the first version, importing the name of the module, *module_name*, enables you to use any function from that module but requires that each use be qualified. Here's an example:

```
import random
n = random.randint(0, 9)
```

You can also import a particular function from a module, in which case it can then be referred to without qualification.

```
from random import randint
n = randint(0, 9)
```

Finally, you can choose to import all function names without qualification, but be careful when you do this. All the names are imported and could potentially conflict with your own function names.

```
from random import *
```

Example 9.3.   *Dice Game (Craps)*

The following program listing implements a complete game of the traditional French dice game of "crabs," which is referred to in casinos all over the world as "craps." The code enables you to play over and over; the only thing it doesn't do is keep score or enable you to place a bet—although that can easily be added and is left as an exercise.

craps.py

```
from random import randint

def main():
    s = ''
    while not s or s[0] in 'Yy':
        play_the_game()
        s = input('Play again? (Y or N): ')

def play_the_game():
    r = roll();
    if r == 7 or r == 11:
        print(r, 'is an instant WINNER!\n')
        return
    if r == 2 or r == 3 or r == 12:
        print(r, 'is an instant LOSER. Sorry.\n')
        return
    print('Your point is now a', r)
    point = r
    while True:
        s = input("Roll again (E=exit)?")
        if len(s) > 0 and s[0] in 'Ee':
            return
```

▼ *continued on next page*

craps.py, cont.

```
        r = roll()
        print('You rolled a', r)
        if r == point:
            print('You\'re a WINNER!\n')
            return
        elif r == 7:
            print('Sorry, you\'re a LOSER.\n')
            return

def roll():
    d1 = randint(1, 6)
    d2 = randint(1, 6)
    print(d1, d2)
    return d1 + d2

main()
```

This is the longest program listing so far in this book, but what it does is straightforward once you thoroughly understand the rules of the game (explained in the next section). The basic idea is to try to roll a 7 or 11 during the first roll of a round—or "game."

If you fail to win or lose on the very first roll of the game, you note your first roll as your "point" and then keep rolling the dice until you either get your "point" again (in which case you win) or roll a 7 (in which case you lose).

So, rolling a 7 either wins the game or loses it, depending on when you roll it.

How It Works

The central function in this program is the play_the_game function. It plays one round of craps, which you can think of as "one game," even though such games sometimes only last for a single roll of the two dice.

The rules themselves, once clearly understood, essentially become the pseudocode for this game.

Roll the dice.

If the roll is a 7 or 11,

    Announce instant winner and end.

If the role is a 2, 3, or 12,

    Announce instant loser and end.

Note the current roll as the "point."

While True,

Roll dice.

If the point is rolled,

Announce "You win" and end.

If 7 is rolled,

Announce "You lose" and end.

This pseudocode for the game serves as a template for the main function, if you just add one more conditional. After `while True`, ask the user if he or she wants to roll the dice or exit immediately. This enables the user to exit at any time.

For all such choices, the default action is to keep on playing. The user can therefore continue just by entering an empty string (pressing Enter without typing any content). Remember that an empty string is equivalent to **None**, which is treated as **False**; but the **not** operator reverses the logical value. Therefore, `not s` is **True** if and only if `s` is an empty string.

```
s = ''
while not s or s[0] in 'Yy':
    play_the_game()
    s = input('Play again? (Y or N): ')
```

This game program involves a total of four functions if you include the three that you enter in the program—`main`, `play_the_game`, and `roll`—as well as the **randint** function imported from the **random** module.

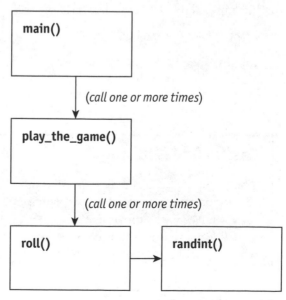

main()

(call one or more times)

play_the_game()

(call one or more times)

roll()   randint()

*From **random** module*

EXERCISES

Exercise 9.3.1.   Several statements in this program use test-for-equality (==) two or more times. Replace these tests by a single test of a value in a string or in a list, such as **s[0] in 'Nn'** or **r in [7, 11]**; make these changes throughout the program.

Exercise 9.3.2.   Revise the dice game so that before each round, the user can specify a bet. Then, depending on whether the user wins or loses the round, add or subtract the bet from the user's current assets. The initial stake should be 100. (Hint: To implement this without the use of global variables, have the play_the_game function return **True** or **False**. Return **True** only if the round is completed and the user wins.) Depending on the value returned, either increase or decrease the user's assets and report the current amount.

Exercise 9.3.3.   Replace the roll function with a more generic version—but then call it correctly so that it still works within the context of the craps.py program. This generic "roll" function should take two arguments: **n**, which determines how many dice to roll; and **sides**, which determines how many sides each die has. No matter how many sides, have the faces run in value from 1 to N. Finally, have the function return two values: the first is a total; the second is a list containing all the dice rolls.

This particular program should simply ignore the second return value (even though the return value might be used by other programs). To do that, create a dummy variable and call the function as follows:

```
r, dummy = roll(2, 6)
```

Finally, specify default values of 2 and 6 for the two arguments so that you can call the function this way:

```
r, dummy = roll()
```

Interlude

Casino Odds Making

The game of craps is played in casinos all over the world. The game has variations and side bets, but the principal bet is "the line," as described in the exercises in the previous section.

If this game were not profitable for the casino, then casinos everywhere would quickly go broke, because people would keep playing until "the

Interlude

▼ *continued*

house" lost everything. On the other hand, if the odds of a player winning were not fairly close to 50/50, then people would stop coming to the casinos, because it would be too difficult to win and players would be discouraged.

The mathematician and philosopher Blaise Pascal (1623–1662) provided all the tools necessary to figure out dice games, as well as many card games. Using a computer language such as Python, it's not too hard to calculate who wins the game of craps.

Remember, you're an instant winner if you roll 7 or 11 on the first roll. There are 6 ways of rolling a 7, so the likelihood of winning by rolling a 7 is 6/36. Likewise, there are 2 ways of rolling an 11, so the likelihood of winning by rolling an 11 on the first roll is 2/36.

Now, what is the probability of winning by 1) rolling a "point" and 2) rolling the "point" again before rolling a 7? That means rolling a 4, 5, 6, 8, 9, or 10, and then rolling that number again before getting a 7. The ways of rolling these six numbers are

▶ Three ways to roll a 4

▶ Four ways to roll a 5

▶ Five ways to roll a 6

▶ Five ways to roll an 8

▶ Four ways to roll a 9

▶ Three ways to roll a 10

In Python, we can summarize this information—the number of ways of rolling each of the "points"—by placing it into a list. According to Pascal, if the dice are fair, the probability of a number coming up is exactly proportional to the number of ways of rolling that number.

```
>>>ways = [3, 4, 5, 5, 4, 3]
```

The probability of winning by rolling and then rerolling any given point is

Prob. = (Prob. of rolling the point on first roll) * (Prob. of rolling it again before 7 is rolled)

The second part of this probability calculation is the tricky part. If the point is a 10, then only rolls of 10 and 7 matter; other rolls are effectively

▼ *continued on next page*

6

▼ *continued*

no-ops. So, what is the probability of rolling another 10 before a 7? Start by ignoring all rolls other than 7 or 10. Then the probability must be

(Ways of rolling that point) / (Total ways of rolling that point OR a 7)

And remember, there are six ways of rolling a 7. Therefore, the next Python statements to enter—which you can do in the interactive environment, by the way—are

```
>>>p = 0
>>>for n in ways:
     p += (n/36) * n/(n + 6)
```

This **for** loop calculates the probability for winning on each of the different "points," 4, 5, 6, 8, 9, 10, and then sums all these individual winning probabilities together by applying the addition-assignment operator (+=) each time through the loop.

For example, the probability that the player will win on a "point" of 6 is the probability of rolling a 6 on the first roll (which is 5/36) times the probability of then rolling a 6 before a 7 (which is 5/(5+6) = 5/11).

Now all that remains is to add in the probability of "instant wins" from a 7 or 11 and then to print the grand total.

```
>>>p += (6/36) + (2/36)
>>>print(p)
0.492929292929293
```

Therefore, the player's probability of winning a "straight line" bet at the dice table in a casino is approximately 49.3 percent. Another way of saying this is that for every dollar a gambler bets in this way, the casino pays out, in the long run, approximately 98.6 cents. So, the "house" is making 1.4 cents for every dollar wagered.

Essentially, a player has *almost* a 50/50 chance of winning any given bet, but in the long run, the "house" wins.

And that is good news for the casinos. The payout is sufficiently good for the players that if a player has an above-average run of good luck, they can walk away a winner. But it also means that—by making 1.4 cents per dollar wagered—the casino, by running the game day in, day out, for years and years, should consistently make money.

If a grand total of a billion dollars were wagered at a casino's dice tables in a year's time, a casino's income from those tables would be in the neighborhood of $14,141,000.

Interlude

Chapter 9 *Summary*

Here are the main points of Chapter 9:

▌ Functions can be defined with any number of arguments—that is, zero or more. The syntax for functions with more than one argument is

```
function_name(argument, argument,…) :
     indented_statements
```

▌ In most function calls, values are passed to function arguments according to position.

▌ Ordinary arguments passed to a Python function are not "reference" arguments in the sense that the function can use them to permanently change the value of a variable passed to it. For example, the following does not do what you want:

```
double_it(n):
     n = n * 2      # This does not work!
```

▌ However, there are a number of ways around this limitation. The simplest way is for the function to return a series of values in the **return** statement.

```
def func():
     return 100, 200, 300
```

▌ The caller of such a function needs to receive the information passed back to it in a meaningful way; that is, the programmer who calls such a function must understand the number and type of each data object passed back.

```
a, b, c = func()
```

▌ Arguments may be passed by name, in the form *arg = value*, such as the following call to the **print** function. Such argument values must be given after other arguments. This technique lets you pass values to arguments without regard to position.

```
print('Stay on the same line', end='  ')
```

▌ Within a function definition, default values may be created by using the *arg = default_value* syntax. This causes the default value to be used if the argument is omitted during a function call. For example, in the following definition, the value 1 is assumed if a second argument is not specified during a function call:

```
def repeat_s(my_string, reps=1):
     # Place indented statements here.
```

9

▶ The syntax for importing a module is

```
import module
```

▶ After you import a module this way, you can refer to any function from that module, but it must be qualified. Here's an example:

```
import random
n = random.randint(0, 9)
```

▶ The syntax for importing a *specific* function within a module is given next. The advantage of this approach is that the function may thereafter be used without the module name as a qualifier.

```
from module import function
```

▶ Finally, you can use the following syntax to permit you to refer to all the functions from the module without qualification. Be careful, however, about name collisions.

```
from module import *
```

Local and Global Variables

One of the issues in programming is *communication*—how do you share information between two functions or between a group of functions? The most direct way is to use global variables.

But Python has idiosyncratic rules about global and local variables. Python likes to do things its own way.

This chapter covers

▶ The difference between local and global variables

▶ The **global** keyword

▶ Using this keyword to prevent "the local variable trap"

▶ Using **global** in programs that encode and decode Roman numerals

Local Variables, What Are They Good For?

What are local variables good for? Plenty, as it turns out. A local variable is visible to only one function at a time. Here's an example:

```
def fact(n):
    prod = 1
    for i in range(1, n + 1):
        prod *= i
    return prod

i = -1
n = fact(5)
print('i and n are', i, 'and', n)
```

These statements print the following:

```
i and n are -1 and 120
```

In the `fact` function just shown, the variable `i` is local—as all function variables are by default; that means the function sees only its own value of `i`. The value of `i` outside the function is –1. And it remains equal to –1.

Because `i` is local, any changes the function makes to this variable have no effect outside the function. Here's what would be printed if `i` were *not* local, meaning visible to the whole program at the same time:

```
i and n are 5 and 120
```

Do you see the problem? The value of `i` ought to be –1, but now the program is reporting a value of 5. That's because if `i` were global everywhere, the function would interfere with the value of `i`, using the **for** loop to set `i` to 1, 2, 3, 4, and finally to 5.

Fortunately, the function uses a local, not a global, version of `i`. Therefore, the function doesn't interfere with what's going on outside. Most of the time, this is desirable behavior.

> When a variable is local, the function sees only its own version of that variable; it cannot use that variable to affect statements outside the function.

Locals vs. Globals

The rule favoring local variables makes programs easier to create and maintain.

Usually, you want functions to be independent. You want a function to carry out a task and tell it, "Use whatever variables you need; don't worry about what other functions are doing." You don't want to create hidden dependencies.

Many years ago, I helped program a complex system in BASICA before Microsoft added support for local variables. A function might change the value of a variable X even though the caller of the function relied on its own copy of X not changing. If you lost track of how many versions of X were running around, it could change without warning. That caused debugging headaches you wouldn't believe.

But sometimes you need variables that are global, not local. This occurs when

▶ Functions need to share information.

▶ It becomes impractical to share all this information through passing long series of arguments and return values.

In these situations, you may need one or more global variables. A global variable has the same lifetime as the program and can be seen by multiple functions.

In the following figure, the variable n can be accessed (or seen) by more than one function. Changes to n in one function affect the value of n in another. As long as a group of functions all use **global n**, then they all see the same version of n.

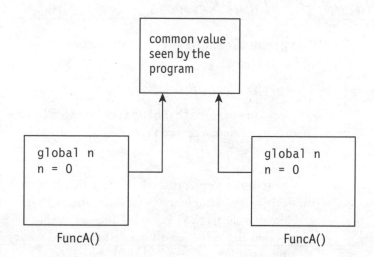

But if n is left as a local variable within a given function, then that function sees only its own version of it. In that case, changes to n in one function do not affect the value of n in another.

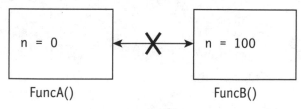

Changes to n in one function
have no effect on value of n
in another function

So, what determines whether a function sees a global variable or a local variable? The rules are

1 Within a function definition, an appearance of a variable name, *var*, is interpreted as local provided that variable exists at the local level—because an assignment statement created it.

10

2 If a local version of *var* does not exist, then a global version of *var* is used, if it exists (but again, it must have been assigned a value somewhere).

3 However, if a **global** *var* statement has been used, then skip step 1; Python looks for a global version only.

Introducing the global Keyword

The **global** keyword has a simple syntax. Place it at the beginning of a function definition.

```
global variable_names
```

This syntax means that **global** is followed by one or more variable names. If there is more than one, then commas are used as separators. Here's an example:

```
global n1, n2
```

The **global** keyword says: within this function, do not recognize a local version of this variable (or variables, if more than one are listed).

Note that the **global** keyword does not create the variable in question, which means that the variable still has to be created somewhere. You can create it by assigning a value at the global level or assigning it a value within a function.

For example, the following statements create two global variables and a local:

```
def a_func():
    global my_thing
    my_thing = 0     # This creates 'a_thing'
    locvar = 0       # Local var: created but ignored


your_thing = 10       # This creates 'your_thing'
```

This example creates two global variables: my_thing and your_thing. The first, my_thing, is created inside the function, but it has global scope, thanks to the **global** keyword. The second, your_thing, is global because it's created outside of any function (the "module level"). Meanwhile, the local variable locvar is also created, but it is local.

The Python "Local Variable Trap"

Consider these statements:

```
n_bank_account = 27333
def reset_funds():
    print('Your bank account holds:', n_bank_acct)
```

Python comes across the variable name, n_bank_acct, and asks whether a local version of n_bank_acct has been created yet. It has not been created within this function, so Python uses the global version of n_bank_acct.

But what if an assignment is added to the function definition?

```
def resent_funds():
    n_bank_acct = 10500    # This creates n_bank_acct.
    print('Your bank account holds:', n_bank_acct)
```

Whoops! Do you see what happened? Suddenly, n_bank_acct is a local variable, because the assignment creates n_bank_acct, and now it can be interpreted as local.

And—here's the problem—this statement, which was intended to change the value of n_bank_acct throughout the program, is of no effect; all this function does now is set a *local* version of n_bank_acct to 10500.

In this situation, the **global** keyword comes to the rescue. It says: don't consider this variable to be local, even if it would otherwise make sense to do so.

```
def resent_funds():
    global n_bank_acct      # This ensures var is global.
    n_bank_acct = 10500     # Now this affects the whole
                            #  program.
    print('You bank account holds:', n_bank_acct)
```

Now the statement n_bank_acct=10500 affects the rest of the program, because the variable is global.

This may seem complex. But the bottom line is that there is one main rule you need to follow regarding global variables.

* If a function uses a global variable and assigns anything to it, use a global statement to prevent the variable from being interpreted as local.

Remember that the **global** keyword does not create a variable; it only prevents it from being interpreted as local.

Interlude

Does C++ Have Easier Scope Rules?

I'm an old C/C++ programmer, and I'm happy to defend these languages—up to a point. Most of the time, Python is easier to use and makes it possible to create powerful programs that do a lot of things in a small space.

▼ *continued on next page*

10

Interlude

▼ *continued*

But once in a while, C++ syntax is easier. The C paradigm for local and global variables, inherited by C++, is sublimely simple:

▶ A variable declared outside all blocks (including functions) is global and static.

▶ A variable declared inside a block is local and temporary.

▶ If there's a name collision, the local variable declared in the innermost block is the one that gets recognized.

Remember, these are the rules for C and C++, not Python!

There! That's easy. There's also the issue of **extern** and **static** declarations, but I won't get into those. You can see how easy and consistent the C/C++ rules are. Here's an example:

```
int my_glob_var = 0;     // my_glob_var defined here.
void a_func() {
    int my_loc = 12;     // Local var defined here.
    my_glob_var = my_loc + 1; // Successful use of
                              // both.
}
```

The position of a variable declaration in C or C++ determines its scope. End of story. The Python rules, in contrast, are more complex. Why? To put the question another way, what does the Python complexity in the area of local vs. global "buy" you?

There is one thing. Python doesn't require you to create global variables at the module level. You can create variables by assigning to them within functions, as long as they have global scope. Such functions can do double duty: you can use them to create the variables, but you can also call the function to reset values by calling this function again.

```
def create_global_vars():
    global n_acct, n_age, n_generation
    n_acct = n_age = n_generation = 0
```

Example 10.1.   *Beatles Personality Profile (BPP)*

This next application is my contribution to the field of amateur psychology. It also illustrates use of a global variable. My theory, using a variation on Jungian archetypes, is that you can classify every person into one of four basic modes of being. These are

▶ **John Lennon**, founder of the Beatles. Walked the line between rebel and leader. He's the classic person to start a new organization if he doesn't like what he sees.

▶ **Paul McCartney**, the "cute" Beatle. Paul is also a leader but makes fewer waves and cultivates popularity. Known today as Sir Paul. Loved by millions.

▶ **George Harrison**, a talented songwriter, but at first he spent time in the shadow of John and Paul. The "quiet Beatle." Serious about his work, mystical, and spiritual.

▶ **Ringo Starr**, the drummer, and most lovable of the Fab Four. Last to join the group. Ringo was happy just to be included and felt that he had three brothers for life.

Which Beatle are you? Take my test, which I've written up as a fairly simple Python program. By analyzing this program, you should be able to see why—at least under its current overall architecture—this program needs to make use of a global variable.

Beatles.py

```
b = ''   # Var. b created (Is this necessary?)
j_str = '''John Lennon. Witty, cheeky, sassy. You like
  to be the leader of your own band.'''
p_str = '''Paul McCartney. You are popular, likable, and
  charismatic. You make a great impression.'''
g_str = '''George Harrison. You are serious, reflective,
  and deeply committed to your work.'''
r_str = '''Ringo Starr. You are lovable and just want
  everyone to get along.'''

def main():
    a = ask_q(
      'Are you more Assertive or Supportive? ','AS')
    if a == 'A':
        are_assertive()
    else:
        are_supportive()
    print('You are a', b)  # Global b assumed.
```

▼ *continued on next page*

Beatles.py, cont.

```python
def are_assertive():
    global b
    a = ask_q(
     'Are you more Intellectual or Social? ','IS')
    if a == 'I':
        b = j_str
    else:
        b = p_str

def are_supportive():
    global b
    a = ask_q(
     'Are you more Intellectual or Social? ', 'IS')
    if a == 'I':
        b = g_str
    else:
        b = r_str



# Ask Q (question) function.
# This function takes a prompt message and a set of
# acceptable choices. Will re-prompt until user gives
# one of the choices...First letter, either case, is
# accepted.
def ask_q(msg, choices):
    while True:
        s = input(msg)
        s = s.upper()    # convert input to uppercase
        if s and s[0] in choices:
            return s[0]
        else:
            print('Enter one of the choices.')
            print('First letter is sufficient.')

main()
```

Here's a sample session:

```
Are you more Assertive or Supportive? A
Are you more Intellectual or Social? I
You are a John Lennon. Witty, cheeky, sassy. You like
to be the leader of your own band.
```

How It Works

In its overall design, this program is simple. It classifies a person into one of four archetypes based on the answers to two questions. This is about as simple an example of a personality profile as you can have, because it asks these questions in a direct way. A more sophisticated program might ask dozens of questions to determine a person's psychological type.

In my analysis, there are two dimensions each with two possible values, so the number of resulting combinations is two times two, which equals four.

These two dimensions are Assertive vs. Supportive and Intellectual vs. Social. The first is really a "leader vs. follower" axis, but I tried to make the choice sound more neutral, without one sounding better than the other. The four types break down as follows:

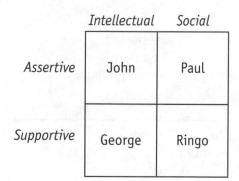

	Intellectual	Social
Assertive	John	Paul
Supportive	George	Ringo

The following pseudocode shows exactly how the program applies these choices.

If you are Assertive,
> *If you are more Intellectual,*
>> *You are a John Lennon.*
> *Else (you are more Social),*
>> *You're a Paul McCartney.*

Else (you are Supportive),
> *If you are more Intellectual,*
>> *You are a George Harrison.*
> *Else (you are more Social),*
>> *You are a Ringo.*

This example illustrates two features. First is the use of the **global** statement to ensure that the variable b is not interpreted as local. If b were local, then it would get set to the desired message, but as soon as the function returned, that message would be ignored…because every function would have its own version of b.

This example also illustrates the **in** keyword. The statement item **in** list or substring **in** string produces a **True** or **False** value, depending on whether the item is an element of the specified object—or in this case, a substring of the specified string.

```
if s and s[0] in choices:
    return s[0]
```

Note the use of s here as the first condition. A string can be tested in this manner; if it is not an empty string, it is interpreted as if **True**. You need to make sure s is not empty before using s[0] to test the first character of input.

Remember that the strings "AS" and "IS" are passed to the choices argument. Therefore, the user is prompted to type A or S (or a word beginning with *A* or *S*) and then the user is prompted to type I or S (or a word beginning with *I* or *S*). The ask_q function keeps prompting until the user responds with one of the responses permitted.

EXERCISES

Exercise 10.1.1. The beginning of Example 10.1 creates the variable b and sets it to an empty string. Is this statement necessary? Why or why not? Try removing the statement, rerun the program, and explain why it still works or why it doesn't.

Exercise 10.1.2. Along the same line, does the statement global b need to be included at the beginning of the main function? Why or why not? Explain your answer in terms of Python's rules regarding local and global rules.

Exercise 10.1.3. Rewrite the whole program in such a way that no global variables are required. One way to do this is to combine are_assertive() and are_supportive() into the main function so it isn't necessary to share information. Another way is to return the value of b.

Example 10.2. *Roman Numerals*

This next sample program converts numbers into Roman numeral form. For example, 2016 is converted into the string "MMXVI." The number 1998 is converted into the string "MCMXCVIII." And here's a simpler example: 152 is converted into "CLII."

This example uses a variable, `amt`, which is declared outside of all functions but needs to be declared "global" inside of the `make_roman` function to prevent it from being interpreted as local.

```
from_roman.py
amt = 0
def make_roman(letter, n):
    global amt
    while amt >= n:
        amt = amt - n
        print(letter, end='')

def main():
    global amt
    amt = int(input('Enter a number: '))
    print('The Roman number is: ', end='')
    make_roman('M', 1000)
    make_roman('CM', 900)
    make_roman('D', 500)
    make_roman('CD', 400)
    make_roman('C', 100)
    make_roman('XC', 90)
    make_roman('L', 50)
    make_roman('XL', 40)
    make_roman('X', 10)
    make_roman('IX', 9)
    make_roman('V', 5)
    make_roman('IV', 4)
    make_roman('I', 1)

main()
```

Here's a sample session:

```
Enter a number: 1308
The Roman number is: MCCCVIII
```

How It Works

This program—although I will show an even better way of doing it in the next section—illustrates the purpose of functions. The program makes many calls to the `make_roman` function.

Although this function is relatively short—only four or five statements long—imagine that instead of calling `make_roman`, you had to repeat the same four statements over and over. You may think the program is long now, but imagine it being five times longer.

The `make_roman` function generates the appropriate Roman numeral—sometimes once, sometimes several times. Take the target number 3,000. The appropriate action is to generate the letter *M* for each quantity of 1,000 that can be successfully subtracted from the target number without producing a negative. The result is then

    MMM

because we can subtract 1,000 three times before exhausting the target number (3,000).

Now, let's take a slightly more challenging example: 3,002. After 1,000 has been subtracted three times, 2 is left over. The program then tries subtracting other quantities and fails, until it gets to this function call:

```
make_roman('I', 1)
```

This function call says, "Subtract 1 as many times as possible," each time generating the letter *I*. The value of `amt` is now only 2. The final result is therefore

    MMMII

This is correct.

So, `make_roman` is a kind of general-purpose function that can generate any letter, or combination of letters, while it looks for one or more instances of the corresponding quantity. For example, it's used to generate "M" for each thousand found and later used to generate "I" for each value of 1 that is left.

The pseudocode for this function is simple.

> *While amt is greater or equal to N,*
>> *Generate the corresponding letter or letters*
>> *Subtract N from amt*

So, for example, if the starting amount is 5,000, this function will subtract 1,000 from the starting amount five times, each time producing an "M" character.

Note that the variable `amt` must be declared **global** because it is the target of an assignment from within the local function, `make_roman`.

Optimizing the Code

This program benefits from the ability to use functions, saving many lines of code, but it may still strike you as too long. All the calls to `make_roman` still take up a good deal of space. Shouldn't there be a way to automate this program further?

There is. Many of the previous chapters have been dedicated to the idea that—especially in Python—the easiest way to perform a lot of calculation is to

1 Put all the data in a list.

2 Process the list.

In this case, we need to process two pieces of information for each call to the function: a string containing a letter (or letters), and a numerical amount corresponding to that string. One solution is to create a list of lists—in effect, a two-dimensional list.

While that approach is fine, you can write a slightly more efficient data structure by creating a list of tuples—in which each tuple contains two values. Tuples are very similar to lists, but they are immutable (cannot be changed) and support fewer methods and functions. But in this case, they suffice.

Let's call this list of tuples `rom_list`.

```
rom_list = [ ('M', 1000), ('CM', 900), ('D', 500),
  ('CD', 400), ('C', 100), ('XC', 90), ('L', 50),
  ('XL', 40), ('X', 10), ('IX', 9), ('V', 5),
  ('IV', 4), ('I', 1) ]
```

All the calls to the `make_roman` function can then be replaced with a **for** statement.

```
for item in rom_list:
    make_roman(item[0], item[1])
```

Now, does the data structure `rom_list` itself need to be global?

Not necessarily. The `make_roman` function itself does not work on or alter this data structure. The function named `main` gets these values and sends them to `make_roman`, which goes about its business without any knowledge of the `rom_list` data structure.

EXERCISES

Exercise 10.2.1.   Revise Example 10.1 by introducing the new code shown in the subsection "Optimizing the Code." Make all the revisions necessary and then verify that the program still works.

Exercise 10.2.2.   Optimize behavior by gathering all the output into a single string and then printing the entire string at the end of the program, by calling **print**. Does this approach cause the program to run appreciably faster or not?

Exercise 10.2.3.   This one is an "extra for experts." You can support quantities larger than 1,000 by first dividing 1,000 and then producing the Roman numeral for quantity. Label this with "(M)" if it is greater than zero. Then process the remaining amount. 1,306,306 would produce "MCCCVI (M) CCCVI".

Interlude

What's Up with Roman Numerals?

Roman numerals are a classic case of a system considered outdated centuries ago that we still can't get rid of.

The Roman numbering system is like most ancient number systems. It's derived from the Latin alphabet, so the Romans didn't have to invent a separate set of characters for numerals. But unlike the superior Hindu-Arabic system, Roman numerals cannot appear in arbitrary positions, making calculations much more difficult.

And that's the problem. Consider how easy it is to add the following Hindu-Arabic numbers, which we use today:

```
      7 4 1
 +    5 3 8
```

You should be able to tell at a glance that the answer is 1279. Now try to add the following Roman numerals:

```
     DCCXLI
 +   DXXXVIII
```

Can you figure out, in your head, that the answer is MCCLXXIX? Can you do this without converting to 741 and 538? Even if you collect all the matching letters and try adding them together (a clever idea), you'll still get the wrong answer, because the Roman numeral is *partly* positional. The X in XL means something different from the X in DX.

It's no surprise, then, that when Fibonacci tried to import the Hindu-Arabic numbering system to Europe in the late Middle Ages, he was at first met with resistance. But the support of one group swung his way: Europe's rising merchant class.

Business was booming, and merchants needed to add, subtract, and multiply numbers on their account books. Governments needed to collect their taxes, and banks needed to collect their interest payments. It was literally a matter of money in the bank.

It was practicality versus tradition, and practicality won out, which is often the case where money is concerned.

▼ *continued*

Yet the legacy of the Roman state and the Church is so great, Roman numerals are still used to mark Highly Important Figures to this day, provided they're figures that don't need to be multiplied or added. Years are good examples, such as MMXVII.

Roman numerals are applied to mark other important numbers as well, such as which *Rocky* or *Star Wars* movie you've seen, or which king or queen we're talking about. I hope you know the difference between Richard II and Richard III. Only one of them said, "A horse, a horse, my kingdom for a horse!"

Example 10.3.   *Decode Roman Numerals*

If there's one thing that's harder than writing Roman numerals, it's reading them. You can imagine a situation in which a program must read a large number of Roman numerals as input and then convert these numerals into actual numbers. This section presents the core of such a program, although it converts only one number at a time.

```
decode_roman.py

rom_list = [ ('M', 1000), ('CM', 900), ('D', 500),
 ('CD', 400), ('C', 100), ('XC', 90), ('L', 50),
 ('XL', 40), ('X', 10), ('IX', 9), ('V', 5),
 ('IV', 4), ('I', 1)]

amt = 0         # Global vars created here.
romstr = ''

def main():
    global romstr
    romstr = input('Enter Roman numeral: ')
    for item in rom_list:
        decode_roman(item[0], item[1])
    print('The equivalent number is', amt)
```

▼ *continued on next page*

decode_roman.py, cont.

```
def decode_roman(letters, n):
    global amt, romstr
    sz = len(letters)
    while len(romstr) >= sz and letters == romstr[:sz]:
        amt += n
        romstr = romstr[sz:]


main()
```

Here is a sample session:

```
Enter Roman numeral: MCDXCII
The equivalent number is 1492
```

How It Works

Not surprisingly, this example uses the same list of data, rom_list, that the previous example did. But in this exercise, the task is to take a string and process it, one or two characters at a time, while building up a total stored in amt.

One issue that could have been a problem in this case was the problem of context. For example, the letter *C* can have a different meaning depending on whether or not it appears before an *M* or a *D* or neither.

CD   'means 400

CM   'means 900

CCC   'each of these mean 100

Fortunately, the logic of the program solves the context issue. Because of the way rom_list is constructed, letter combinations are checked out in a particular order. The program first looks for the appearance of "CM" and "CD" at the beginning of the input string. Only if neither of these combinations can be found does the program interpret *C* as meaning 100. In that case, the program reads as many Cs as it can, each time adding 100 to the total answer.

Here is the pseudocode of the decode_roman function. Basically, all it does is look for a particular one or two-letter string, such as "M" or "CD" at the very beginning of the string. If these characters are found, then the corresponding quantity is added to the amount (amt), the target characters are stripped from the beginning of the string, and the action repeats.

> *Set sz to length of the string named "letter"*
> *While length of romstr is greater or equal to sz AND*
> > *letter string matches beginning of romstr,*
> > *Add n to amt*
> > *Remove sz characters from the front of romstr*

Finally, note that slicing is used here effectively. The expression

```
letters == romstr[:sz]
```

...compares the string named `letters` to the first `sz` characters of the string named `romstr`. But what is `sz`? It's the length of `letters`, which we established on the previous line by using the **len** function.

```
sz = len(letters)
```

Therefore, these statements determine whether `letters` is a substring that appears at the beginning of `romstr`!

Optimizing the Code

The line of code

```
while len(romstr) >= sz and letters == romstr[:sz]:
```

can be replaced with the following, even while keeping every other line of code the same:

```
while romstr.startswith(letters):
```

The **startswith** method compares two strings; if the second string `letters` in this case) appears at the beginning of the first string, the method returns **True**.

EXERCISES

Exercise 10.3.1. The decode_roman function includes **global** statements for two variables: amt and romstr. Would the program still work properly without these statements? Why or why not?

Exercise 10.3.2. The main function includes a **global** statement for the variable romstr. Would the program work properly without this statement? Why or why not?

10

Exercise 10.3.3.   Using Example 10.1 as a model, write a program that takes any number of roman numerals, entered one at a time, and then gives their total. This is a "Roman numeral adding machine," possibly the first the world has ever known (except for the fact that I wrote it and made it work first).

Chapter 10   *Summary*

The major ideas of Chapter 10 are

▶ Variables in Python can be either local or global. A local variable can only be "seen" by the function it's part of. For example, two different functions can have a local variable named i, and the value of i in one function doesn't affect the value of i in the other.

▶ Most variables in functions should be left as local variables. If all your variables are global, then the changes made by one function's internal calculations may interfere with what happens in other functions, causing debugging headaches.

▶ Remember that the most important rule in Python is this: an assignment creates a variable if it does not already exist.

```
a_var = 100    # Create a_var as a new variable,
               #  it doesn't exist already
```

▶ When Python comes across a variable name, it asks if the variable already exists at the local level—that is, was there an assignment to that value within the current function? If so, the variable is interpreted as local.

▶ If a variable does not exist at the local level—because there was no assignment to it within the current function—Python must interpret it as global. But as soon as there is an assignment to this same variable, then it is interpreted as local, and that in turn means the variable is no longer shared with the rest of the program.

▶ However, a **global** *var* statement alters this process by telling Python, "Do not interpret this variable as local—even if there is an assignment to it." This statement has this simple syntax, in which variables is one or more names, and commas separate them if there is more than one.

```
global variable, variable, ...
```

▶ A global statement does not create a variable. One way to create a global variable is to assign a value to it, provided that is done when it has global scope (thanks to the **global** keyword).

```
global my_acct
my_acct = 0        # Create this if it does not exist.
```

▶ Another way to create a global variable is to assign it a value outside of any function (in what is sometimes called *module-level code*).

▶ The best general rule is this: if a function assigns a value to a variable and that variable needs to be the global, not local, version, then you need a **global** *var* statement. (And if there's any possibility you *might* assign a value to this variable, it's a good policy to declare it **global** just to be safe.)

11

File Ops

In programming, there's no getting away from disk files—or rather just "files," because these days files are not necessarily restricted to disk files. In any case, they're essential, because they store data that doesn't go away after the program ends. Everything from credit databases to police records depend on file storage.

Python facilities for reading and writing to files are especially easy. Some take advantage of the Python concept of *iterable*, which makes everything easier once you understand it.

In this chapter, I'll introduce simple techniques for reading and writing text files.

▶ Text vs. binary files

▶ The op system (os) module

▶ Writing to text files

▶ Reading text files

Reading and writing binary files is an advanced topic to be covered in another book. Many of the issues in reading and writing to text files apply to binary files as well. However, the Python facilities for text files are especially easy to use, so I recommend you get your feet wet by working with text files first.

Text Files vs. Binary Files

But what do I mean by "text file"? If you've programmed in other languages before, you're probably familiar with this term, so you can skip this section and go right to the next, "The Op System (os) Module."

Disk files tend to come in two major kinds: text files and binary files. Text files are intended to be written to and read from as if you were reading or writing to the console. All the data consists of printable characters.

For example, if you read the sentence "1,000 years" from either a text file or the console, you're reading a text string 11 characters in length. The first character happens to contain the numeral 1, and the third, fourth, and fifth characters happen to contain the numeral 0, but all of it consists of printable text.

As we've seen in earlier chapters, a string such as 1,000 can be entered at the console like any other; after all, your keyboard lets you type a digit character such as 1 or 5 just as you can type a letter. But a string has to be converted to numeric format before you can actually perform arithmetic on it.

Binary files are different. They can contain text strings, but they mostly contain data in a format that is not readable to human eyes.

A text file, in essence, is one long text string, although, as we'll see, it can be broken up with newlines.

A binary file consists of raw data that may not mean anything at all unless you know how to read it. Microsoft Outlook can understand binary files written by Outlook. Microsoft Excel can understand binary files written by Excel, and so on.

You cannot successfully read a binary file without knowing *in advance* how the information is formatted.

Text file	Binary file
To be, or not to be That is the question Whether 'tis nobler in the mind to suffer the slings and arrows of outrageous fortune Hamlet Act 3	09 18 E3 FF 03 7A FE 00 33 76 67 8B 32 99 38 E0 87 27 E3 95 03 7A FE 00 25 76 67 EE 76 8B E0

The Op System (os) Module

Before you read or write to files, you may want to be able to figure out what files actually reside on your disk.

Python provides a powerful module for interacting with files and directories, called **os**, which is short for "operating system." Importing the module—which gains access to all its functions—is easy.

```
import os
```

You can give this command from within a program or within the interactive environment. In the latter case, the next thing you may want to do is get help on this module.

```
>>>import os
>>>help(os)
```

The help listing for **os** is quite long. Fortunately, the Python interactive environment enables you to scroll up and down so that you can view this information one screen at a time. It shows that there are many functions you can call from this module.

For example, you can list the contents of the current directory. On my computer, Python sets the default directory to my principal Documents folder, which is huge.

```
>>>file_list = os.listdir()
>>>for item in file_list:
    print(item)
```

In my case, I have hundreds of files, and printing out the directory another way could cause long delays. Incidentally, you can figure out the number of items by using the **len** function.

```
>>>len(file_list)
356
```

So, there are 356 files in my current directory (also called a *folder*). Whew! I need to delete or move some files!

I recommend you do what I did: under this directory (folder), use your operating system to create a subdirectory specifically for use with reading and writing text files with Python. I created a subdirectory called Python Txt. You can easily create such a subdirectory with either Windows or Macintosh systems.

From within Python, you can then switch to this directory with the **chdir** function, which takes one string argument.

```
>>>os.chdir('Python Txt')
```

You can then get the full path name for the current working directory. (Don't worry; I'll summarize all these commands at the end of the section.)

The command that does this is **os.getcwd**, which is short for "GET Current Working Directory."

```
>>>os.getcwd()
'/Users/brianoverland/Documents/Python Txt'
```

The function name is easy to misspell, so enter it carefully. The output of this function is a string that you may, if you want, assign to a variable. In any case, this string shows the full path name of the directory you want to work in.

Alternatively, you can select a directory as your Python directory and then for each project create a subdirectory.

The path name you get on your computer will of course be different. I recommend that whatever this name is, you make it the working directory of programs that read and write text. You can put the following at the beginning of each program—bearing in mind that *your* path name will be different.

```
import os
os.chdir('/Users/brianoverland/Documents/Python Txt')
```

Here's a summary of the **os** functions used so far.

SYNTAX	NAME/DESCRIPTION
import os	Import the **os** module.
help(os)	From within the interactive environment, this prints a list of os functions and other features.
os.listdir()	List directory. Returns a list, each element of which is a string containing a file name.
os.chdir(*string*)	Change directory. The string can contain either a relative or a full path name.
os.getcwd()	Get Current Working Directory. Returns the full path name of the current directory, in a string.

The following figure illustrates the move from a directory to a subdirectory. The string "Python Txt" is a *relative*, not a full, path name; it does not begin with a slash (/).

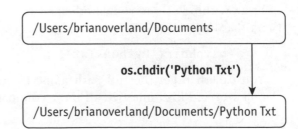

Interlude

Running on Other Systems

My programs refer to the particular directory that I use, and your programs can refer to your own dedicated Python-text-file directory. But what happens when you give your programs to someone else to run on their computer?

You have several options. The simplest is to let your Python programs run in the default directory on every computer, whatever it is, and hope for the best.

Another choice is to have your program install a new, dedicated directory, possibly just under the root. This is a little risky, because you're assuming you can make changes to the directory structure of the host computer. For example, if your program was the "Delta" program, it could check to see if a /delta directory existed on the host computer, and if it did not, create that directory itself.

This is one reason standard Python installations include the **os** module... because that module enables you to do many operations involving the reading, changing, and creation of new directories.

Finally—and this is what many large commercial applications do—you could purchase dedicated "Setup" software that you can use to write a customized setup script. This script will take the end user through the process of properly installing the software you've written, including the installation of required directories and subdirectories.

Open a File

All input/output operations on a file, no matter how complex, boil down to a three-step process.

1 Open the file.

2 Read information, write information, or both.

3 Close the file.

Opening a file is critical, because when you tell Python to write or read information to a file, it has to know *which file you mean*. It would be extremely inefficient to do this for each individual read or write operation. The operating system has to do quite a bit of work to find a file and set up internal information for it, such as read/write mode and file pointers, so it should never have to open a particular file more than once or twice per session.

The second step is to read or write to the file, which is usually the interesting part. We'll get to that in the next section.

Finally, the file must be closed. Until you close a file, the information you *thought* you wrote may only partially be written to the disk file. Closing the file forces the last of the write operations, if any, to be physically sent to the file.

Let's assume that the current working directory is the one you want to be in. Here's the syntax for opening a file for writing:

> *file_obj_name* = **open(***file_name*, **'w')**

Here are some examples that open three different files and create three different file objects:

```
f = open('read.txt', 'w')
f1 = open('brian.txt', 'w')
f2 = open('My Biography', 'w')
```

This is a simple syntax, but you must remember to include the w string as the second argument, assuming you want to write to the file.

Opening a file for writing is fairly simple, because it works whether or not the file already exists. There's a danger, however. If the file doesn't exist, a new one will be created. But if it does exist, the old contents are destroyed and replaced with the new text you write.

So be careful. This is one reason I advise learning about file operations by creating a new directory, where you can't destroy any existing files needed by other programs.

Look at the first file opening again.

```
f = open('read.txt', 'w')
```

The f is a variable name just like any other. Because this is an assignment, it creates f as a new variable; and if f already exists, the old association is broken. You might choose to use a more descriptive name.

```
in_file = open('read.txt', 'w')
```

The value returned is a file object. You don't need to understand all about objects yet—just keep in mind that this variable just created, in_file in this case, will be used to read from the file.

Remember that after you're done working on a file, it's important to close it. No arguments are involved.

```
f.close()
```

Let's Write a Text File

After a file has been opened in write mode, it's easy to write out text—although there are one or two caveats.

```
file_obj.write(string)
```

Let's open a file, write a line of text, and close it.

```
out_file = open('hamlet.txt', 'w')
out_file.write('To be or not to be')
out_file.close()
```

Now if you use your operating system to look in the current working directory, and you click the file `hamlet.txt`, the system's default text editor should display the following:

```
To be or not to be
```

So far, so good. Now, let's try to write two lines instead of one.

```
out_file = open('hamlet.txt', 'w')
out_file.write('To be or not to be')
out_file.write('That is the question')
out_file.close()
```

Now when you click the file `hamlet.txt`, you should find that the old contents were entirely deleted, replaced (not appended) by the new content. This is what you'll see:

```
To be or not to beThat is the question
```

Oops. What happened? The **write** method does not automatically append a newline character to advance to the next line.

However, you can add a newline by adding the characters \n to the end of each string. So unless you want text to be put together on the same line, you should make the following calls instead of the ones just shown. I added comments for emphasis.

```
f.write('To be or not to be\n')    # Note the \n.
f.write('That is the question\n')  # Note the \n.
```

When you run the fixed version of the program, here's what gets put in the `hamlet.txt` file:

```
To be or not to be
That is the question
```

Example 11.1.   *Write File with Prompt*

The following application opens a file and writes to a file named `stuff.txt`. The user enters as many lines as he or she wants and enters a blank line to quit.

```
writefil.py
    def main():
        out_file = open('stuff.txt', 'w')
        while True:
            s = input('Enter>>')
            if not s:
                break
            out_file.write(s + '\n')
        out_file.close()
        print('Done!')

    main()
```

This is a simple program, in which the basic operation is just a loop that prompts for input and then—unless the input is a blank line—writes the input out as string, appending a newline, and prompts again. (Remember that not s returns **True** if the string is blank.)

Here's a sample session:

```
Enter>>To be or not to be
Enter>>Whether tis nobler in the mind
Enter>>To suffer the slings and arrows
Enter>>Of outrageous fortune
Enter>>
Done!
```

How It Works

Inside the main function, the first action is to attempt to open a file. Because this attempts a "write file" opening, the file does not need to previously exist. It therefore always succeeds unless you use an illegally formed file name. But `stuff.txt` should present no problems.

```
    out_file = open('stuff.txt', 'w')
```

Now a simple loop is executed, in which the user is prompted, the text is written to the file, and the loop does not quit until a blank string is entered— meaning that the user pressed Enter after entering no text.

```
while True:
    s = input('Enter line: ')
    if not s:
        break
    out_file.write(s + '\n')
```

Note that it's the last line that does the interesting work: writing to the file. We can represent this loop through the following pseudocode:

While true (loop always):

    Set s to user input after prompting

    if s is an empty string,

        Exit loop

    Write s to the file, appending a newline

This program logic might present one little defect if you're staying alert here. What if the user wants to enter a completely blank line? How would she do that? Fortunately, there's at least one obvious answer: the user can just type a single blank space and then press Enter. A string consisting of one blank space is different from a completely empty string, but if you look at the contents of the file later, the difference is not noticeable to the human eye.

Other solutions are possible. For example, you could use a special code to indicate that user should exit, such as @.

Finally, it's important to close the file, or the data won't be written out.

```
out_file.close()
```

EXERCISES

Exercise 11.1.1. Instead of having the program exit when the user enters a blank line (''), have it exit in response to a special code such as @. Remind the user of this in the input prompt.

Exercise 11.1.2. Prompt the user for a file name rather than using `stuff.txt`.

Exercise 11.1.3. Example 11.1 writes a string to the output file by directly appending a newline character (\n). Instead of doing this in the main function, offload this job to a dedicated `write_line` function that automatically adds a newline.

Exercise 11.1.4.   This example writes lines to a file, one at a time. Instead of writing the text directly, place each new line into a list of strings. Then create one composite string out of this list and write the entire string to the file in one operation. (Hint: You may find it useful to use helper functions from Chapter 7, "Python Strings.")

Read a Text File

Reading a text file is about as easy as writing to a file, but when you open a file, you need to make sure it already exists, or the result is something called an *exception*, which we'll deal with in the next section.

For now, try to be sure that a file exists before you open it. You can use an optional second argument that specifies read mode.

```
in_file = open('hamlet.txt', 'r')
```

However, this second argument is not necessary, because read mode is assumed by default, as is text mode.

```
in_file = open('hamlet.txt')
```

If all goes well, you now have a file object for the disk file named `hamlet.txt`, created earlier in this chapter.

At this point, you actually have several choices for how to read a file. Python is a language highly organized around the idea of *iterables*, which are data collections from which you can read one element at a time, by asking for "the next one."

Even a text file can be treated as an iterable. When used with a **for** statement, each element corresponds to a line of the file, that is, separate strings delineated by newline characters (\n).

The following statements, therefore, print one line of the file at a time.

```
for a_line in in_file:
    print(a_line)
```

The results for a version of `hamlet.txt` containing two lines of text are

```
To be or not to be

That is the question
```

What happened? The problem is that Python prints each line entirely—including the newline character (\n). The solution is simple: suppress the print function's default behavior, which is to print an additional newline.

```
for a_line in in_file:
    print(a_line, end='')
```

And now the result is what we want:

```
To be or not to be
That is the question
```

Note ▶ If you try reading a file more than once, you might be frustrated, because after the first time through a file, the *file pointer* is at the end and there's nothing more to read. The operating system uses the file pointer to determine what part of the file to read or write next.

To reset the file pointer to the beginning of the file, use this statement:

```
f.seek(0)
```

But as long as your file isn't too large, I recommend reading all the lines into a list, where they can be easily managed. The **readlines** method reads the entire file at once, placing each line (including the newline, remember) into a different element in a list of strings. Here's an example:

```
str_list = in_file.readlines()
for a_line in str_list:
    print(a_line, end='')
```

As I pointed out in the previous note, if you want to try all these approaches, reset the file pointer after each read.

```
in_file.seek(0)
```

Finally, if you want the simplest way to just display the contents of the file as they are, you can read the entire contents into a single string and just print that string.

```
print(in_file.read())
```

Always remember, when you are finished with the file, close it.

```
in_file.close()
```

Files and Exception Handling

One of the difficulties with opening a file in read mode is that the file must already exist. If it doesn't, you can't proceed.

In some programming languages (such as C and C++), a failed attempt at opening a file just returns a null pointer. But Python raises an exception: specifically, a runtime error of type **FileNotFoundError**.

If you want to handle the possibility of such an exception, you need to write an exception-handling control structure, which has this general syntax:

```
try:
    try_statements
except error_type:
    except_statements
```

Incidentally, you may have more than one "except" block, each one is looking for a different class of exception.

The *try_statements* are executed unconditionally. (They can be interrupted by an exception, of course, but that's always true.)

The *except_statements* are executed if and only if an exception is raised during the execution of the *try_statements*.

In either case, execution resumes after the end of the **try/except** block. More statements may follow, or you might be at the end of the program.

The use of this syntax makes it easy to recover gracefully from a "file not found" error. In the following example, the program fails to go forward if a file is not found, but at least it does so by printing a friendly error message.

```
try:
    f = open('hamlet.txt')  # Open hamlet for reading
    print(f.read())
    f.close()
except FileNotFoundError:
    print('Sorry; "hamlet.txt" not found.')
```

The problem with this approach is that it doesn't give the user a chance to reenter the name or find a name that does work. If the user enters a file name and commits a typo, she might want a chance to reenter the name. We can therefore put the code into a **while** loop and reprompt the user until she enters the name of an existing file.

```
while True:
    try:
        fname = input('Enter file name: ')
        if not fname:
            break
        f = open(fname)  # Attempt file open here.
        print(f.read())
        f.close()
        break
    except FileNotFoundError:
        print('File could not be found. Re-enter.')
```

The **try/except** block in this example says essentially, "Try to open a file using the file name entered by the user. If this succeeds, then print the file and be done. Otherwise, print a friendly error message."

So how do I get the user to reenter the file name? Simple. The entire **try/except** block is placed inside a `while` loop. That loop continues until something is done to break it. A successful read operation breaks it by using the **break** keyword. But a failed read does nothing but print a message; and because nothing is done to break the loop in that case, the `while` loop executes again.

This code also enables a user to get out directly by just typing an empty string (Enter without entering any text).

Interlude

Advantages of try/except

Exception handling, for the most part, is a special kind of error handling, although it is occasionally used for other situations.

Why use this technique? After all, one perfectly good approach would be for a file-open function to return an error code if it failed. The program could then test the value returned to determine if there is an error. After all, C and C++ do in fact use that technique. For example, to open a disk file in C, you'd use code something like this:

```
fp = file_open("hamlet.txt", 'rb');
if (fp) {
    /* read the file */
} else {
    puts("File could not be opened.");
}
```

One problem with this approach is that no specific information is given as to why the file open failed. Was it that the name was badly formed to begin with? Was the name valid but it wasn't found in the directory? Or did some other process have exclusive rights to the file?

Another, more general problem is that large programs can get very complex. The "main" function might call `FuncA`, `FuncA` might call `FuncB`, and so on. If error detection and handling is based on error codes handed back the obvious way, then an error code might have to be propagated all the way back to the highest level, where the code actually interacts with the user.

The beauty of exception handing is that errors and other special events can be handled in one central location, regardless of where they occur. Control of the program automatically transfers "all the way back up" to the exception-handling block.

▼ *continued on next page*

▼ *continued*

Interlude

In short, one part of your program, if you want, can deal with all the exceptions you anticipate, and the rest of the program can be much cleaner as a result. The rest of the program can be completely free of error detection and propagating error codes by returning values up through a chain of function calls.

The following figure illustrates how a function can call another function, which calls yet another function, but no matter where the problem occurs, control "pops back up" all the way to the **except** block, where it is dealt with.

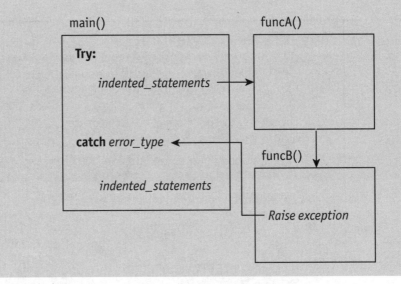

Example 11.2. *Text Read with Line Numbers*

The following program queries a user for a file name and then prints the contents of the file after reading it. It also prints line numbers.

readfil.py

```python
in_file = None

def main():
    if open_file():
        fss = '{:>2}. {}'
        str_list = in_file.readlines()
```

```
            for i, item in enumerate(str_list, 1):
                print(fss.format(i, item), end='')
            in_file.close()

    # Open file function: return True if file is found...
    # Return False if user wants to quit early.
    def open_file():
        global in_file
        while True:
            try:
                fname = input('Enter file name: ')
                if not fname:
                    return False
                in_file = open(fname)  # Attempt file open.
                return True
            except FileNotFoundError:
                print('File not be found. Re-enter.')

    main()
```

Here's a sample session:

```
Enter file name: hamet.txt
File could not be found. Re-enter.
Enter file name: hamlet.txt
  1. To be or not to be
  2. Whether tis nobler in the mind
  3. To suffer the slings and arrows
  4. Of outrageous fortune
```

How It Works

This example brings together a number of features introduced in previous chapters. First, the variable in_file is created at the module level, making it global, but relying on a **global** statement to make sure that it is treated as such.

```
in_file = None
```

Actually, this statement is unnecessary. If you truly understand the rules for global variables, you can leave out this initial, module-level assignment to in_file. The open_file returns a valid setting to in_file if successful—that is, it returns a value other than **None**.

This is the only function that needs the **global** statement, because it assigns a value to in_file; main() does not. By the time in_file is referred to in main, the open_file function has been executed and *it has assigned a value to in_file*, thus creating in_file as a global variable!

The main function turns over the jobs of querying the user, and then finding and opening the chosen file, to the open_file function. This function returns **True** if the file was successfully opened, and **False** otherwise; in the latter case, the user decided to quit early, so main does nothing more.

If the file was successfully opened, the program first uses the **readlines** method to fill up a list and then uses the **enumerate** function to turn each of the lines into line number/string pairs, which are then printed. A format specification string (fss) is used to ensure that the numbers and text lines are nicely spaced, with numbers being right-justified.

```
if open_file():
    fss = '{:>2}. {}'
    str_list = in_file.readlines()
    for i, item in enumerate(str_list, 1):
        print(fss.format(i, item), end='')
    in_file.close()
```

The call to the **readlines** method reads the entire file, placing each line of input into a separate string—with all the strings together placed in a list. The variable str_list is then used to refer to this list.

The **enumerate** function is then used to generate a series of number/text pairs, beginning with the number 1.

The open_file function seems to do a lot of work, but all it does is continue to query the user until one of two conditions happen:

1 The user enters a blank string by just pressing Enter, in which case no file is selected and the open_file function returns False.

2 The open method returns a legitimate file object without raising an exception. In that case, the variable in_file is associated with this object and the open_file function returns **True**.

Note that in_file is created by an assignment in this function; therefore, since in_file is meant to be accessed by both functions, it must be explicitly declared **global**:

```
global in_file
```

EXERCISES

Exercise 11.2.1. Revise Example 11.2 so that instead of making `f_obj` a global variable, make `f_obj` a value that is passed back by the `file_open` function. Revise the statements in the caller, `main()`, accordingly. (Hint: you might need to pass back more than one value.)

Exercise 11.2.2. Revise the example so it continues operation, until the user presses Enter after a blank line. This way, the user can view any number of text files before terminating the program.

Exercise 11.2.3. Alter the print format so that the example displays lines in the format *nnn>>*, where *nnn* is a print field three spaces wide (enough to print up to line 999 without losing vertical alignment).

Exercise 11.2.4. Revise the program to prompt for a *range* of line numbers to print. Test the numbers carefully to confirm that they are valid indexes and then print the range shown. Take input in the form *begin*, *end* and parse it, using string functions from Chapter 7. For example, if the user enters **5, 15**, print all the lines from line 5 up to and including line 15.

Other File Modes

So far, I have presented only two modes: text-file read and text-file write. You can actually open a file in a number of different modes.

MODE	DESCRIPTION
r	Open text file for reading. (Default.)
w	Open text file for writing.
w+	Open text file for both reading and writing. Unlike the "w" mode, this mode does not destroy existing contents.
rb	Open binary for reading.
wb	Open binary for writing.
w+b	Open binary file for both reading and writing. Unlike the "w" mode, this mode does not destroy existing contents.

Chapter 11   *Summary*

Here are the basic ideas of Chapter 11:

▌ You can import the **os** module to read the current directory, change directory, and perform many other operations related to disk file operations.

```
import os
```

▌ As with other modules, you can get help on the features of the **os** module.

```
help(os)
```

▌ File operations are generally a three-step process: 1) open a file, 2) read or write to the file, and 3) close the file.

▌ The Python **open** method returns a file object if successful, which you can assign to a variable.

```
my_file = open('hamlet.txt')
```

▌ The file object can then be used to read or write, depending on the mode. (Note that the default is read mode on a text file.)

▌ Text-file operations are different from binary-file operations because text files assume that the entire file consists of printable characters—including numbers, which are represented as numerals.

▌ For example, "100,000" in a text file is not an integer but rather a string six-characters long.

▌ The Python **write** method simply writes out a string of text.

```
out_file.write('To be or not to be.')
```

▌ This method does not automatically append a newline character (\n), so you need to do that if you want to write separate lines.

```
out_file.write('To be or not to be.\n')
```

▌ After you are done working with a file, remember to use the **close** method.

```
out_file.close()
```

▌ To open a file for reading, you must specify the r mode.

```
in_file = open('hamlet.txt', 'r')
```

▶ An attempt to open a file for reading fails if the file cannot be found. The best way to respond to this possibility is to set up a **try/except** block that "catches" the **FileNotFoundError** exception.

▶ There are several ways to read a file. One way is to treat the file as an iterable and read one line at a time.

```
for in_str in in_file:
    print(in_str, end= '')
```

▶ Another way to read a file is to treat it as a series of lines and read it into a list of strings:

```
a_list = in_file.readlines()
```

▶ Finally, you can use a call to the read file to read in the entire contents of the file as one large string.

```
print(in_file.read())
```

▶ If you want to return to the beginning of the file (in order to re-read it), you can reset the file pointer by using the **seek** function.

```
my_file.seek(0)
```

Dictionaries and Sets

How would you like to be able to give a key value—such as a name—and have Python find the corresponding value for you? How would you like to be able to have the language carry out searches at lightning speed?

That's what Python *data dictionaries* do. They potentially solve many programming problems by creating something like a rudimentary database.

This chapter explores dictionaries and sets by covering the following topics:

▶ Setting up a simple dictionary

▶ Loading and saving to disk files

▶ Operations on sets

Why Do We Need Dictionaries, Ms. Librarian?

With a Python list, you access data by index number in the range 0 to N-1. For example, if you taught a small class, you might record the grades as follows:

```
grade_list = [2.0, 3.5, 4.0, 3.8, 2.5]
```

There's a big limitation here. How do you know which grade belongs to which student? What you'd really like to do is assign grades by name, not by index number, which is almost meaningless. Assume names are in alphabetical order. Instead of writing this:

```
grade_list[0] = 4.0
```

...you'd prefer to use a more meaningful index, such as a student name. That's exactly what you can do with Python dictionaries.

```
grade_dict['Alan Anderson'] = 4.0
```

When a value such as Alan Anderson is used this way, it's called a *key*. The number 4.0 is its corresponding value.

You create a data dictionary—or just "dictionary"—as a group of key-value pairs. Here's an example:

```
grade_dict = { 'Alan Anderson': 4.0,
               'Betsy Baron': 2.8,
               'Tom Swift': 3.5 }
```

These keys happen to be listed here in alphabetical order, but order has no significance in data dictionaries. I could have the same key-value pairs in a different order, and the dictionaries would be considered equivalent.

```
grade2_dict = { 'Tom Swift': 3.5,
                'Betsy Baron': 2.8,
                'Alan Anderson': 4.0 }
```

This equivalency can be tested from within the interactive environment.

```
>>>grade_dict == grade2_dict
True
```

Order is not significant because the internal storage of the database items has no direct relation to how items are accessed. Remember, items in a dictionary are accessed by key value, not by position. As for how a key is found, for now you should consider that "magic."

The following syntax summarizes how to create and initialize a dictionary.

```
dictionary = { key : value, key : value, ...}
```

You can have zero or more key-value pairs. Starting with an empty dictionary, which has zero of these pairs, is perfectly valid.

```
employee_dict = { }
```

Having created a dictionary, you want to know how to do the following:

▶ How do I add and change key-value pairs?

▶ How do I use a key to access a value?

▶ How do I test the existence of a key?

The next few sections provide the answers.

Adding and Changing Key-Value Pairs

Once a dictionary exists, you can add any number of key-value pairs by using the following syntax:

```
dictionary[key] = value
```

The dictionary must already exist, although it may be empty to begin with. If the key does not yet exist in the dictionary, it is added along with its corresponding value. If the key *does* exist, it is given the new value.

The following statements initialize the dictionary called grades as empty and then add three entries:

```
grade_dict = {}
grade_dict['Alan Anderson'] = 2.0
grade_dict['Tom Swift'] = 3.2
grade_dict['Betsy Baron'] = 3.5
```

Each statement, after the first, adds a key-value pair. The order in which these are added is not relevant. You can add new key-value pairs at any time. Here's an example:

```
grade_dict['Bill Gates'] = 3.9
```

Here we've given Bill a high grade. But suppose we want to go back and give him an even higher grade later? The answer is: we use the same syntax for *changing* values as for creating new ones.

```
grade_dict['Bill Gates'] = 4.0
```

There were four key-value pairs before this statement, and there continue to be four. The effect of this last statement is to alter one of the values. This produces the following dictionary:

key	value
'Alan Anderson'	2.0
'Tom Swift'	3.5
'Betsy Baron'	3.2
'Bill Gates'	4.0

grades dictionary

Accessing Values

You use a similar syntax to access existing values.

> *dictionary*[*key*]

This expression, appearing on the right side of an assignment, or another context such as a **print** statement, produces the value corresponding to the key. For example, we could print all four values as follows:

```
print(grade_dict['Alan Anderson'])
print(grade_dict['Tom Swift'])
print(grade_dict['Betsy Baron'])
print(grade_dict['Bill Gates'])
```

When you print the contents of the dictionary this way, each key—in this case the name of a student—must currently exist. Use of a key that does not already exist results in a runtime error. Specifically, Python raises a **KeyError** exception.

If you want to print out the entire contents of the dictionary, without knowing ahead of time what the existing keys are, you can use a **for** statement.

```
for key in grade_dict:
    print(key, '\t', grade_dict[key])
```

Dictionaries, when iterated, return a series of keys, which you can then use to get corresponding values. The effect of this loop is to print the following:

```
Alan Anderson   2.0
Tom Swift       3.5
Betsy Baron     3.2
Bill Gates      4.0
```

You can think of each *dictionary*[*key*] reference this way: the key is the input; the dictionary returns the corresponding value.

This is how the reference to `grade_dict['Bill Gates']` produces the value 4.0:

grade_dict['Bill Gates']

Value produced is 4.0

'Alan Anderson'	2.0
'Tom Swift'	3.5
'Betsy Baron'	3.2
'Bill Gates'	4.0

Searching for Keys

Although key-value pairs can be assigned new values at any time, you cannot print or refer to a key-value pair if the key does not already exist. So the following is perfectly valid, assuming the grade_dict dictionary exists:

```
grade_dict['Bill Sykes'] = 2.0
```

But this next statement will cause a **KeyError** exception to be raised, assuming that "Sky" is a typo.

```
print(grade_dict['Bill Sky'])
```

There are several ways to deal with this problem. One is to use **try** and **except** to deal with such situations when they arise. Another solution is to search for a key before using it to access a value. Here is the relevant syntax:

key **in** *dictionary***.keys()**

This expression returns **True** if the specified *key* currently exists in the dictionary; it returns **False** otherwise.

For example, we could search for the key "Bill Sky" before trying to use that key to access a value.

```
k = 'Bill Sky'
if k in grade_dict.key():
    print(k, 'has the grade', grade_dict[k])
else:
    print(k, 'not in the database')
```

Another, more efficient approach, is to the use the **get** method, which has this syntax:

*dictionary***.get(***key, default_val***)**

This expression produces the value corresponding to the *key*, if found. Otherwise, it returns the default value.

The *default_val* argument is itself optional and has **None** as *its* default value. This means that if **get** returns the special value **None**, the key wasn't found. So the search can be written as follows:

```
k = 'Bill Sky'
v = grade_dict.get(k)    # Look-up is performed here.
if v:          # If v is not None...
    print(k, 'has the grade', v)
else:
    print(k, 'not in the database')
```

This is an efficient approach, because it performs only one lookup.

Dictionaries, in some ways, are the most flexible and powerful Python collection we've seen so far. But they have some restrictions.

▶ Each key in a dictionary is unique, appearing at most once, but the associated values can contain any number of duplicate values. For example, every student must have a unique name, but everyone could be given a grade of 4.0 if you chose.

▶ Once you choose a data type to use for your keys, this data type must not vary. Only certain types can be used, as described in the upcoming interlude. Values can have any data type, although it is a good idea to use a consistent type for those as well.

Interlude

What Explains Dictionary "Magic"?

In a way, dictionaries are magic. You specify the key value you're interested in, and you get an associated value back. Common sense suggests that some kind of searching is going on under the covers and that nothing is ever really free.

And yet, the Python encourages you to think of the process as instantaneous: specify a key and get back a value. Python syntax treats this as a direct access, not a search.

There is in fact a kind of magic involved with key-value access. The underlying values are not stored in a simple list or array. Instead, the values are accessed through something called a *hash table*. A mathematical formula is applied to each key to determine the actual location of the value (called a *bucket*). Then Python is able to access that value almost instantly.

Another way to achieve this kind of "instant searching" effect is to use a binary tree, but Python uses hash tables for dictionary collections, and hashing is even faster.

But for this process to work, the keys must be "hashable"—that means that Python must be able to apply a mathematical formula to each key. Not all data types are hashable, which restricts your choice of data type. The main requirement is that the type is immutable. You can therefore use a numeric field (integer and floating-point values supported) and strings. You can even use tuples of numbers and/or strings, but you cannot use lists as keys.

Example 12.1.   *Personal Phone Book*

This example is a rudimentary database application that keeps track of phone numbers, letting you access them by typing in the subject's name.

The key for this dictionary is the name of a person whose phone number you want to retrieve. The value is a string containing the phone number itself.

```
phone_book1.py

phone_dict = { }

# Main function. Prompts for next command and executes.
def main():
    while True:
        prompt = 'Enter command: 1. data entry, '
        prompt += '2. query, 3. exit >> '
        s = input(prompt)
        if not s:     # If string empty, break
            break
        cmd = int(s)
        if cmd == 3:
            break
        if cmd == 1:
            add_entries()
        elif cmd == 2:
            display_entries()

# Add Entries function. Prompts for key-value pairs
# until user wants to exit. Adds key-value to dict.
def add_entries():
    while True:
        key_str = input(Input name (ENTER to exit): ')
        key_str = key_str.strip()
        if not key_str:  # If key_str empty, return
            return
        val_str = input('Enter phone no: ')
        val_str = val_str.strip()
        if not val_str:
            return
        phone_dict[key_str] = val_str

# Display Entries function. Prompts for name & prints
# corresponding value. Re-prompts if key not found.
def display_entries():
    while True:
        key_str = input('Enter name (ENTER to exit): ')
```

▼ *continued on next page*

phone_book1.py, cont.

```
        key_str = key_str.strip()
        if not key_str:  # If string empty, return
            return
        val_str = phone_dict.get(key_str)
        if val_str:
            print(val_str)
        else:
            print('Name not found. Re-enter.')

main()
```

This program, although simple, creates a database. It does not contain any facilities for loading from and saving to a disk file, which normally you'd need for the application to be useful. But those features will be added later in this chapter. Here's a sample session:

```
Enter command: 1. data entry, 2. query, 3. exit >> 1
Enter name (ENTER to exit): John Bennett
Enter phone no: 555-2000
Enter name (ENTER to exit): Jane Austen
Enter phone no: 555-1212
Enter name (ENTER to exit):
Enter command: 1. data entry, 2. query, 3. exit >> 2
Enter name (ENTER to exit): John Bennet
Name not found. Re-enter.
Enter name (ENTER to exit): John Bennett
555-2000
Enter name (ENTER to exit): Jane Austen
555-1212
Enter name (ENTER to exit):
Enter command: 1. data entry, 2. query, 3. exit >> 3
```

How It Works

Despite its length, this is actually a simple program. All the main function does is give the user a choice between executing one of several commands and then call the appropriate function.

The dictionary, called `phone_dict` is created as an empty dictionary at the beginning of the program.

```
phone_dict = {}
```

Most of the statements in this program perform actions that you've seen performed many times in this book: prompt the user, get input, make modifications to the input as appropriate, and then respond.

The `add_entries` function prompts for two strings: `key_str` and `val_str`. After the function gets these strings, it's easy to add them as a key-value pair.

```
phone_dict[key_str] = val_str
```

The `display_entries` function prompts for a key string and then displays the corresponding value, checking to see if the key currently exists in the phone book. The code is written so as to perform only one lookup per item, which makes it efficient. If the specified key is not found, the **get** method returns **None**; we therefore test to see if this value is not **None**.

```
val_str = phone_dict.get(key_str)
if val_str:
    print(val_str)
else:
    print('Name not found. Re-enter.')
```

EXERCISES

Exercise 12.1.1. Revise Example 12.1 so that it uses strings to store a command rather than actual numbers. The virtue of this approach is that it doesn't risk an exception by using to use an **int** conversion. (Hint: you can still test the first character to see what digit it contains, if any.)

Exercise 12.1.2. If the phone book is empty and the user selects command number 2 (query), return immediately after stating that it's empty. (Hint: use the **len** method.)

Exercise 12.1.3. Write a similar application for a grades dictionary, in which the value field is stored as floating-point. Remember to change user prompts as appropriate.

Converting Dictionaries to Lists

Python dictionaries support a number of operations, and these are different from the ones supported for lists—although both support the **len** function.

From within the interactive environment, you can get a list of dictionary abilities by typing the following:

```
>>>help(dict)
```

Note that Python uses the word `dict` to refer to the general type that all dictionaries have.

So far, I've mentioned the use of the **get** method and the **len** function. Another useful method is the **items** method, which returns all the contents of the dictionary in a list format. Each element of this list is a tuple in (key, value) format. Here's an example:

```
>>>print(phone_dict.items())
dict_items([('John Bennett', '555-1000'),
            ('Jane Austen', '555-1212')])
```

But what is this strange thing called `dict_items`? It's not a list in the strict sense, but it is an *iterable*, which means you can loop through it. For example, you can print all the contents.

```
for i in phone_dict.items():
    print(i)
```

This might produce output such as the following:

```
('John Bennett', '555-1000')
('Jane Austen', '555-2000')
```

You can refer separately to keys and values if you want. Remember that the items method returns a series of tuples of the form (key, value).

```
for k, v in phone_dict.items():
    print('Key: {}, Value: {}'.format(k, v))
```

This loop prints

```
Key: John Bennett, Value: 555-1000
Key: Jane Austen, Value: 555-2000
```

Example 12.2. *Reading Items by Prefix*

This example is essentially the same as Example 12.1, but it adds one important function: the ability to select items based on their first few characters.

When using a phone book, I might not be able to remember the exact spelling of a certain name. Was it John Bennet or John Bennett? I can never remember. Sometimes it would be much easier just to tell the computer, "Give me a list of every name beginning with *J*." That's what the function in the next code listing does.

```
phone_dict2.py
```

```python
# Get by Prefix function. Prompt and search dict.
def display_by_prefix():
    while True:
        s = input('Enter prefix (ENTER to exit): ')
        s = s.strip()
        if not s:
            return
        for k, v in phone_dict.items():
            if k.startswith(s):
                print(k, '\t', v)
```

This function, of course, needs to be linked into the main program through a function call. We can let the user access this function through another command—let's call it the `prefix` command and assign it the number 4. The following bold lines represent new or altered statements.

```python
# Main function. Prompts for next command and executes.
def main():
    while True:
        prompt = 'Enter command:\n1. data entry, '
        prompt += '2. query, 3. exit, 4. prefix >> '
        s = input(prompt)
        if not s:
            break
        cmd = int(s)
        if cmd == 3:
            break
        if cmd == 1:
            get_entries()
        elif cmd == 2:
            display_entries()
        elif cmd == 4:
            display_by_prefix()
```

Here's a brief excerpt from a sample session:

```
Enter command:
1. data entry, 2. query, 3. exit, 4. prefix >> 4
Enter prefix (ENTER to exit): J
Jane Austen    555-1212
John Bennett   555-2000
Joseph Bloe    555-3333
```

How It Works

This example relies heavily on the **startswith** string method, which has the following syntax:

string.**startswith**(*prefix_str*)

This expression returns **True** if the first X characters of string match the characters in *prefix_str*, in which X is the length of the prefix. This method also has optional arguments that specify starting and ending positions to search.

This is a case-sensitive comparison.

string.**startswith**(*prefix_str, start, end*)

Most often, however, you'll use this method without the optional arguments. The **startswith** method enables the following loop to select everything that starts with the characters in **s**, the input string:

```
for k, v in phone_dict.items():
    if k.startswith(s):
        print(v, '\t', itm[1])
```

EXERCISES

Exercise 12.2.1. Revise Example 12.2 in such a way as to guarantee that the output is in sorted order. (Hint: Step through the items in such a way as to build a list, and then use the **sort** method on this list.)

Exercise 12.2.2. Write the answer to Exercise in 12.2.1 so that it makes at least one use of list comprehension.

Exercise 12.2.3. Write and test a "substring" function, which prints all items whose keys contain a substring entered by the user.

Example 12.3. *Loading and Saving to a File*

The next block of code adds two additional functions, for loading from a file and saving to a file. These capabilities help make the phone-book application truly useful, by enabling you to save the data semipermanently.

```
phone_book3.py
# Load files function.
# Use try/except to re-prompt if file not found.
def load_file():
```

phone_book3.py, cont.

```
        phone_dict.clear()   # This dict created earlier.
        while True:
            try:
                fname = input('Enter file to load: ')
                in_file = open(fname, 'r')
                a_list = in_file.readlines()
                for i in range(0, len(a_list), 2):
                    key_str = (a_list[i]).strip('\n')
                    val_str = (a_list[i + 1]).strip('\n')
                    phone_dict[key_str] = val_str
                print(fname, 'successfully loaded.')
                in_file.close()
                break
            except FileNotFoundError:
                print('File not found. Re-enter.')

    # Save file function.
    # Prompt for name of a file and then write out
    # key/val pairs.
    def save_file():
        fname = input('Enter file to save to: ')
        out_file = open(fname, 'w')
        for k in phone_dict:
            out_file.write(k + '\n')
            out_file.write(phone_dict[k] + '\n')
        out_file.close()
```

In addition to adding to these two functions, you would also need to modify the main function so that it provides access to these functions through command choices. One way to do this is to create a global list that contains tuples, each with a command number and name.

```
commands = [(1, 'Enter Records'), (2, 'Query'),
    (3, 'Load File'), (4, 'Save'), (5, 'Exit')]
```

You can also add in a list-by-prefix command if you want to incorporate the code from Example 12.2.

With this list in place, you can then print out a command list as follows:

```
for i, s in commands:
    print(i, s)
```

How It Works

This example introduces one method that may be new to you. But what it does is obvious: it clears the existing contents of phone_book, if any. This is optional, but usually it makes sense to do this before loading a new file.

```
phone_dict.clear()
```

Most of what the code in this example does is lifted from similar functions shown in Chapter 11, "File Ops." But Example 12.3 doesn't just read and write lines of text; it "reads" and "writes" these lines by reading or writing them into the dictionary named phone_dict.

For example, the load_file function reads pairs of text lines: the first line is read as a key, and the next as its corresponding value. Note that the **for** loop advances two lines at a time.

```
a_list = f.readlines()
for i in range(0, len(a_list), 2):
    key_str = (a_list[i]).strip('\n')
    val_str = (a_list[i + 1]).strip('\n')
    phone_book[key_str] = val_str
```

Notice how the **readlines** method reads all the lines of a text file into a list. The length of that list controls how many iterations of the loop are executed. Each iteration creates one key/value pair.

Similarly, the save_file function has a loop that writes two lines—one containing a key, the one after that containing the associated value—for each key/value pair. It's necessary to append a newline character (\n) so that each such **write** operation writes out a separate line.

```
for k in phone_dict:
    out_file.write(k + '\n')
    out_file.write(phone_book[k] + '\n')
```

After each of these loops, the **close** method is called on the file object (f) so that a file is kept open only as long as necessary.

```
out_file.close()
```

The following figure illustrates how two key/value pairs would be stored in a file:

'John Bennett\n'	first key
'555-1000\n'	first value
'Jane Austen\n'	second key
'555-1212\n'	second value

EXERCISES

Exercise 12.3.1. Put together all the code just described and test it, to make sure the application works. For extra credit, build a single print string, preferably using the **join** method, and then print that string rather than printing each command separately.

Exercise 12.3.2. When a file is loaded, save the name in a global string variable. Revise the `save_file` function so that it automatically saves to this same file. However, if no file has been previously loaded (so that you are dealing with a "new" file, so to speak), then when the `save_file` function is called, it prompts for a file name. If you're really ambitious, provide both a Save and a Save File command.

Exercise 12.3.3. Add a default file name to the application, such as `phone_data.txt`. At the beginning of the program, load this file if it exists. Then, when the user saves to a file, use this file name. In addition to a Save command, which uses the default file, maintain a separate Save As command so that the user can save to a different file.

All About Sets

Another type of data collection, closely related to the Python dictionary (`dict`) type, is the Python notion of set. Several things to keep in mind are

▶ Instead of "keys," a set has simple elements, very much as a list does.

▶ As with dictionary keys, these elements are always unique. Adding a value to a set that already contains that value has no effect.

▶ But unlike dictionaries, Python elements have no associated values. A set contains elements, not key-value pairs.

One basic idea should make it very easy to understand sets: a Python set is close to the concept of sets in mathematics. For example, you can get unions and intersections.

But there's at least one little "gotcha." Sets use a notation that looks much like a dictionary: they use curly braces, which mathematicians sometimes call *set braces*.

```
set_name = { value1, value2, value3… }
```

There's a limitation. This notation works only when there is one or more elements, or values. So the following all work, as ways of creating sets:

```
lucky_nums = { 3, 7, 11, 27, 9 }
friends_set = {'John', 'Pete', 'Ken', 'Jane'}
fav_num_set = { 5 }
```

But a problem occurs when you use an empty set of braces: Python considers that to designate an empty dictionary.

```
a_set = {}
```

This looks innocent enough, but consider the following behavior, which you can test from within the interactive environment:

```
>>>a_set = {}
>>>type(a_set)
<class 'dict'>
```

You should be able to see that you're already in trouble. The **type** function indicates that you've created a dictionary (dict), not a set.

Fortunately, Python provides an easy way to create an empty set.

empty_set_name = **set()**

Here's an example:

```
a_set = set()
```

Operations on Sets

The biggest single difference between sets and lists is that sets maintain unique values. You can attempt to keep adding a duplicate value to a set, but that operation is simply ignored. As I first explained in Chapter 6, "List Comprehension and Enumeration," there are times this is exactly the behavior you want, and we'll take advantage of it in the upcoming Example 12.4.

Another difference is that ordering in a set does not matter. So the following two sets are equivalent:

```
>>>a_set = {1, 2, 3}
>>>b_set = {3, 2, 1}
>>>a_set == b_set
True
```

Set collections support a number of methods that are unique to sets. First, remember that you can always add and remove members. This is similar to the **append** method for lists.

```
>>>beat_set = {'John', 'Paul', 'George', 'Pete'}
>>>beat_set.remove('Pete')
>>>beat_set.add('Ringo')
>>>beat_set
{ 'George', 'Paul', 'John', 'Ringo' }
```

Remember that the ordering a set is given has no significance.

Some of the other most important operations on sets include intersection, union, and difference. There are many other operations, which you can learn about by typing **help(set)** from within IDLE.

Assume the following two sets:

```
a_set = {1, 2, 3, 4, 5, 6}
b_set = {4, 5, 6, 10, 20}
```

Given these definitions, we can picture the union of the two sets through a traditional set-theory diagram (Venn diagram). The union produces the set {1, 2, 3, 4, 5, 6, 10, 20}. An element is in the union if it is a member of *either or both* sets.

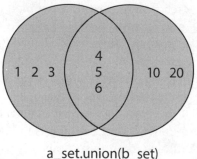

a_set.union(b_set)

We can do the same thing with intersections. An element is in the intersection if it is a member of *both* sets. Therefore, the intersection of these two sets is {4, 5, 6}.

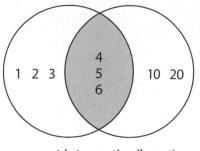

a_set.intersection(b_set)

Finally, the difference between the sets is either "a_set − b_set" or "b_set − a_set"; in the former case, it consists of all elements of a_set *that are not elements* of b_set. That operation produces the set {1, 2, 3}.

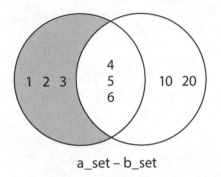

a_set − b_set

Interlude   **What's So Important About Sets?**

Back in the 1960s and 1970s, many mathematics textbooks at the elementary school level introduced something called "The New Math." What this meant was mostly that students would be exposed to set theory early on.

Set theory had taken on special significance a number of decades earlier, around the turn of the previous century. A group of mathematical philosophers—especially Frege, Russell, and Whitehead—were looking for a more solid basis on which to base mathematics and logic. They found what they were looking for in set theory, or thought they did. For example, the number 2, they thought, could be defined as the set of all dualities.

But alas, there were logical problems even in the heart of set theory. Russell himself famously realized that if a set could contain itself, this led to an unsolvable logical paradox—and the only solution was to declare that a set could not be a member of itself.

Set theory is still considered useful in mathematics, for example, in classifying rational and irrational numbers as members of different sets: sets that, surprisingly, have different properties even though both are infinite. But in recent decades, set theory has been eclipsed to a large extent by group theory. That's another story.

Example 12.4.   *Revised Sieve of Eratosthenes*

This example uses the Python set-collection capability to provide a more efficient version of the sieve of Eratosthenes example in Chapter 6.

```
sieve3.py

nums = set(range(2, 20))
comps = {j for i in nums for j in range(i*i, 20, i)}
primes = nums - comps
print(primes)
```

When properly entered and executed, this short program prints the following set of prime numbers, which begins with 2 and continues up to but not including 20.

{2, 3, 5, 7, 11, 13, 17, 19}

How It Works

Although this program is incredibly short, it has some subtle features. First, the **range** keyword is used to help generate a set beginning with 2, up to but not including 20.

{2, 3, 4, 5… 19}

The problem is that the **range** keyword produces a list, not a set. It might be tempting to make a set by putting it inside braces.

```
nums = { range(2, 20) }   # ERROR! Wrong way to do this.
```

The problem with that approach is that it simply creates a set with one element; and that element is a list! Instead, the proper way to create a set from a range is to use the **set** keyword to do a conversion. This produces the set we actually want.

```
nums = set(range(2, 20))  # Right way to make a set.
```

Another subtle feature is the use of list comprehension, although here it is actually "set comprehension." Look again at the longest statement in the program.

```
comps = {j for i in nums for j in range(i*i, 20, i)}
```

This statement is equivalent to the following:

```
comps = set()
for i in nums:
    for j in range(i * i, 20, j):
        comps.add(j)
```

The reason the set-comprehension approach works is that the expression between the braces is not a list but actually an *iterable*, which is a series of values that you can get one at a time, and an iterable can be made into a list or a set, depending on whether brackets or braces are used.

As explained in Chapter 6, this nested for loop causes j to be set to the multiple of each number in the set nums. Each such value of j—which represents the multiple of some number i, starting with i * i—is added to the set named comps, which forms the set of composite numbers.

And it makes far more sense to make comps a set rather than a list, because in some cases, a number would be added for inclusion more than once (12, for example), and it's more efficient to automatically avoid maintaining duplicate values, which is what sets do.

Finally, to get the prime numbers in the interval between 2 and 19, inclusive, we simply "subtract out" the composite numbers by using the set-difference operation.

```
primes = nums - comps
```

EXERCISES

Exercise 12.4.1.   Two of the statements in Example 12.4 can be combined in a very easy and trivial way to save a line. Carry out this fix.

Exercise 12.4.2.   Revise Example 12.4 so that it prompts the user to enter a number N; then find and print all the prime numbers up to but not including N.

Exercise 12.4.3.   Write a program that uses sets, as much as possible, to contain all the even numbers between 1 and 25. Then use the set "difference" operation to produce a set containing all the odd numbers in that range.

Chapter 12   *Summary*

Here are the major points of Chapter 12:

▶ A Python dictionary (type dict) is a collection type that a series of key/value pairs. Here's an example:

```
my_dict = {'one' : 1, 'two' : 2, 'three' : 3}
```

▶ Keys are maintained so that they are always unique.

▶ Values can contain any number of duplications relative to each other. For example, the same value, 4.0, can be assigned to many different keys.

12

▶ The following syntax can be used either to add a new key/value pair or to change the value associated with an existing key.

```
my_dict['four'] = 4
```

▶ You can also use this expression on the right side of an assignment or in another context, provided that the key already exists. The result is to produce the associated value.

```
n = my_dict['four']
```

▶ But this syntax raises a **KeyError** exception if the key can't currently be found in the dictionary.

▶ The **get** method returns the value associated with a key; if the key does not exist in the dictionary, then **get** returns the special value **None**. This return value can be tested to see if the key does or does not exist, but it will not raise an exception.

```
n = my_dict.get('four')
```

▶ Once you choose a type for keys, use it consistently. The associated values can have any type, but it is usually a good idea to pick a consistent data type for values as well.

▶ Sets are similar to lists but contain no duplicate members, and the ordering within a set has no significance.

▶ To declare an empty set, you must use a set conversion, not just empty braces.

```
empty_set = set()
```

▶ You can also use braces to specify a set, but that notation must include at least one element; otherwise it creates an empty dictionary.

```
a_set = {1, 2, 3}
```

▶ Thereafter, you can use the **add** and **remove** methods to add or remove new elements. If you try to add an element that duplicates an existing element, that has no effect.

▶ The methods supported by sets include **union**, **intersection**, and **difference**.

▶ The subtraction operator (-) performs a set difference operation, yielding all the elements that are members of the first set (nums) but not the second (comps).

```
primes = nums - comps
```

▶ The **len** function works on dictionaries and sets, just as it works on lists.

Matrixes: 2-D Lists

Python lists can contain almost any kind of Python data, including other lists. So what would you call a list of lists?

The answer is a two-dimensional list, also called a *matrix*. Many applications—and game programs in particular—depend on the use of matrixes.

This chapter covers several aspects of matrixes.

▶ Creating small matrixes

▶ Creating large, N*M matrixes

▶ Rotating a matrix

Simple Matrixes

With Python, you can easily create small matrixes (two-dimensional lists) by direct initialization. For example, to create a three-by-three matrix, in which all elements initialized to 0, you could use this statement:

```
list2D = [[0, 0, 0], [0, 0, 0], [0, 0, 0]]
```

For clarity, I could also enter the statement this way. Remember that this works because a statement with an open parenthesis or bracket automatically extends onto the next line.

```
list2D = [ [0, 0, 0],
           [0, 0, 0],
           [0, 0, 0] ]
```

You can, of course, initialize the elements to any values you want. Here's an example:

```
list2D = [ [1, 3, 2],
           [50, 50, 66],
           [-1, -2, -3] ]
```

These values are all integers. But you can use any kind of data you want. You could use floating-point numbers or strings, for example. But for this chapter, we'll stick with numeric data, just to keep things simple.

Accessing Elements

If you've programmed in another language such as C, C++, or Java, this next section should be obvious to you. To access an element of a two-dimensional list, use the following syntax:

```
list_name [row_num] [col_num] = n
```

For example, to assign 67 to the first element of the first row, you'd use this statement:

```
mat[0][0] = 67
```

Within Python, index numbers—whether for lists, tuples, or other data collections—are always zero-based, and this extends to any number of dimensions. Zero-based numbers run from 0 to N-1, where N is the length of the dimension.

So in a three-by-three matrix, the index numbers are as shown here:

m[0][0]	m[0][1]	m[0][2]
m[1][0]	m[1][1]	m[1][2]
m[2][0]	m[2][1]	m[2][2]

Once a matrix has been created, you can both assign to and assign from array elements all you want, as long as none of the indexes go out of range.

```
mat[2][1] = mat[0][1] + mat[1][1]
```

This statement assigns a value to one element by adding up the values of two other elements. Essentially, this particular statement sums the middle column's top two rows and enters the result in the bottom row.

mat = [[0,5,0], [0,3,0], [0,0,0]]

0	5	0
0	3	0
0	8	0

└── mat[2][1] = mat[0][1] + mat[1][1]

Irregular Matrixes and Length of a Row

Python makes it easy to create irregular-shaped matrixes. Here's an example:

```
>>>mat = [ [-1, -2, -3],
           [10, 20],
           [1, 2, 3, 4, 5] ]
```

This matrix doesn't have a simple *rows* × *cols* shape but instead has rows of size 3, 2, and 5. How, in general, do you determine the size (or sizes) of such a matrix?

You can get the length of a matrix directly, but doing so just gives the number of rows.

```
>>>len(mat)
3
```

The variable matr refers to a list that happens to contain three other lists. Each of these lists can be thought of as a "row." These rows, in turn, have length 3, 2, and 5.

```
>>>len(mat[0])
3
>>>len(mat[1])
2
>>>len(mat[2])
5
```

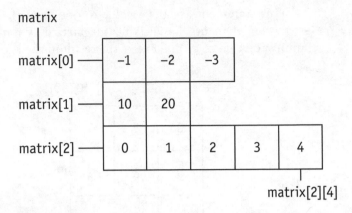

Multiplication (*) and Lists

Once you've been programming for a while, you'll want to know how to create larger, N*M matrixes—matrixes of arbitrarily large size. This is almost trivial to do in other languages but requires special techniques in Python.

First, however, you need to understand how the multiplication operator (*) affects lists. Suppose you want to create a string made of hyphens (-) without typing them all out. In Python, you can do that this way:

```
border_str = '-' * 40
```

This statement creates a string consisting of 40 hyphens. It's a useful technique in itself, and we'll make use of it in Chapter 17, "Conway's Game of Life."

You can do something similar with lists. A long list can be created out of a shorter list, efficiently creating a list of any size.

```
z_list = [0] * 9
```

Now z_list is a list of length 9, initialized to all 0s. Valid indexes run from 0 to 8. It's still a one-dimensional list that you can use just like any other. And you can print it out.

```
>>>z_list = [0] * 9
>>>print(z_list)
[0, 0, 0, 0, 0, 0, 0, 0, 0]
```

This technique enables you to build arbitrarily large lists from smaller lists of any size. Here's an example:

```
>>>z_list = [0, 1] * 5
>>>print(z_list)
[0, 1, 0, 1, 0, 1, 0, 1, 0, 1]
```

But so far, we've only been able to create (or rather, extend) one-dimensional lists. To get a *list of lists* is another matter. You might imagine you could do it this way:

```
mat = [ [0] * 4 ] * 4
```

And this actually does create a list of lists—in a sense. But it's not usable. Why not?

The Python Matrix Problem

The problem with the statement at the end of the previous section is that it does create several rows—but it's the same row created over and over. Here's another example:

```
>>>mat = [ [0] * 3 ] * 3
```

You can print it out. But watch what happens if you set an element and then print it again:

```
>>>print(mat)
[[0, 0, 0], [0, 0, 0], [0, 0, 0]]
>>>mat[0][0] = 555
>>>print(mat)
[[555, 0, 0], [555, 0, 0], [555, 0, 0]]
```

What happened? We set one element to 555, and yet 555 occurs three times! If you experiment, you'll discover that whatever setting you make to any row of the matrix automatically affects *every other row.*

Here's the problem: The expression [[0] * 3] * 3 was supposed to create a three-by-three matrix. Instead, it created one row and then created *three references* to it. Instead of getting three separate rows, you get one row, but it's referred to three times. This is not what we want.

Here's another way to understand this problem. In Python, a statement such as

```
mat = [[0] * 3] * 3
```

…has the same effect as if you'd entered the following:

```
row = [0] * 3
mat = [row, row, row]
```

How to Create N*M Matrixes: The Solution

The problem is that, unlike many other languages, Python has no data declarations. If it did, it would've been easy for the designers of the language to come up with a multidimensional list syntax.

Instead, you have to create, or rather build, a multidimensional list from the ground up. Here's the simplest way to do that:

```
name = [ [val] * cols  for i in range(rows)]
```

Here are some examples. These create a 3-by-3, 10-by-10, and a 20-by-12 matrix.

```
m1 = [[0] * 3  for i in range(3)]
m2 = [[0] * 10 for i in range(10)]
m3 = [[0] * 12 for i in range(20)]
```

In this last case, there are 12 columns and 20 rows, because the left part of the expression creates a single row ([0] * 12) and then replicates it 20 times. The last element of that matrix is m3[19][11].

This syntax uses list comprehension, first introduced in Chapter 6. The reason it works—to take the last example—is because it is equivalent to the following:

```
m3 = []
for i in range(20):
    m3.append([0] * 12)
```

Here's the critical point: this loop generates a *new instance* of [0] * 12 each time it executes. You therefore get 20 independent rows rather than getting the same row over and over.

If you want, you can initialize all the values of the matrix to a value other than 0. For example, the following assignment initializes all the values to –1:

```
m4 = [[-1] * 10 for i in range(10)]
```

You can even initialize every row to different values.

```
m5 = [[i] * 4 for i in range(4)]
```

By now, you should be able to predict what you'll see if the matrix, m5, is printed.

But if you want to initialize every element of the matrix to a unique value, you have no choice but to use nested list comprehension. Here's an example:

```
m6 = [[i * j for j in range(5)] for i in range(5)]
```

Here's a "pretty" display loop followed by the results:

```
>>>for i in m6:
    print (i)

[0, 0, 0, 0, 0]
[0, 1, 2, 3, 4]
[0, 2, 4, 6, 8]
[0, 3, 6, 9, 12]
[0, 4, 8, 12, 16]
```

Can you create matrixes of three, four, or even more dimensions?

Yes. The technique requires you to keep adding uses of list comprehension. So, a two-dimensional matrix is created this way:

```
mat_2d = [[0] * 10  for i in range(10)]
```

A three-dimensional array (each dimensional also equal to 10) is created this way:

```
mat_3d = [[[0] * 10 for i in range(10)]
                    for j in range(10)]
```

You should be able to see that by adding list-comprehension clauses, you can increase the matrix to have as many dimensions as you want. It's not even necessary to use variables on the right side, by the way. You can use an underscore (_) to indicate a "blank" variable.

```
mat_3d = [[[0] * 10 for _ in range(10)]
                    for _ in range(10)]
```

And a *four*-dimensional list? You could create it with the following statement, although I am reducing each dimension to five elements each, because this matrix is starting to occupy a great deal of space!

```
mat_4d = [[[[0] * 5 for _ in range(5)]
                    for _ in range(5)]
                    for _ in range(5)]
```

Interlude

Why Isn't It Easier?

The previous section should be the response to anyone who says the reason for learning Python is "It's easier."

It's certainly easier to do many, many things in Python. You can sit down and program without having to declare anything. You don't have to worry about semicolons and braces, for the most part. Best of all, you're provided with many powerful built-in functions.

▼ *continued on next page*

Interlude

▼ *continued*

But creating large matrixes is, sadly, not easier in Python. In a supposedly "harder" language such as C or C++, you can create a matrix of any size just by declaring it.

```
int my_matrix[20][50];
```

If this declaration is at the global level (not inside a function), all the values are initialized to zero for you, courtesy of C!

Why can't the Python technique for creating matrixes be as easy as the technique in C or C++?

The answer is that this is part of the price one pays for Python's declaration-free language. As this book has stated many times, the way you create a variable is by assigning it a value. To create an array, therefore, it's necessary to append one row at a time and one element a time. The list-comprehension syntax, in effect, sets up loops that do just that…. but do it in a relatively small amount of space.

Example 13.1.   *Multiplication Table*

This application builds a matrix that contains the values of a multiplication table and prints them out.

```
mult_tab.py

def main():
    rows = cols = 8
    mat = [[(i + 1) * (j + 1) for j in range(cols)]
                              for i in range(rows)]
    # Print out matrix
    for i in range(rows):
        for j in range(cols):
            print('{:>2} '.format(mat[i][j]), end='')
        print()

main()
```

This application produces an 8-by-8 multiplication table that shows the results of multiplying values ranging between 1 and 8. You can easily make it bigger if your screen has the room.

Here's the output:

```
1  2  3  4  5  6  7  8
2  4  6  8 10 12 14 16
3  6  9 12 15 18 21 24
4  8 12 16 20 24 28 32
5 10 15 20 25 30 35 40
6 12 18 24 30 36 42 48
7 14 21 28 35 42 49 56
8 16 24 32 40 48 56 64
```

How It Works

This program stores multiplication values in a matrix and then prints out the values. If that's all you need a program to do, it would make more sense to just print the values on the screen without bothering to store them.

However, this example features some important coding techniques we're going to utilize in upcoming sections. First, the program begins by creating an 8-by-8 matrix. We could have created a matrix initialized to all zeroes and set the values later, using a nested loop. But that would have been inefficient.

```
# This is the less efficient way.
m = [[0] * cols for i in range(rows)]
```

As long as we're going to the trouble of creating the array, why not initialize it with the correct values from the beginning? The program therefore uses the following statement to generate and set up the multiplication table in one fell swoop:

```
m = [[(i + 1) * (j + 1) for j in range(cols)]
                        for i in range(rows)]
```

The values i + 1 and j + 1 create a 1-based table rather than a 0-based table, because multiplication by zero isn't interesting.

The program uses a nested loop to print out the contents of the matrix.

```
for i in range(rows):
    for j in range(cols):
        print('{:>2} '.format(m[i][j]), end='')
    print()
```

Notice the use of the **format** string method, which right-justifies each element in a print field two characters in size. The string {:>2} fixes this formatting pattern.

Note, also, that it's necessary to print a newline after each row of the table is printed. This does not happen automatically. Instead, the final line, which calls **print** again with no arguments, prints a newline at the end of each row.

EXERCISES

Exercise 13.1.1.   Revise Example 13.1 so that it prints a 12-by-12 multiplication table. Make sure everything still aligns nicely; this will require a change to the formatting code.

Exercise 13.1.2.   What advantage, if any, is there to using the variables rows and cols, instead of "hard-coding" 8 and 8 or 12 and 12?

Exercise 13.1.3.   Instead of using fixed sizes for the dimension of the table, prompt the user for these values: number of rows and number of columns.

Exercise 13.1.4.   Remember that making many calls to the **print** function slows down performance time substantially. Instead of making many such calls, build up a large print string and then print it at the end. (Hint: Remember that you can represent a newline as \n.)

Exercise 13.1.5.   Create a four-dimensional matrix, each dimension length 2 in size. Set every element to the product of i * j * k * m, where each value is an index of the element plus one (because we're simulating one-based indexes). Use list comprehension as shown in this chapter rather than direct specification of values.

If you're really ambitious, figure out an elegant way to print this four-dimensional matrix. This may take some thought.

Example 13.2.   *User-Initialized Matrix*

The next step in mastering two-dimensional (matrix) technology is to let the user enter any and all the values of the elements. We'll assume a five-by-five matrix size.

This program, in turn, will prove to be a slick little utility for entering any numbers the user likes into the matrix; and it will be useful in the next sections, when we rotate the matrix.

```
mat_enter.py

    def main():
        rows = cols = 5
        mat = [[0] * cols for i in range(rows)]
        for i in range(rows):
            s = input('Enter a row of values: ')
```

mat_enter.py, cont.

```
            a_list = s.split()
            for j, item in enumerate(a_list):
                if j >= cols:
                    break
                mat[i][j] = int(item)
        print_mat(mat)


    # Print_mat function. This is written in such a way
    # that size information (row, col) does not need to
    # to be passed in as extra arguments.

    def print_mat(mat):
        s = ''
        for a_row in mat:
            for item in a_row:
                s +='{:>3} '.format(item)
            s += '\n'
        print(s)

    main()
```

How It Works

The program starts by creating a five-by-five matrix in which each element is initialized to 0. This initialization is desirable in this case, because we want the default value for each element to be 0.

```
rows = cols = 5
mat = [[0] * cols for i in range(rows)]
```

The rest of the main function consists of an input-values loop. For each row in the matrix—in this case, there are five rows—the user is prompted to enter a set of values. The approach here is meant to be "idiot proof."

Specifically, let's suppose that N is the number of items entered, while Cols is the number of columns in a row.

▶ If N is smaller than Cols, then the last Col-N elements are left set to 0.

▶ If N is greater than Cols, then the last N-Col entries are ignored.

Here is pseudocode that summarizes what the statements do.

For each i from 0 to rows–1,

    Prompt user for a line of input

    Split that input line into a list of strings

    For each item in this list,

        If the max. number of items have been entered, break.

        Assign item to appropriate matrix element.

The **enumerate** function, first introduced in Chapter 6, is useful here. Remember that this function returns an index/item pair—which in turn provides direct access to individual elements as well as getting an index number "for free." There are other ways to write this, but **enumerate**, in this situation, enables you to write cleaner code.

```
for j, item in enumerate(a_list):
    if j >= cols:
        break
    m[i][j] = int(item)
```

Optimizing the Code

The snippet of code at the end of the previous section works, but we can improve on it. Remember the problem: to read as many items from the input line as possible, provided the number of items read does not exceed the column size (5 in this case).

Really, then, we'd like to just get up to the first five items—or rather the first `cols` items—but no more. We can do this through slicing.

```
for j, item in enumerate(a_list[:cols]):
    m[i][j] = int(item)
```

The expression `a_list[:cols]` says, "Get all the elements up to but not including the element indexed by `cols`." In other words, get the first five elements.

But what if the user entered fewer than five elements? That's not a problem, because in that case, `a_list[:cols]` simply gets all the elements. Therefore, `a_list[:cols]` really says, "Get at most the first five elements," which is exactly what we want.

EXERCISES

Exercise 13.2.1. At the beginning of the program, prompt the user for the number of rows and the number of columns to use.

Exercise 13.2.2. Revise the program so that as soon as the user enters a number larger than 1000, the size of the print field is increased. Also, increase the print field if the number entered is less than –99. How general can you make this solution?

Exercise 13.2.3. Revise the program so that it converts negative entries into positive ones.

Exercise 13.2.4. Can you write the program in such a way that it avoids using a range in the outer loop? Specifically, after the matrix exists, can you replace

```
for i in range(rows):
```

with a more direct form of iteration? You still need to make the program work correctly.

How to Rotate a Matrix

Now that you know how to create a matrix and let the user enter values for it, you can create an application that does something interesting: rotating a matrix entered by a user.

Rotating a matrix clockwise 90 degrees is a classic problem in computer science. Complex "in-place" solutions are possible, so I'm going to present the approach that is by far the easiest: build a new matrix from an old one and then just replace the first.

Python, as you'll see, makes this whole process easy. First, examine what happens to the coordinates of a cell as it's rotated clockwise 90 degrees.

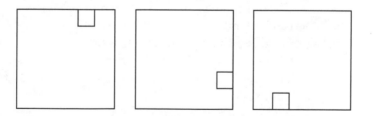

During these two rotations, the coordinates of a typical cell (element) transform as follows—to which I've added two more rotations:

```
[0] [3]
[3] [4]
[4] [1]
[1] [0]
[0] [3]
```

From observation, you can see a pattern for each pair of coordinates, [i][j]:

▶ The new value of i gets the old value of j.

▶ The new value of j gets 4 minus the old value of i.

Therefore, to create a new matrix out of the old one, the correct transformation for each cell is

```
new_matrix[j][4 - i] = old_matrix[i][j]
```

This rotation rule can also be expressed as follows (and we'll find this useful later):

```
new_matrix[i][j] = old_matrix[4 - j][i]
```

But how do we create a whole new matrix and use it to replace the old? Ideally, we want to be able to perform this entire operation over and over, so the old matrix has to be discarded after each rotation.

The solution is essentially a three-step process:

1   Create a new matrix of the same dimensions as the first; we can label this new matrix mat2.

2   Assign new values to each individual mat2 element, using the transformation formula we just arrived at.

3   Assign the "current matrix" value, mat, to refer to the same matrix as mat2. This is accomplished by the simple statement mat1 = mat2.

The third step is the interesting one. It has a couple of effects. First, it causes mat1 to refer to the same data in memory that mat2 does. This operation happens lightning fast, as no actual data is copied other than a simple reference to mat2. The second effect is that the old data is now an "orphan," in a sense. It's still there, but nothing refers to it. There's no way for the program to get at it anymore.

And in C, that would be a problem, because of the danger of "memory leaks"—sections of memory that are no longer used but take up space that could be used other programs.

Fortunately, Python magically solves this problem through a process called *garbage collection*. When a piece of data exists for which there is no reference, the Python engine deletes it. It's "magic" because you don't have to pay attention to it.

The bottom line is that mat1 now refers to the post-rotational data—which is what we want—and the old data will be deleted from memory automatically.

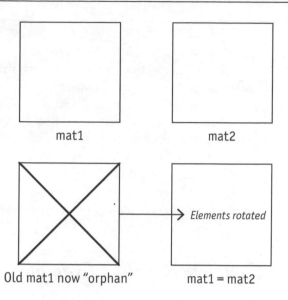

mat1   mat2

Old mat1 now "orphan"   mat1 = mat2

Interlude

Pros and Cons of Garbage Collection

The "garbage collection" approach to matrix rotation, presented in the previous section, is the easiest from a Python programming perspective. However, it does involve the constant creation of a new matrix, followed by the copying of element values into their new positions, and followed by the automatic deletion of the old matrix in memory. For most purposes, this is fine.

But if you're dealing with very large matrixes and if performance time is an issue, you might want to look for a more efficient solution.

One such solution would be to maintain exactly two matrixes in memory at all times and then switch between them after each rotation. This is a good solution, and it is left as one of the exercises later in this chapter.

But what if you're happy with the "garbage collection" solution, in which the old matrix is automatically deleted by some background process?

Is such a solution doable in C?

As a matter of fact, yes. But it requires a great deal more work on the part of the programmer. The C coder has to explicitly allocate memory when he or she wants to dynamically create a new object in memory. That memory, in turn, has to be referred to something called a *pointer*, which in C is the only way to refer to new objects in memory. Finally, the C programmer has to explicitly delete the memory when it's no longer in use, or the program can and will create memory leaks.

▼ *continued on next page*

Interlude

▼ *continued*

Modern programmers who program in Python, Java, or C# have come to appreciate the freedom from worry that automatic garbage collection gives them. "Let the programming environment itself worry about garbage collection," they might say. "That's what it's there for."

That is one way to look at it. But a typical C programmer has a different way of looking at it. Because garbage collection isn't hidden from the programmer by being taken care of automatically, the C programmer can get garbage collection only by making a deliberate decision to use it. This is an advantage to having a C-language background. It forces you to think about implementation and performance issues.

Example 13.3. *Complete Rotation Example*

The following major example is the culmination of everything in this chapter. It demonstrates how to create a matrix, let the user initialize any and all values, and finally rotate it any number of times.

```
rotate.py

n = 5
mat1 = [[0] * n for i in range(n)]

def main():
    enter_mat_vals()
    print_mat()
    s = ''
    while not s or s[0] not in 'Nn':
        rotate_mat()
        print('Here is the rotated version:')
        print_mat()
        s = input('Rotate matrix again? (Y or N): ')

def rotate_mat():
    global mat1
    mat2 = [[0] * n for i in range(n)]
    for i in range(n):
        for j in range(n):
            mat2[j][n - 1 - i] = mat1[i][j]
```

rotate.py, cont.

```python
        mat1 = mat2

def enter_mat_vals():
    for i in range(n):
        s = input('Enter a row of values: ')
        a_list = s.split()
        for j, item in enumerate(a_list[:n]):
            mat1[i][j] = int(item)

def print_mat():
    s = ''
    for i in range(n):
        for j in range(n):
            s +='{:>3} '.format(mat1[i][j])
        s += '\n'
    print(s)

main()
```

13

Here is a sample session:

```
Enter a row of values: 1 2 3 4 5
Enter a row of values: 20
Enter a row of values: 30
Enter a row of values: 0 0 0 66
Enter a row of values: 0 55
  1   2   3   4   5
 20   0   0   0   0
 30   0   0   0   0
  0   0   0  66   0
  0  55   0   0   0

Here is the rotated version:
  0   0  30  20   1
 55   0   0   0   2
  0   0   0   0   3
  0  66   0   0   4
  0   0   0   0   5

Rotate matrix again? (Y or N): N
```

How It Works

This program consists of four functions: main, enter_mat_vals, rotate_mat, and print_mat. The main function does something only mildly interesting: it sets up a loop that continues until the user indicates they'd like to quit the programming by typing **No**, **N**, or just **n**.

The main program executes the "Should I continue?" test at the top of the loop.

```
s = ''
while not s or s[0] not in 'Nn':
```

The expression not s is tested first, because if the input string is empty, then testing the first character would cause an error. By the way, because of how this is written, the default command (selected by just pressing Enter) is to do another rotation.

The enter_mat_vals and print_mat functions execute lines of code that have already been described earlier in this chapter, in Example 13.2. The interesting new function, therefore, is the rotate_mat function.

```
def rotate_mat():
    global mat1
    mat2 = [[0 for j in range(n)] for i in range(n)]
    for i in range(n):
        for j in range(n):
            mat2[j][n - 1 - i] = mat1[i][j]
    mat1 = mat2
```

This function requires a **global** statement, because there's a global variable named "mat1" that needs to be seen by the entire program. As explained in Chapter 10, "Local and Global Variables," when Python sees an assignment, it tries to determine whether the variable could be interpreted as a local. In this case, mat1 *could* be interpreted as local because

 An assignment to a variable creates that variable if it does not exist already.

But the **global** statement prevents Python from interpreting mat1 as local, thereby forcing it to recognize the global version.

```
global mat1
```

Coming to our aid here is another Golden Rule of Python. As Chapter 10 pointed out, there is one principle that determines when you must use the **global** statement to avoid error.

 If a function uses a global variable, and if that function assigns data to the variable, then use a "global" statement to prevent it from being local.

Now, what about the `enter_mat_vals` function? This function assigns data to an element within `mat`:

$$mat1[i][j] = int(item)$$

This statement is permitted because Python lists are mutable, and therefore list elements can be changed. But this is a change to an element, not a reassignment to `mat1` itself. Therefore, a **global** statement is not needed.

But consider this statement:

```
mat1 = mat2
```

This statement breaks the association `mat1` has with the old matrix and makes it an alias for the new data, stored in `mat2`.

What happens to the old matrix, the one that holds data before rotation? It no longer has any variable referring to it. Therefore, Python will eventually delete that old data from memory when it has a chance, thanks to Python *garbage collection.*

To summarize, here are the statements in the `rotate_mat` function:

The "global" statement ensures that changes to mat1 affect the entire program.

Create mat2 as a new 5 by 5 matrix, taking up 25 places in memory.

For i in range 0 to 4,

For j in range 0 to 4,

Copy mat1[i][j] to a rotated position in mat2

Assign mat1 to refer to the new matrix, mat2

Optimizing the Code

In the `rotate_mat` function, I broke down everything into a series of discrete steps. However, by using list comprehension, it's possible to combine many of these steps.

```
def rotate_mat():
    global mat1
    mat2 = [[mat1[n - 1 - j][i] for j in range(n)]
                                for i in range(n)]
    mat1 = mat2
```

This does everything the longer version of the function does, but it does some of it implicitly. A new matrix is created, and the variable `mat1` is associated with this new data object in memory. The effect is therefore the same: the old matrix is orphaned and will be the target of garbage collection. All this happens without having to name a new matrix (mat2). You can now replace all occurrences of mat1 with just mat if you wish.

To make this work, I had to reverse the coordinates for rotation. The list comprehension in this case implicitly does the following:

```
new_matrix[i][j] = old_matrix[n - 1 - j][i]
```

EXERCISES

Exercise 13.3.1.   Revise the print_mat function in this example to use the simpler, more direct for loops used earlier, in Example 13.2. Test everything to make sure it still works.

Exercise 13.3.2.   Revise Example 13.3.1 so that it rotates the matrix counterclockwise during each rotation.

Exercise 13.3.3.   Revise the example so that it gives the user three choices: 1) horizontal inversion, 2) vertical inversion, and 3) quitting. *Inversion* should flip the matrix either horizontally or vertically, changing the matrix into its reflection.

Exercise 13.3.4.   Revise the example so that instead of creating a new matrix each cycle, it switches back and forth between two matrixes in memory. Alternately, either mat1 or mat2 is the "current" matrix, and the other becomes the new matrix to be written to.

Chapter 13   *Summary*

Here are the main points of Chapter 13:

▶ Python supports lists inside of lists, which become two-, three-, and higher-dimensional matrixes.

▶ You can create small arrays by declaring all the elements of the two-dimensional lists (matrixes) this way:

```
my_matrix = [[0, 0, 0], [0, 0, 0], [0, 0, 0]]
```

▶ To create larger matrixes, you need to use a declaration such as the following, which creates a matrix of size *rows* by *cols*:

```
m = [[v] * cols  for i in range(rows)]
```

▶ You can also use

```
m = [[v for j in range(cols)] for i in range(rows)]
```

▶ You can refer to an individual element of a matrix as follows; remember that in each dimension, indexes run from 0 to N-1, in which N is the size of the dimension.

```
mat[4][5] = n
```

▶ To print or reset all the values of a matrix, use a nested loop. Here's an example:

```
for i in range(rows):
    for j in range(cols):
        mat[i][j] = n
```

▶ If you're not going to be setting or resetting matrix values, you can loop this way:

```
for a_row in mat:
    for item in a_row:
        print(item, end=' ')
```

▶ If the only variable referring to a block of data, such as a matrix, loses its association to the data, that data becomes an "orphan" that no longer is accessible by the program.

▶ Python automatically looks for and deletes such orphans from memory. This process is called *garbage collection*.

▶ Remember the general principle that the fewer separate calls a program makes to the **print** function, the faster will be the runtime performance.

13

14 Winning at Tic-Tac-Toe

One of the most universally played childhood games is Tic-Tac-Toe. In a three-by-three matrix, each player takes turns marking an X or an O until one player gets three in a row, horizontally, vertically, or diagonally.

Sounds simple, doesn't it? But to handle all aspects of the game is far from trivial. This chapter attacks the problem in several steps.

▶ Creating the board and permitting moves

▶ Determining the winner

▶ Implementing a complete strategy for a computer player

Design of a Tic-Tac-Toe Board

As we implement a Tic-Tac-Toe game, the use of character-based graphics is fine for now. This version of the game will print out a simple display, prompt the user for a move, and then print the new board. Here is the game board at the beginning:

```
  1 2 3
1 . . .
2 . . .
3 . . .
```

There are two players, the X player and the O player. Player 1 (the X player) goes first. Let's say she enters the coordinates 2, 2 to take the center. The refreshed board is then

```
  1 2 3
1 . . .
2 . X .
3 . . .
```

Player 2 (the O player) chooses to go one square above—coordinates row 1, column 2. This results in the following board:

```
  1 2 3
1 . O .
2 . X .
3 . . .
```

So far, so good. But the X player (player 1) gets the next move. She takes the corner (1,1), threatening a win on the diagonal (1,1), (2,2), (3,3).

```
  1 2 3
1 X O .
2 . X .
3 . . .
```

Now the O player has no choice but to block the threatened win. He plays in the opposite corner: (3,3).

```
  1 2 3
1 X O .
2 . X .
3 . . O
```

X now plays the *coup de grâce*. Placing the X in the space (2,1) threatens two wins: there's the vertical win with (1,1), (2,1), (3,1), and there's the horizontal win with (2,1), (2,2), (2,3). Player 2 cannot block both.

```
  1 2 3
1 X O .
2 X X .
3 . . O
```

There's a critical point here you may need to remind your users: when a move is entered in the form 2, 2 (for example, to take the center), you need to use a consistent scheme such as the "row, column" scheme I'm adopting here. For the rest of the chapter, we'll assume that the row coordinate comes first and that user input—except when stated elsewhere—uses 1-based indexes.

Column Number (Enter Second)

	1	2	3
1	1, 1	1, 2	1, 3
2	2, 1	2, 2	2, 3
3	3, 1	3, 2	3, 3

Row Number (Enter First)

Plan of This Chapter

The ultimate goal of this chapter is to create a game in which the computer plays X. The user will take the role of the O player. Ideally, we should build a computer strategy that achieves a win whenever possible. The plan of this approaches the task in three stages.

Phase 1

The program maintains the game board and invites two human players to make a move. It must reprompt the user over and over if 1) the input is not in the right format, 2) the coordinates entered are out of range, or 3) the user tries to play in a square that is no longer available. The program prints out the current board state after each move.

Phase 2

In this phase, the program operates as it did in Phase 1, except for one major difference: if one of the two players gets three in a row, the computer announces the winner and terminates the game.

Phase 3

Using insights gleaned in Phase 2, this version replaces one of the human players with a computer player, which should play optimally. The program in this chapter will make the first move; but I'll describe a strategy for the computer if it goes second.

Python One-Line if/else

One of the tasks of the program in Phase 1 is to alternate between the X and O players. The program will employ a variable named num_moves to keep track of whose turn it is; if num_moves is odd, then it's X's turn; if this variable is even, then it's O's turn.

Here's an obvious way to write the program logic, using the condition num_moves % 2 to determine whether the number of moves (turn number) is even or odd.

```
if num_moves % 2 > 0:
    player_ch = 'X'
else:
    player_ch = 'O'
```

But there's a more compact way to write this, using a one-line version of if and else.

```
player_ch = 'X' if num_moves % 2 > 0 else 'O'
```

For clarity's sake, I can put parentheses around the condition, making the purpose of **if** and **else** more obvious.

```
player_ch = 'X' if (num_moves % 2 > 0) else 'O'
```

This is an example of the Python "ternary" or "conditional" operator, which has the following syntax:

value1 **if** *condition* **else** *value2*

This expression produces *value1* if the condition evaluates to **True** and *value2* otherwise.

Version ▶ The conditional operator was introduced in Python 2.5. If you're running an earlier version of Python, you can use the following statement, which has the same effect in this case:

```
player_ch = ['O', 'X'][num_moves % 2]
```
◀ **Version**

Example 14.1. # Simple Two-Player Game

The following example implements a simple two-player game but only permits legal moves in the required "row, col" format. It reprompts as necessary and reprints the board after each move. The program terminates automatically when all nine squares have been filled in or if the user enters 0 to exit immediately.

```
ttt1.py

n = 3
mat = [['.'] * n  for i in range(n)]

# Main function: alternately prompt the two human
# players — 'X' and '0' — by calling get_move function.
#
def main():
    num_moves = 0
    print_mat()
    print('Moves are r, c or "0" to exit.')
    exit_flag = False
    while not exit_flag:
        num_moves += 1
        if num_moves > 9:
            print('No more space left.')
            break
        player_ch = 'X' if num_moves % 2 > 0 else '0'
        exit_flag, r, c = get_move(player_ch)

# Get Move function.
# Prompt and re-prompt human player ('X' or '0')
# until a valid move of form 'row, col' has been
# entered at an available square. Then enter move
# into the grid and re-print the grid display.
def get_move(player_ch):
    while True:
        prompt = 'Enter move for ' + player_ch + ': '
        s = input(prompt)
        a_list = s.split(',')
        if len(a_list) >= 1 and int(a_list[0]) == 0:
            print('Bye now.')
            return True, 0, 0   # Throw 'EXIT' flag
        elif len(a_list) < 2:
            print('Use row, col. Re-enter.')
```

▼ continued on next page

```
            else:
                # First, convert to 0-based indexes.
                r = int(a_list[0]) - 1
                c = int(a_list[1]) - 1
                if r < 0 or r >= n or c < 0 or c >= n:
                    print('Out of range. Re-enter.')
                elif mat[r][c] != '.':
                    print('Occupied square. Re-enter.')
                else:
                    mat[r][c] = player_ch
                    print_mat()
                    break
        return False, r, c   # Do not throw 'EXIT' flag

def print_mat():
    s = '  1 2 3\n'
    for i in range(n):
        s += str(i + 1) + ' '
        for j in range(n):
            s += str(mat[i][j]) + ' '
        s += '\n'
    print(s)

main()
```

How It Works

This is the simplest form of the Tic-Tac-Toe game. All it does is alternately ask two different human players for moves. Yet there still is a good deal to do on the housekeeping side.

First, it's necessary to create a true three-by-three matrix. The first two statements do that using the techniques of Chapter 13, "Matrixes: 2-D Lists." Each element in the array has the starting value of a string containing a dot (.), which indicates a blank space.

```
n = 3
mat = [['.'] * n  for i in range(n)]
```

The main function then alternates between X and O by calling the get_move function.

The `get_move` function returns **True** if and only if the user types 0 to terminate the game early. When that happens, the `exit_flag` variable is switched on (set to **True**) within the main function, and the program terminates.

The main function also terminates the game if nine moves have been made.

```
while not exit_flag:
    num_moves += 1
    if num_moves > 9:
        print('No more space left.')
        break
    player_ch = 'X' if num_moves % 2 > 0 else 'O'
    exit_flag, r, c = get_move(player_ch)
```

The program prompts and reprompts until it gets valid input. The function returns three values: `exit_flag`, `r`, and `c`. The last two, `r` and `c`, aren't used in this version of the program but will be useful in Phase 2.

The **split** method is extremely helpful in reading user input. As explained in Chapter 7, "Python Strings," it conveniently splits an input line into a list of individual strings.

```
def get_move(player_ch):
    while True:
        prompt = 'Enter move for ' + player_ch + ': '
        s = input(prompt)
        a_list = s.split(',')
        if len(a_list) >= 1 and a_list[0] == '0':
            print('Bye now.')
            return True    # Throw 'EXIT' flag
        elif len(a_list) < 2:
            print('Use row, col. Re-enter.')
        else:
            ...
    return False    # Do not throw 'EXIT' flag
```

The **else** clause is reached if input is in the form `r, c`: a comma-separated list of two items. The statements in this clause test the other conditions necessary to accept the move. Note that this **else** clause has a nested **else** clause of its own.

```
r = int(a_list[0]) - 1
c = int(a_list[1]) - 1
if r < 0 or r >= n or c < 0 or c >= n:
    print('Out of range. Re-enter.')
elif mat[r][c] != '.':
    print('Occupied square. Re-enter.')
```

```
            else:
                mat[r][c] = player_ch
                print_mat()
                break
```

The first thing this block of code does is to interpret the two items entered, converting 1-based index numbers to 0-based indexes. Valid moves run from (1,1) to (3,3), and these are converted to actual coordinates, running from (0,0) to (2,2).

If the input passes all tests, the program places an X or O into the grid as appropriate, calls the `print_mat` function, and breaks the re-prompting cycle.

Note ▶   Python lists evaluate to **None** if empty; therefore, when tested as conditions, they are equivalent to **False** if empty and **True** otherwise. This means that the following line of code:

```
        if len(a_list) >= 1 and a_list[0] == '0':
```

Can be replaced by this shorter line:

```
        if a_list and a_list[0] == '0':
```

Doing that replacement is left as an exercise.

◀ Note

EXERCISES

Exercise 14.1.1.   Revise the `print_mat` function to use the **join** method. It should be used to join all the input on a line, using a blank space to separate items. It should also be used to join output lines together, using newlines to separate them. (This approach is a more efficient approach to building a string, but unless you are joining hundreds of strings, you probably won't notice a big difference in performance.)

Exercise 14.1.2.   Revise the example so that instead of using an exit code of 0, accept an exit code consisting of the word *exit*. Enable the program to recognize any word as meaning exit if the first character is *E* or *e*.

Exercise 14.1.3.   Revise Example 14.1 so that it plays on a four-by-four square. Remember that the total number of moves is now larger than nine. (Hint: there are only a few changes that need to be made, but there are several of them, scattered throughout the program.)

Exercise 14.1.4.   Revise Example 14.1 so that it plays on a six-by-six square.

14

Interlude

Variations on Tic-Tac-Toe

Tic-Tac-Toe may be the simplest game that has a visual component. But it's just the beginning. You could, for example, implement a game of four or five in a row, on a larger board. And you're not limited to two dimensions.

```
   1 2 3      1 2 3      1 2 3
 1 X . .      . . .      . . .
 2 . . .      . X .      . . .
 3 . . .      . . .      . . X
    (1)        (2)        (3)
```

In this three-dimensional version, each of the grids is one "plane" or "slice" of a cube. Winning combinations include the one shown here: (1, 1, 1), (2, 2, 2), (3, 3, 3).

This three-by-three-by-three game is too easily won by whoever goes first, but other games are possible. What about a four-by-four-by-four game in which a player wins by getting four in a row?

The count Method for Lists

Much of Python's programming power comes from its list-handling abilities. The rest of the chapter makes use of another list method, **count**.

```
n = list.count(value)
```

The call to **count** generates an integer value. For example, suppose you have the following list of single-character strings:

```
a_list = ['X', 'X', '0', '.', 'X, '0']
```

The **count** method makes it easy to count the number of occurrences of Xs, Os, and dots, which will be useful in this chapter. Here is a sample session from within the interactive environment that demonstrates this method:

```
>>>a_list.count('X')
3
>>>a_list.count('0')
2
```

Example 14.2. *Two-Player Game with Win Detection*

This next phase adds one element to the game, but it's an important one: after each move, detect whether either player has achieved three in a row.

The reason this phase is so important is that in detecting a three-in-a-row situation, we have begun to give the program a certain intelligence: if the program can detect wins, then it also can detect *when someone is about to win*, and such awareness can be used in creating an optimal computer-player strategy, which we'll do in Phase 3.

Most of the statements in this version are the same as in Phase 1. The new lines are in bold.

```
ttt2.py
n = 3
mat = [['.'] * n  for i in range(n)]

win_list = [[1, 2, 3], [4, 5, 6], [7, 8, 9],
            [1, 4, 7], [2, 5, 8], [3, 6, 9],
            [1, 5, 9], [3, 5, 7]]

# Main function: alternately prompt the two human
# players — 'X' and 'O' — by calling get_move function.
#
def main():
    num_moves = 0
    print_mat()
    print('Moves are r, c or "0" to exit.')
    exit_flag = False
    while not exit_flag:
        num_moves += 1
        if num_moves > 9:
            print('No more space left.')
            break
        player_ch = 'X' if num_moves % 2 > 0 else 'O'
        exit_flag, r, c = get_move(player_ch)
        if (not exit_flag) and test_win(r, c):
            print('\n', player_ch, 'WINS THE GAME!')
            break

# Get Move function.
# Prompt and re-prompt human player ('X' or 'O')
# until a valid move of form 'row, col' has been
# entered at an available square. Then enter move
# into the grid and re-print the grid display.
def get_move(player_ch):
```

```
        while True:
            prompt = 'Enter move for ' + player_ch + ': '
            s = input(prompt)
            a_list = s.split(',')
            if len(a_list) >= 1 and int(a_list[0]) == 0:
                print('Bye now.')
                return True, 0, 0
            elif len(a_list) < 2:
                print('Use row, col. Re-enter.')
            else:
                # First, convert to 0-based indexes.
                r = int(a_list[0]) - 1
                c = int(a_list[1]) - 1
                if r < 0 or r >= n or c < 0 or c >= n:
                    print('Out of range. Re-enter.')
                elif mat[r][c] != '.':
                    print('Occupied square. Re-enter.')
                else:
                    mat[r][c] = player_ch
                    print_mat()
                    break
    return False, r, c

def print_mat():
    s = '   1 2 3\n'
    for i in range(n):
        s += str(i + 1) + ' '
        for j in range(n):
            s += str(mat[i][j]) + ' '
        s += '\n'
    print(s)


# Test Win function.
# win_list = List of all winning combinations.
# ttt_list = an individual list, such as [1, 2, 3],
#    that holds one winning Tic-Tac-Toe combination.
# my_win_list = list of all ttt_list instances
#    that contain the current cell.
# Function tests all the combos in my_win_list.
# A combo returns True if it has 3 Xs or 3 Os.
#
```

▼ *continued on next page*

ttt2.py, cont.

```
def test_win(r, c):
    cell_n = r * 3 + c + 1    # Get cell num. 1 to 9.
    my_win_list = [ttt_list for ttt_list in win_list
                    if cell_n in ttt_list]
    for ttt_list in my_win_list:
        num_x, num_o, num_blanks = test_way(ttt_list)
        if num_x == 3 or num_o == 3:
            return True
    return False

def test_way(cell_list):
    letters_list = []
    # Create list of the form ['X', '.', 'O']
    for cell_n in cell_list:
        r = (cell_n - 1) // 3
        c = (cell_n - 1) % 3
        letters_list.append(mat[r][c])
    num_x = letters_list.count('X')  # How many X's?
    num_o = letters_list.count('O')  # How many O's?
    num_blanks = letters_list.count('.')
    return num_x, num_o, num_blanks

main()
```

How It Works

The first thing this version does is to create a matrix called ways, which lists all eight ways the game can be won. I could have used row-column coordinates such as "(0,0), (0,1), (0,2)," representing the top row, but for Tic-Tac-Toe, it's easier to use cell numbers 1 through 9, at this point, and then translate into row-column coordinates as needed.

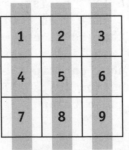
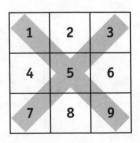

The ways of winning the game are therefore summarized by the following combinations. In detecting win conditions, the program is only interested in these combinations of cells.

```
win_list = [[1, 2, 3], [4, 5, 6], [7, 8, 9],
            [1, 4, 7], [2, 5, 8], [3, 6, 9],
            [1, 5, 9], [3, 5, 7]]
```

The `test_win` function takes a coordinate pair—`(r, c)`, which is expressed in zero-based indexes—and produces a cell number from 1 to 9.

```
cell_n = r * 3 + c + 1  # Get cell # 1-9
```

We need to find winning combinations that contain this cell number. The variable `ttt_list` refers to a member of `win_list`: that is, each `ttt_list` is a three-number combo such as [1, 2, 3] or [4, 5, 6] that refers to one Tic-Tac-Toe combination.

From this list of lists (`win_list`), we build `my_win_list`, a group of lists to be tested.

```
my_win_list = [ttt_list for ttt_list in win_list
                 if cell_n in ttt_list]
```

This means the following: if, for example, the cell number is 1, we want to find all the Tic-Tac-Toe combinations that include 1. So we get the following list of lists, by (in effect) saying, "Use all lists from `win_list` that contain the number 1."

```
[[1, 2, 3], [1, 4, 7], [1, 5, 9]]
```

As another example, if the cell number is 5, we want to find all the Tic-Tac-Toe combinations that include the cell number 5. So, we get the following list of lists by saying, "Use all lists from `win_list` that contain the number 5."

```
[[4, 5, 6], [2, 5, 8], [1, 5, 9], [3, 5, 7]]
```

To make this (potentially) cryptic code more obvious, consider that the Python list-comprehension statement shown earlier is a compact way of writing this:

```
my_win_list = []
for ttt_list in win_list:
    if cell_n in ttt_list:
        my_win_list.append(ttt_list)
```

In other words, look at each of the lists inside `win_list` (itself a list of winning combinations); append a list onto `my_win_list` if and only if it contains `cell_n`, the cell number.

Each of these three-element lists is then passed to the test_ways function. That function returns the number of Xs, Os, and blanks in the combination passed to it. If three Xs or three Os are found, then there is a winner. Congratulate the winner and terminate!

For example, if positions 1, 5, and 9 all contain an X, then the X player wins. These positions are converted to matrix elements $(0, 0)$, $(1, 1)$, and $(2, 2)$; then we detect how many Xs and Os are at these positions.

1		
	5	
		9

1 → (0, 0)

5 → (1, 1)

9 → (2, 2)

The test_ways function does the actual counting of letters, looking for three of the same kind. First, it builds up a list called letters_list, which contains individual characters X, O, and ., found in the corresponding matrix squares. The **count** method makes it easy to return the three counts—the number of Xs, the number of Os, and the number of dots. A typical return value might be 1, 1, 1, which means that one of each type of letter was found.

```
def test_way(cell_list):
    letters_list = []
    # Create list of the form ['X', '.', 'O']
    for cell_n in cell_list:
        r = (cell_n - 1) // 3
        c = (cell_n - 1) % 3
        letters_list.append(mat[r][c])
    num_x = letters_list.count('X')  # How many X's?
    num_o = letters_list.count('O')  # How many O's?
    num_blanks = letters_list.count('.')
    return num_x, num_o, num_blanks
```

A return value of 3, 0, 0 would mean three Xs were found. A return value of 0, 3, 0 would mean that three Os were found. Clearly, when three Xs or three Os are found in any winning combination—such as in the list [1, 2, 3]—someone has won the game.

EXERCISES

Exercise 14.2.1. Write two additional functions, make_cell_n and make_ rc_coords, to perform the translation back and forth between cell number (such as 5) and corresponding 0-based coordinates (such as 2,2). Then revise Example 14.2 accordingly, to use these functions as needed. Some of the functions should now be shorter.

Exercise 14.2.2. Instead of using positional numbers 1 to 9, just use tuples directly. For example, instead of [1, 2, 3] denoting a horizontal row, use [(0,0), (0,1), (0,3)]. This will be a good deal more work initially, but it will save work later in the program and permit you to collapse a number of statements.

Introducing the Computer Player

Phase 2 of the Tic-Tac-Toe game introduced the ability to detect a win condition. It involved finding three Xs or three Os in any of the eight winning combinations.

The final step is to use this ability—count the Xs and Os in winning combinations—to come up with a winning strategy for a computer player. Then the game can be rewritten so that the user plays against the computer. We want to give the computer a solid strategy.

We need a hierarchy of principles, of "heuristics." First, if the computer can win anywhere on the board, it should make that move immediately, regardless of all other considerations. To keep the program simple, let's assume that the computer is the X player.

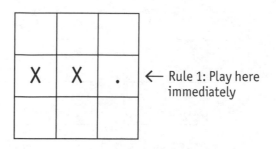

← Rule 1: Play here immediately

Second, if no immediate win is possible, the computer's next priority is to prevent an immediate win by the opponent (the human player). This is a "blocking" situation, and it occurs anywhere there are two Os in a winning combo along with an open space, signified by a dot (.).

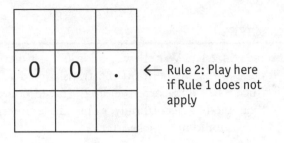

← Rule 2: Play here if Rule 1 does not apply

But if no side has an immediate win, we need to look for other winning opportunities. The best opportunity is a "double threat." We look for an open square that, if played, creates two winning combs, only one of which can be answered. This guarantees a win.

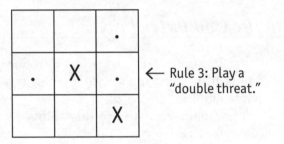

← Rule 3: Play a "double threat."

But we need still more rules. Fortunately, there are general principles that win in Tic-Tac-Toe. Assume we're going first. Then the winning strategy is to play in a corner on the first turn and the opposite corner the next turn (turn 3). Otherwise, play in the first available corner. This gives us a winning strategy most of the time.

X		0
	?	
		X

X	?	X
		0

X		?
		0
		X

First two positions force 0 to repond in such a way as to let X win; third position keeps hope for a win alive

In the games shown here, X has either forced a win or still has a possible win. In all three cases, if O plays in the "?" position, then X has a winning move in the bottom-left corner.

But if it's turn 3 and if opponent has responded by playing in a *side space* (2, 4, 6, or 8), then the winning move is to play in the center (5). This is a "special rule." It can be implemented by examining the human players' most recent move.

We can construct a priority list. Select the first available square from the following list of moves. This "default" rule plays in a corner first. Then it plays in the opposite corner next, if available; otherwise, it takes first available corner.

```
pref_list = [1, 9, 3, 7, 5, 2, 4, 6, 8]
```

So, we can summarize the rules as follows. Remember that these are a hierarchy and must be evaluated in precisely this order:

1 If the turn number is 3 and the opponent has played in a side space, play the center. (This is the "special rule.")

2 If an immediate win is possible anywhere, take it.

3 If the opponent has an immediate win possible, play to block him.

4 If it's possible to play a double threat, do so.

5 Otherwise, play the first available cell number indicated in the preference list.

Example 14.3. *Computer Play: The Computer Goes First*

The following code listing contains new functions only; otherwise, it is nearly identical to the previous example, 14.2.

ttt3.py

```
# Get Computer Move function.
# For each blank cell in the grid, test it according to
# the three rules; 1) look for win, 2) look to block,
# 3) look for double threat. If none of these work,
# use pref. list
def get_comp_move(num_moves, opp_cell):
    # If it's turn 3 and opponent played in a side
    # space, play the center.
    if num_moves == 3 and opp_cell in [2, 4, 6, 8]:
        return 1, 1    # Take the center
```

▼ *continued on next page*

ttt3.py, cont.

```python
    # Get a list of all available (blank) cells
    cell_list = [(i, j) for j in range(n)
                 for i in range(n) if mat[i][j] =='.']

    # Test every avail. cell for "to win" condition
    for cell in cell_list:
        if test_to_win(cell[0], cell[1]):
            return cell[0], cell[1]

    # Test every avail. cell for "to block" condition
    for cell in cell_list:
        if test_to_block(cell[0], cell[1]):
            return cell[0], cell[1]

    # Test every avail. cell for "double threat" cond.
    for cell in cell_list:
        if test_dbl_threat(cell[0], cell[1]):
            return cell[0], cell[1]

    pref_list = [1, 9, 3, 7, 5, 2, 4, 6, 8]
    for i in pref_list:
        r = (i - 1) // 3
        c = (i - 1) % 3
        if mat[r][c] == '.':
            return r, c


# Test To Win: Test every win combo for the cell...
# If two Xs are present, this cell will win!
def test_to_win(r, c):
    cell_n = r * 3 + c + 1
    my_win_list = [ttt_list for ttt_list in win_list
                   if cell_n in ttt_list]
    for ttt_list in my_win_list:
        num_x, num_o, num_blanks = test_way(ttt_list)
        if num_x == 2:
            print('Watch THIS...')
            return True
    return False


# Test to Block: Test every win combo for the cell...
```

```
# If two Os are present, this cell must be blocked
def test_to_block(r, c):
    cell_n = r * 3 + c + 1
    my_win_list = [ttt_list for ttt_list in win_list
                    if cell_n in ttt_list]
    for ttt_list in my_win_list:
        num_x, num_o, num_blanks = test_way(ttt_list)
        if num_o == 2:
            print('Ha ha, I am going to block you!')
            return True
    return False


# Test Double Threat: Test all win combos for the cell;
# If there are two threats, play this cell.
def test_dbl_threat(r, c):
    threats = 0
    cell_n = r * 3 + c + 1
    my_win_list = [ttt_list for ttt_list in win_list
                    if cell_n in ttt_list]
    for ttt_list in my_win_list:
        num_x, num_o, num_blanks = test_way(ttt_list)
        if num_x == 1 and num_blanks == 2:
            threats += 1
        if threats >= 2:
            print('I have you now!')
            return True
    return False
```

14

Remember that these functions are *additions* to the Phase 2 version of the game (Example 14.2). Place them anywhere in the program, but include them before the final call to main().

Also, replace the definition of main with the version shown next. Altered and new statements are in bold.

```
def main():
    r = c = 0
    num_moves = 0
    print_mat()
    print('Moves are r,c or "0" to exit.')
    exit_flag = False
```

```
while not exit_flag:
    num_moves += 1
    if num_moves > 9:
        print('No more space left.')
        break
    if num_moves % 2 > 0:
        cell_n = 3 * r + c + 1
        r, c = get_comp_move(num_moves, cell_n)
        mat[r][c] = 'X'
        print('\nOkay, my move...\n')
        print_mat()
        if test_win(r, c):
            print('\nX WINS THE GAME!')
            break
    else:
        exit_flag, r, c = get_move('O')
        if (not exit_flag) and test_win(r, c):
            print('\nO WINS THE GAME!')
            break
```

How It Works

Even though this chapter has presented the longest and (in some ways) the most complicated Python code in the book so far, the heuristics supported by the get_comp_move function are reasonably simple.

The logic of the computer player can be summarized in the following pseudocode:

If it's the third turn and the opponent has played in a side space,

    Return 1, 1, the center position.

Get a list of all available squares (squares currently containing a dot)

For every cell in this list,

    Return this cell if it would score an immediate win.

For every cell in this list,

    Return this cell if it would block opponent's win.

For every cell in this list,

    Return this cell if it would create a "double threat."

Return first available cell from the preference list.

Notice how this logic works: all available cells are tested for a direct-win opportunity (two Xs already present); only after all those cells are checked does the program move on to check all cells for a block (two Os already present). Finally, if no cell passes the "to win" or "to block" tests, all available cells are checked for a double-threat opportunity, which would guarantee a win in two turns.

When any of these tests succeed, the `get_comp_move` function returns immediately, so the remaining tests are not performed. Only when all the tests fail does the program pick a move from the preference list. The program selects the first available position from the list.

```
for i in pref_list:
    r = (i - 1) // 3
    c = (i - 1) % 3
    if mat[r][c] == '.':
        return r, c
```

Playing Second

Of course, for a complete game, you'd want to be able to have the computer play second.

But a change in strategy is required. The three main heuristics still apply. But now we need a different preference list. When going second, the computer's overriding goal is to avoid losing. The correct first move is therefore to take the center, if available; if it isn't, the computer should play in any corner. Here is the preference list if going second:

```
pref_list = [5, 1, 9, 3, 7, 2, 4, 6, 8]
```

We also need a special rule. If the opponent plays in a corner, the computer responds by taking the center, and the human opponent plays in the opposing corner, this sets up a trap.

← Play in opposing corner; 0 in corner now fatal

It's important now to not play in a corner. The special rule is to avoid playing a corner in this situation. I'll write it in pseudocode. The implementation is left as an exercise.

If num_moves is equal to 4,

If opponent played in both 0,0 and 2,2 or

opponent played in both 0,2 and 2,0,

Return 1,0 (play a side space)

EXERCISES

Exercise 14.3.1.   Revise the example so that instead of starting in the center every time, it randomly selects from a group of starting positions including the center and all four corners. Note that several numbers in the preference list may need to be changed as a result, as the second move should favor playing in the opposite corner.

Exercise 14.3.2.   Revise the example so that the computer plays second, as the O player. (Or, you can take the approach that X is always the computer and O is always the user; this simplifies a number of problems.) Changes to strategy should be made as described in the previous section. All three heuristics remain the same, but the preference list should be different, and a new special rule is needed.

Exercise 14.3.3.   Expand the example so that when the program begins, it offers the human player the choice of going either first or second. The computer adjusts strategy as appropriate. (Hint: Again, it may simplify things to always make the computer the X player, whether going first or second, but you can make the program more flexible than that if you choose.)

Interlude

The Art of Heuristics

For the computer to give you a good game, it must employ strategy and tactics. This is called *heuristics*, and it's the closest thing to "making a judgment" you'll find in this book. By employing heuristics, the program makes a kind of judgment as to what would be a superior play. And yet—here's the paradox—each decision is the result of tiny, limited decisions, which just compare two quantities.

This again raises the philosophical question of whether computers, which at the lowest level do nothing but follow mechanistic, predetermined rules, can in any real sense be intelligent or exercise judgment.

Interlude

▼ *continued*

Still, if you play against the computer many times, you can almost feel the computer plotting against you, outmaneuvering and outsmarting you. I'll leave the philosophical questions on the table for now.

The art of heuristics is a fascinating field unto itself, and people have devoted years to it. Much of it comes down to two major techniques, both demonstrated in this chapter: *look-ahead* and *playing for position*.

Look-ahead, sometimes called *brute force*, determines the quality of a move by directly looking ahead to its consequences, in which the computer seeks to achieve wins and avoid losses. The program in this chapter applies a primitive example, looking ahead one move, to discover a possible win, loss, or a guaranteed win.

The program also gives an example of playing for position. If there are no immediate win or loss opportunities, the program chooses on the basis of a preference list. The computer does not *deduce* this preference list; it is just told that certain positions have greater strategic value.

Super-chess playing programs use more refined examples of these two techniques. IBM's Big Blue, which can defeat the best human chess players in the world, can look ahead 10 or 20 moves to evaluate the effects of moves. But Big Blue does not look ahead to play out all possible games; if it did, the entire planet Earth might not be big enough to house all the processors and memory circuits needed. Instead, at some point Big Blue must value some positions as simply being better than others. It therefore plays for position, as well as evaluating whether certain moves would result directly in a win.

For Tic-Tac-Toe, I challenged a programmer friend of mine, extremely skilled in Python, to write a 100 percent brute-force look-ahead solution for the game. If it worked, it would be guaranteed to play the absolute perfect game of Tic-Tac-Toe in every possible situation.

With some feedback from me, he got his program to work. It took 20 seconds to make its first move. That may sound tolerable, but imagine the game were played on a three-dimensional board or a larger matrix, such as four in a row played on a six-by-six board. Faced with a more sophisticated game, the pure "look-ahead" program would likely take many minutes, hours, or more, sitting there "thinking," before it made its first move!

Similarly, a computer could completely "solve" chess—if it were big enough (it might have to be bigger than Earth)—but even if such a complete brute-force solution to chess could be produced, it might take millions of years to make its first move...maybe far longer!

And this is why game-playing programs need heuristics, strategies based on high-level principles.

Chapter 14   *Summary*

Here are the main points of Chapter 14:

▶ A game program, even a simple one such as Tic-Tac-Toe, often requires a matrix, that is, a two-dimensional list. Remember to use the matrix-creating syntax from Chapter 13.

```
mat = [['.'] * n for i in range(n)]
```

▶ Remember that in Python, indexes always run from 0 to N-1, where N is the length of the dimension. But it's often easier for users to use 1-based indexes rather than 0-based. This may require you to convert back and forth.

▶ This chapter introduced the use of the conditional, one-line **if/else** operator. The expression produces *value1* if the *condition* is true, and *value2* otherwise.

```
player_ch = 'X' if (num_moves % 2 > 0) else 'O'
```

▶ This chapter also introduced the **count** method. This is a method applied to lists that counts how often a specified value occurs.

```
row_vals = ['X', 'X', 'O']
num_of_Xs = row_vals.count('X')
```

▶ The art of designing computer strategy is called *heuristics*. Two of the most common techniques are "brute-force looking ahead" and "playing for position."

Classes and Objects I

Object orientation is one of the most interesting topics in computer programming. Classes, objects, and the object-oriented paradigm are especially important in Python because they underlie everything done in the language.

But in this chapter, as elsewhere, I'll focus on a functional, hands-on approach: creating interesting but relatively simple applications. The topics include

▶ Basic object-oriented techniques

▶ Using objects in a database application

▶ A multidimensional point class

What's an Object?

Believe it or not, you've been using Python objects from the beginning of this book.

Strings are objects, and they support methods. Methods are similar to functions, but they apply to specific objects through the dot notation (.). What a method does, in effect, is send a message to an object, to which it then responds. Here's an example:

```
my_str = '   Henry VII    '
a_str = my_str.strip()
print(a_str)    # print 'Henry VIII'
```

These statements call the **strip** method of a string object, `my_str`. The object responds by sending back a version of the string that is stripped of leading and trailing spaces.

Now, here's a mind-blowing fact...

In Python, *every* data item is an object! This includes built-in data types such as **int** and **float**, in addition to **string**, as well as data types you create

295

yourself. Even instances of **int** and **float** are objects, and they even support methods. Here's a method called on two data objects: the integers 5 and 33.

```
>>>(5).bit_length()
3
>>>(33).bit_length()
6
```

Can you guess what the bit_length method does? It's a method of the **int** class, which says, "Return the minimum number of bits necessary to represent this integer in binary format."

Classes in Python

In Python, all data items are objects, and each object is an instance of a class. The importance of classes is: by defining your own class, you define a fundamental new data type.

A class is like an object factory. A class determines what data will be stored in each object. The class also determines what methods, if any, each object supports. There is a one-to-many relationship. You define a class and then crank out as many objects as you want.

CLASS   **OBJECTS**

If you've programmed classes and objects in another language before (such as C++), these basic concepts should be familiar to you, although the syntax will be new. With that in mind, let's explore several questions:

- ▶ How do I define a simple class?
- ▶ How do I use that class to create objects?
- ▶ How do I attach data to objects?
- ▶ How do I write methods?

How Do I Define a Simple Class?

The **class** keyword is one of the simplest Python keywords to use. In the beginning, at least, there's almost nothing to it.

```
class class_name:
    method_definitions
```

In general, there are zero or more method definitions. Here's a simple class without any definitions at all. Usually, you will want at least one method definition, but the following is legal:

```
class Dog:
    pass
```

That's it. Type this into the environment, and you've created your first Python class.

The keyword **pass** is a kind of placeholder. It says, "There's nothing more to do here for now; I'll come back and add things later." Or, you might just use it as a permanent no-op (no operation). Occasionally this is needed because Python has no statement terminator; therefore, it has no way to specify a blank statement other than **pass**.

How Do I Use a Class to Create Objects?

Once you've defined a class, creating an object is a breeze. It uses this syntax:

```
obj_name = class_name(args)
```

For example, given that we've defined a Dog class, it's easy to create Dog objects. Right now, there are no arguments involved, but we'll add those later.

```
my_dog = Dog()
your_dog = Dog()
top_dog = Dog()
```

Remember to always include the parentheses in this context, even when there are no arguments. If you omit the parentheses, something strange happens: you create an alias for the class itself. At this point in your Python career, there's no reason you'd want to do that.

To see the difference, consider this session:

```
>>>a = Dog()          # Right way!
>>>a
<__main__.Dog object at 0x1041499e8>
>>>b = Dog            # Wrong way!
>>>b
```

```
<class '__main__.Dog'>
>>>c = b()               # Weird consequence(!)
>>>c
<__main__.Dog object at 0x1041c7438>
```

Do you see what happened? The variable named a became attached to an object, meaning that (once we write some more code) that object will give all the information we need on a particular dog.

But when b was created, I forgot the parentheses, so instead of representing a particular dog, b became *an alias for the Dog class itself.* This caused the strange, and probably unintended, effect of making "b" another name for Dog. You should generally avoid that.

As another example of how to do things the right way, consider another class, Cat:

```
class Cat:
    pass

my_cat = Cat()
your_cat = Cat()
top_cat = Cat()
```

Finally, it isn't always necessary to assign an object to a variable, as these last three statements do. You can create an object "on the fly," so to speak, which is sometimes done for arguments and return values.

```
return Cat()   # Return a cat object.
```

Note ▶ Python is a dynamic language, and there is no rule about the order things are defined in, except one: a class, just like a function, must be defined before you execute statements that refer to it.

In practice, this means you shouldn't have to worry about forward references. To be safe, just put all your class definitions early in the source file, before you execute any statements.

◀ Note

How Do I Attach Data to Objects?

In this section, I show the easiest way to attach data to individual objects, which is the "ad hoc" approach. (But even though it's easy, it enables different objects of the same class to have different data structures—which is a drawback I'll discuss later.)

With any object, I can attach a data field (or rather, *instance variable*) directly to it at runtime. Here's an example:

```
my_dog = Dog()
my_dog.name = 'Skyler'
my_dog.breed = 'Great Dane'
my_dog.age = 7
```

Three pieces of information—name, breed, and age—are now attached to my_dog. We can do the same thing to another dog object, this time using different values.

```
your_dog = Dog()
your_dog.name = 'Handsome Dan'
your_dog.breed = 'Bulldog'
your_dog.age = 12
```

All this information can now be used anywhere appropriate, by again using the dot notation. Here's an example:

```
print('My dog\'s name is', my_dog.name)
print('Your dog\s name is', your_dog.name)
```

This prints

```
My dog's name is Skyler
Your dog's name is Handsome Dan
```

Consequently, we end up with two objects—my_dog and yr_dog—each of which supports three pieces of information.

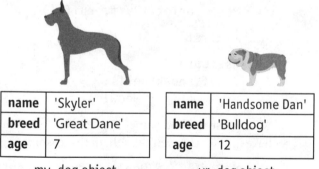

name	'Skyler'
breed	'Great Dane'
age	7

my_dog object

name	'Handsome Dan'
breed	'Bulldog'
age	12

yr_dog object

But there's a limitation. Creating instance variables on an ad hoc basis does nothing to guarantee that all objects of the same class include the same instance variables. Here's an example:

```
top_dog = Dog()
top_dog.name = 'Alfie the Alpha'
top_dog.breed = 'Border Collie'
print(top_dog.age)      # ERROR! 'Age' never created!
```

The problem in this case is that just because the other dogs were given an age variable doesn't mean that Alfie was. In an upcoming section, I'll show how to ensure that all the objects support the same instance variables (data fields).

How Do I Write Methods?

Writing a method is how we give objects of a class the ability to respond to messages; another way of saying this is that methods give objects of a class *behavior*.

One of the most important rules in object orientation, in every language I've seen, is that methods are always written at the class level, even though data is mostly stored at the instance level. That's important enough to state as a golden rule:

In Python, as elsewhere, methods are functions defined inside class definitions— even though they may be called through an object (an "instance method").

The general syntax is

```
class class_name:
    def method_name(self, other_args):
        statements
```

Here's an example for the Dog class:

```
class Dog:
    def speak(self):
        print('Ruff, ruff!')
```

And another for the Cat class:

```
class Cat:
    def speak(self):
        print('Meow!')
```

With these method names in place, we can create both Dog and Cat objects that behave differently, even though (in this case) they both support a speak method.

```
d = Dog()   # Don't forget parentheses when
c = Cat()   #  creating objects!
```

So we get behavior like this, which you can enter within the interactive environment:

```
>>>d.speak()
Ruff, ruff!
>>>c.speak()
Meow!
```

To review:

1 The variable d is an object of the Dog class, and c is an object of the Cat class.

2 Each of these two classes defines its own speak function.

3 When you use dot notation (.) to call a method through an instance, Python looks up the method defined for that particular object's class and then calls that method.

4 So d.speak() calls the speak method defined in the Dog class, and c.speak() calls the speak method defined in the Cat class.

This illustrates one of the most important aspects of object orientation. In Python, you get it for free: methods are automatically *polymorphic*, which means you can write one function and have it interpreted an unlimited number of ways by different objects.

For example, in the following statements, the cry function automatically calls the right version of the speak method for any object passed to it. The only requirement is that, at run time, the object in question must support the method. So, and this is the key to polymorphism, *any* object that supports a speak method can be passed to this function. Python automatically does the right thing at runtime.

```
>>>def cry(x):       # Define cry, a new function.
   x.speak()
   x.speak()

>>>cry(d)
   Ruff, ruff!
   Ruff, ruff!
>>>cry(c)
   Meow!
   Meow!
```

The All-Important __init__ Method

Python has a number of special method names. These names are effectively reserved words, and they start and end with double underscores (__). By convention, a leading underscore (_) indicates that a member is private, although the language does not enforce private access.

But if you use a combination of leading *and trailing* double underscores (__), you may conflict with one of the reserved names, such as **__init__**.

The `__init__` method is one of the most important methods. It is an initialization method, called just after an object of the class is created. This is the ideal place to create instance variables. The initialization method ensures that all objects of the class support a common group of variables. Here's the general syntax:

```
class class_name:
    def __init__(self, other_args)
        self.var_name = arg
        self.var_name = arg
        self.var_name = arg
```

For example, the Dog class can automatically create three instance variables for each and every Dog object created.

```
class Dog:
    def __init__(self, name, breed, age):
        self.name = name
        self.breed = breed
        self.age = age
```

Given this definition, you can create a Dog object as follows—either by using positional arguments or by using "keyword" arguments, specifying the argument name. There's an advantage to using keyword arguments—and you get this feature of Python "for free." The advantage is you don't have to remember the position of the args.

```
a_dog = Dog('Speedy', 'Greyhound', 5)
b_dog = Dog(breed='Poodle', name='Toots', age=3)
```

Interlude

Why This self Obsession?

If you're new to Python, the use of self may be surprising. What exactly does it do?

The word self is just a symbolic name that could—in theory—be anything you want. You could use fred if you really wanted. But Python programmers use self by convention, and going against that convention makes your code far less readable by other people.

When Python evaluates a method called through an object, it automatically passes a hidden argument: a reference to the object itself. But this argument is not hidden within the method definition, which is why (generally speaking) a method definition will have a total of N+1 arguments, where N was the number explicitly passed.

Within a definition, when you see a variable modified by self, you know that this is a reference to an instance variable. So, statements such

▼ *continued*

Interlude

as the following cannot be misinterpreted. The left side is an instance variable; the right is an argument.

```
self.name = name
```

Design for a Database Class

One way to think of an object is a "data record plus." By this, I mean that—at minimum—a class does everything a data record does. For example, with an employee data record, we might want to have the following fields:

▶ Employee name

▶ Employee job name

▶ Employee job rank

▶ Employee salary

This is typical of a class: it consists of four different fields with different data formats. We could realize these as two strings, an integer, and a floating-point number. You can think of this data format—this class—as follows:

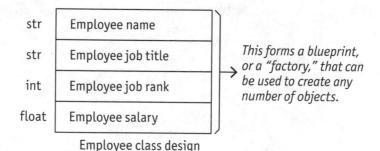

Employee class design

Now, to create this class, we write a class definition, including one method declaration, for the method called __init__.

```
class Employee:
    def __init__(self, name, jname, jrank, salary):
        self.name = name
        self.jname = jname
        self.jrank = jrank
        self.salary = salary
```

C++ Classes Compared to Python

Python is not a language for systems programming or sophisticated commercial software. It is a language for quick development, writing solutions in a small number of lines. It's popular in web development and IT departments. It might seem strange, therefore, that at first the Python classes seem more complex. Consider this small Python class:

```
class Point:
    __init__(self, x, y):
        self.x = x
        self.y = y
```

This might seem like more work than the C++ version.

```
class Point {
    double x, y;
};
```

But wait! C++ recognizes three levels of access: public, private, and protected. Without at least one public member, the C++ version is useless. Another problem is that until recently, C++ could initialize only by using a constructor. So the minimal C++ version would be

```
class Point {
  public:
    double x, y;

    Point(double new_x, double new_y) {
        x = new_x:
        y = new_y;
    }
};
```

Class syntax in C++ provides a feature that many OOP programmers swear by: private data access, as well as protected. Use of private data lets you construct classes and objects as "black boxes," in which no outsider can make assumptions about internals.

Python has a different philosophy. It's a language for smaller projects in which the goal is to get things working quickly. The emphasis in Python is on *fast turn-around* and *easy access*.

Python has a weaker concept of private data. Presumably you're only letting people on the project you trust. To improve ease of access, Python makes everything public. Such an attitude, in C++ circles, would be deemed heresy, punishable by spending eternity in Purgatory debugging poorly commented code.

Example 15.1.   *Tracking Employees*

So far, we've used classes as passive data-record types. That functionality is enough to write a rudimentary database for keeping track of employees.

This program will look much like the phone book application in Chapter 12. But now, instead of the value in a dictionary being a string containing a phone number, the value will be an object having multiple attributes.

Each object will be a complete employee record, including employee name—even though the name is also going to be the key. This is not as inefficient as it seems, as I'll explain.

So, for example, we create three Employee objects:

```
emp1 = Employee('Steve Balmer', 'President', 10,
                300888.66)
emp2 = Employee('Bill Gates', 'CEO', 12, 1700444.75)
emp3 = Employee('Brian O.', 'Prog.', 5, 29000.89)
```

The objects can then be attached to the database as follows:

key	value			
'Steve Balmer'	'Steve Balmer'	'President'	9	300888.66
'Bill Gates'	'Bill Gates'	'CEO'	12	1700444.75
'Brian O.'	'Brian O.'	'Programmer'	5	29000.89

Employee DB combining string key with
class/object value field

Even though it looks like this scheme duplicates some of the information, it doesn't really, because the key string and the employee name field, as you'll see, are references to the same data in memory.

Here's the complete program—although the find-by-prefix, save to file, and load from file features are yet to be added.

```
db1.py

emp_dict = {}
prompt='Select: 1. data entry, 2. query, 3. exit>> '
```

▼ *continued on next page*

```python
class Employee:
    def __init__(self, name, jname, jrank, salary):
        self.name = name
        self.jname = jname
        self.jrank = jrank
        self.salary = salary

# Main function. Prompts for command and executes.
def main():
    while True:
        s = input(prompt)
        if len(s) == 0:
            break
        cmd = int(s)
        if cmd == 3:
            break
        if cmd == 1:
            add_entries()
        elif cmd == 2:
            display_entries()

# Add Entries function. Prompts for key-value pairs
# until user wants to exit. Adds key-value to dict.
def add_entries():
    while True:
        key_str = input('Input name (ENTER to exit): ')
        key_str = key_str.strip()
        if not key_str:
            return
        jname = input('Enter job name: ')
        jrank = int(input('Enter job rank: '))
        salary = float(input('Enter salary: '))
        emp_dict[key_str] = Employee(key_str, jname,
                                jrank, salary)

# Display Entries function. Prompts for a name and
# prints values. Re-prompts if key not found.
def display_entries():
    while True:
        key_str = input('Input name (ENTER to exit): ')
```

db1.py, cont.

```
                    key_str = key_str.strip()
                    if not key_str:
                        return
                    emp_obj = emp_dict.get(key_str)
                    if emp_obj is None:
                        print('Name not found. Re-enter. ')
                    else:
                        print('Name:', emp_obj.name)
                        print('Job title:', emp_obj.jname)
                        print('Job rank:', emp_obj.jrank)
                        print('Salary:', emp_obj.salary)

main()
```

How It Works

The critical parts of this example include: the class definition, the statements that insert a new object, and the statements that read and print an object.

First, the beginning of the program creates the `Employee` database as an empty dictionary. As the user enters employee records, the dictionary increases in size.

```
emp_dict = {}

class Employee:
    def __init__(self, name, jname, jrank, salary):
        self.name = name
        self.jname = jname
        self.jrank = jrank
        self.salary = salary
```

These statements create an `Employee` class. Remember that the purpose of a class is to create a blueprint (or a factory, if you prefer) from which to generate any number of instances (or "objects").

In this program, each `Employee` object will contain data for one employee, including employee name, which is also the key.

The function that enters new employee records is simple. It gets an employee name, which becomes a key in the dictionary. It collects the other information for that employee and puts it in an Employee object. That object is the value associated with the key.

```
jname = input('Enter job name: ')
jrank = int(input('Enter job rank: '))
salary = float(input('Enter salary: '))
emp_dict[key_str] = Employee(key_str, jname,
                          jrank, salary)
```

This last line is the critical one. It could have been written a little more simply, at the cost of using an extra line:

```
emp_obj = Employee(key_str, jname, jrank,
                salary)
emp_dict[key_str] = emp_obj
```

Then there's the function that queries for data. First, it prompts the user for an employee name, which is a key. Then it verifies whether that key exists in the database by testing the value returned from **get**. If that value is not **None**, then the key exists, and the rest of the record (that is, the object) is printed out.

```
emp_obj = emp_dict.get(key_str)
if not emp_obj:
    print('Name not found. Re-enter')
else:
    print('Name:', emp_obj.name)
    print('Job title:', emp_obj.jname)
    print('Job rank:', emp_obj.jrank)
    print('Salary:', emp_obj.salary)
```

EXERCISES

Exercise 15.1.1.   Create an application similar to Example 15.1 but designed for a Kennel Club. For this rudimentary database, store the following information on each dog, in addition to the dog's name: breed (a string), owner name (a string), and age (an integer). Change all the prompts so that they communicate the correct information to the user.

Exercise 15.1.2.   Go back to Example 15.1, but add a user command that searches for values by prefix.

Exercise 15.1.3.   Add user commands to save information to a file and to load from file.

Exercise 15.1.4.   Add all these user commands (from the last two exercises) to the Kennel Club database application specified in Exercise 15.1.1.

Defining Other Methods

So far, I've discussed simple classes that have just one method: initialization. But you can write others. Methods empower objects to provide services to the user. With ordinary functions, you need to specify all the information the function needs by passing arguments—potentially a very long list.

But when you invoke a method, you assume that the object already contains most of the information to be worked on...or at least a great deal of it. Methods can also have arguments, but their argument lists tend to be shorter.

For example, let's add a `promote` method to the `Employee` class. This method will 1) increment job rank, 2) increase salary by $20,000, and 3) print a message.

```
class Employee:

    # Put the __init__ method definition here.

    def promote(self):
        self.jrank += 1
        self.salary += 20000
        print('Send a congratulatory message.')
```

If we're using the database from Example 15.1, then here's how this method could be called in the context of that application:

```
emp_obj = emp_dict.get('Bill Gates')
emp_obj.promote()
```

In coming up with method names, you should avoid starting with underscores (__), because Python has a number of reserved method names that have special meaning. One of these is **__init__**.

Another special method name is **__str__**, which determines what happens when the object is converted to **string** format; the method does this by returning a string.

This method provides a default printing format. For example, we might add the following **__str__** method to the `Employee` class:

```
    def __str__(self):
        ls = [self.name,
              'Job title:' + self.jname,
              'Job rank:' + str(self.jrank),
              'Salary:' + str(self.salary)]
        return ', '.join(ls)
```

When this definition is added to the class, then you can print objects automatically.

```
emp_obj = Employee('Bill Gates', 'CEO', 13,
                    1955888.5)
print(emp_obj)
```

This prints

```
Bill Gates, Job title: CEO, Job rank: 13,
Salary: 1955888.5
```

Notice that, as with all methods that work on instances, the first argument in the definition is self.

Note ▶ The **__repr__** ("represent") method name fulfills a purpose similar to **__str__**. If you define both, then the string returned by **__repr__** determines the display format recognized by the Python interpreter (for example, when printed from within IDLE). In contrast, the **__str__** method is used by the **print** function. If you define **__repr__** but not **__str__**, then **__repr__** is used by the **print** function as well.

As with other instance methods, remember to make self the first argument in the method definition.

◀ Note

Design for a Point3D Class

Classes and objects come in many shapes in sizes. For the rest of this chapter, we'll use a Point3D class, which will support three instance variables: x, y, and z. It will also support the following methods:

▶ **__init__**, to create the instance variables x, y, and z

▶ **__sub__**, which determines how to subtract one point from another

▶ **__eq__**, which determines how to compare two points for equality

We could also, if wanted, create a print format by defining a **__str__** method.

These methods, in turn, will be extremely useful when we want to determine whether a group of points is linear. More specifically, a function will answer the question, "Do a group of three points exist along a single straight line?"

Here's a picture of the class design:

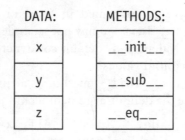

Design for the Point3D Class

Here's the class definition, which includes a document string. (Document strings provide information in response to the **help** command.)

```
class Point3D:
    ''' Three dimensional point class, supporting
        subtraction and comparison. '''

    def __init__(self, x, y, z):
        self.x = x
        self.y = y
        self.z = z

    def __sub__(self, other):
        d1 = self.x - other.x
        d2 = self.y - other.y
        d3 = self.z - other.z
        return Point3D(d1, d2, d3)

    def __eq__(self, other):
        return (self.x==other.x and self.y==other.y
                and self.z==other.z)
```

Given this class definition, you could perform the following operations, creating point objects and then subtracting them (thanks to the **__sub__** and **__eq__** methods).

```
pt1 = Point3D(5, 5, 10)
pt2 = Point3D(4, 4, 9)
pt1 - pt2 == Point3D(1, 1, 1)
```

The last statement produces the Boolean value **True**.

Point3D Class and Default Arguments

If you've programmed in C++ or Java before, the Python initialization method, `__init__`, may not seem flexible. What if you want to have the nearest equivalent of a "default constructor," which is called when the user specifies no initial values?

But the `__init__` method is a function like any other, and therefore you can use the default-argument technique to achieve the same result.

```
def __init__(self, x=0, y=0, z=0):
    self.x = x
    self.y = y
    self.z = z
```

When the `__init__` method is written this way, you can create objects of the class without specifying arguments. But it's always necessary to use parentheses after the class name.

```
pt1 = Point3D()
```

The object is now initialized to all zero values. So given these statements:

```
fss = 'The value of the point is {}, {}, {}.'
print(fss.format(pt1.x, pt1.y, pt1.z))
```

the following is printed:

```
The value of the point is 0, 0, 0.
```

Of course, it would be easier to print this data if you wrote a `__str__` method for the class; that's left as an exercise. Remember, that method needs to return a string.

Three-Dimensional Tic-Tac-Toe

How do we make practical use of a three-dimensional point class? A good way to use it is to solve problems related to a three-dimensional game of Tic-Tac-Toe. I won't show an entire solution to the game in this chapter, but I'll give some clues.

As I showed in Chapter 14, a three-dimensional game consists of three planes, indexed as 1, 2, or 3. Each individual point consists of coordinates running from $(1, 1, 1)$ to $(3, 3, 3)$. Assume coordinates are read in this way: plane-row-column.

```
    1 2 3         1 2 3         1 2 3
1   . . .     1   . . .     1   X . .
2   . . .     2   . X .     2   . . .
3   . . X     3   . . .     3   . . .
      (1)           (2)           (3)
```

However, for ease of programming, we instead use zero-based, instead of one-based, coordinates, so that point coordinates run from $(0, 0, 0)$ to $(2, 2, 2)$.

So the winning combination is $(1,3,3)$, $(2,2,2)$, $(3,1,1)$. Or, in zero-based coordinates, this is $(0,2,2)$, $(1,1,1)$, $(2,0,0)$. It would be nice to have a function that determined whether a group of positions does, in fact, constitute a win.

To do that, in turn, the function needs to see if the three points are "linear," meaning all along the same line within three dimensions. And because every position exists inside a three-by-three-by-three cube, we can make some simplifying assumptions.

Example 15.2. *Looking for a 3-D Win*

The following program prompts the user for three positions in a three-by-three-by-three Tic-Tac-Toe game and reports whether or not these constitute a winning combination.

```
points2.py

class Point3D:
    ''' Three dimensional point class, supporting
        subtraction and comparison. '''

    def __init__(self, x, y, z):
        self.x = x
        self.y = y
        self.z = z

    def __sub__(self, other):
        d1 = self.x - other.x
        d2 = self.y - other.y
        d3 = self.z - other.z
        return Point3D(d1, d2, d3)

    def __eq__(self, other):
        return (self.x==other.x and self.y==other.y
                and self.z==other.z)

def main():
    s = ''
    while not s or s[0] in 'Yy':
        p1 = get_point()
```

▼ *continued on next page*

```
            p2 = get_point()
            p3 = get_point()
            if is_win(p1, p2, p3):
                print('Is a winning combination.')
            else:
                print('Is not a win.')
            s = input('Do again (Y or N)?')

def get_point():
    s = input('Enter point in x, y, z format: ')
    ls = s.split(',')
    x, y, z = int(ls[0]), int(ls[1]), int(ls[2])
    return Point3D(x, y, z)

def is_win(p1, p2, p3):
    if (p3 - p2 == p2 - p1
      or p2 - p3 == p3 - p1
      or p3 - p1 == p1 - p2):
        return True
    else:
        return False

main()
```

Here's a sample session:

```
Enter point in x, y, z format: 0, 0, 0
Enter point in x, y, z format: 1, 1, 1
Enter point in x, y, z format: 2, 2, 2
Is a winning combination.
Do again? N
```

How It Works

Most of this example is straightforward. All it does is prompt for the information needed to create three Point3D objects, determine if those points together form a winning combination, and then ask the user if she wants to go again.

As long as you understand the Point3D class, the only thing that needs to be explained is the is_win function. If three points in a three-by-three-by-three grid are all aligned, then we can assume the following: if we can find the midpoint, then the points on either side are equidistant.

Therefore, three tests are performed. Each time, a different midpoint is assumed. Here I've added comments to clarify which point is being tested as the midpoint.

```
def is_win(p1, p2, p3):
    if (p3 - p2 == p2 - p1     # p2 is midpoint
        or p2 - p3 == p3 - p1   # p3 is midpoint
        or p3 - p1 == p1 - p2)  # p1 is midpoint
        return True
    else
        return False
```

EXERCISES

Exercise 15.2.1.   Example 15.2 assumes that the three different points entered are all different. If any of them are equal, the analysis does not hold up. Alter is_win so that it returns False immediately if any two of the three points are equal.

Exercise 15.2.2.   Alter the get_point function so that it reprompts the user until the three coordinates are in the correct format and each ranges between 0 and 2, inclusive.

Exercise 15.2.3.   Write another method to the Point3D class. (Suggestion: if nothing else, write an __**add**__ method that enables two points to be added together with the plus sign.)

Example 15.3. *Calculating Ways of Winning*

This example uses the Point3D class for another but related purpose. Before you write a 3-D Tic-Tac-Toe game, you might want to determine this: how many different ways are there to win in this three-dimensional game?

There are a number of ways to arrive at this answer. Many such approaches, however, are error-prone. But there's a foolproof technique that, if followed correctly, must produce the right answer. Here is the technique:

1   Produce a list of all possible locations (Point3D objects) in the three-by-three-by-three game. Call this list all_pts.

2   Produce a list of all *trios* of such locations, but do it in an ordered way that does not repeat any combinations. Call this list combos. This is a list in which each element has a trio of points.

3   Finally, eliminate all elements of combos that are not linear—that do not represent three points in a straight 3-D row, column, or diagonal.

Here is the program listing:

```
points2.py
   class Point3D:
       ''' Three dimensional point class, supporting
           subtraction and comparison. '''

       def __init__(self, x, y, z):
           self.x = x
           self.y = y
           self.z = z

       def __sub__(self, other):
           d1 = self.x - other.x
           d2 = self.y - other.y
           d3 = self.z - other.z
           return Point3D(d1, d2, d3)

       def __eq__(self, other):
           return (self.x==other.x and self.y==other.y
                   and self.z==other.z)

   def is_linear(t):
       p1, p2, p3 = t
       return p3 - p2 == p2 - p1

   all_pts = []
   for a in range(3):
       for b in range(3):
           for c in range(3):
               all_pts.append(Point3D(a, b, c))

   n = len(all_pts)
   print('The number of positions is', n)
   combos = []
   for i in range(n):
       for j in range(i+1, n):
           for k in range(j+1, n):
               combos.append((all_pts[i], all_pts[j],
                               all_pts[k]))
   my_combos = [i for i in combos if is_linear(i)]
   print('Number of winning combos is', len(my_combos))
```

When the program is run, it produces this output:

```
The number of positions is 27
The number of winning combos is 49
```

In other words, in a three-by-three-by-three board there are 27 places you can place an X or O, and there are 49 combinations of all Xs (or all Os) that represent "three in a row" (or three in a diagonal, or a column), for example, (0,0,0), (0,1,0), and (0,2,0). Order in which points are listed is not a factor.

How It Works

If you read the earlier description, this program is straightforward. It creates a list containing all positions, or points. From that list, it creates a list called `combos` that consists of all unique combinations of three points. Each such combination is a tuple.

The combos list is the following size:

27 x 26 x 25

From this larger list, we eliminate every combination except those that represent a win. Such combinations are linear—all three points line up. Moreover, if the combination is linear, p2 will always be the midpoint and the other two points will be equidistant from.

You may be able to grasp that fact intuitively: that because of how the "combos" list is built, p2 will automatically be the midpoint. This assumption simplifies things greatly.

In this function, there is one expected argument, `t`. But it is a tuple with three members; therefore, Python always you to assign it to a three-element series, in this case, the three points p1, p2, and p3.

```
def is_linear(t):
    p1, p2, p3 = t
    return p3 - p2 == p2 - p1
```

Finally, a single line selects only those tuples in the `combos` list that passes the `is_linear` test.

```
my_combos = [i for i in combos if is_linear(i)]
```

Optimizing the Code

You can improve the code by putting the `Point3D` class definition in its own file and name it `point3d.py`. You can then import the file easily, in each and every application in which you want to use the class, by including this line:

```
from point3d import Point3D
```

This relieves you from having to cut and paste a chunk of code whenever you want to include the class definition.

EXERCISES

Exercise 15.3.1.   Replace the first and second loops with list comprehension statements, if possible.

Exercise 15.3.2.   Revise Example 15.3 so that it tests how many winning combinations there are in a four-by-four-by-four game of Tic-Tac-Toe. In this game, there are four units in each direction, and to win, you have to get four points in a row that line up. The logic is similar, but now you have to test combinations of *four* points. However, the class Point3D should still be usable without change.

Chapter 15   *Summary*

Here are the major points of Chapter 15:

▶ You can think of a Python class as a "data record plus." It can do everything a passive data record can do—store a series of data fields in different formats—but potentially much more.

▶ An instance of a class is called an *object*. This means that there is a one-to-many relationship between classes and objects. For each class, you can create zero or more objects.

```
an_obj = ClassName(args)
another_obj = ClassName(args)
```

▶ A function defined within a class is called a *method*. In this chapter, we dealt with instance methods, which operate on a single object at a time.

▶ A reference to the object itself is passed as the first argument to such a method. By convention, this argument is named self. It should be placed at the beginning of each method definition.

```
def method_name(self, other_args):
    statements
```

▶ However, when you call an instance method, you do not include the self argument. That is passed automatically.

```
object.method_name(args)
```

▶ Classes generally have at least one method: **__init__**, which creates instance variables recognized by every object of the class.

```
def __init__(self, other_args):
    self.var1 = value
    self.var2 = value
    self.var3 = value
```

▶ Other special methods include **__str__**, which produces a string representation used by the **print** function. This method must return a string. Still other special methods are **__add__**, **__eq__**, and **__sub__**.

▶ You can also create any number of your own method names. Use of a leading underscore or two (_) is encouraged as a way of signaling that the member should be regarded as private. However, you should avoid using the *combination* of leading and trailing double underscores, as in **__init__**, because that convention is used by special method names.

▶ All references to an instance variable from within the class definition must be accessed as *self.name*.

▶ Remember to use the dot notation (.) to access instance variables as well as methods.

15

Classes and Objects II

Classes are a big topic in Python. Chapter 15 introduced most of the basic syntax, but there's much more involved. Python provides many ways to make your classes and objects expressive, convenient, and powerful.

The object-oriented topics we'll look at in this chapter include such "Pythonic" features as

▶ Doc strings

▶ Testing types at run time

▶ Inheritance

▶ Class methods and variables

Getting Help from Doc Strings

As I mentioned earlier in the book, you can get help from within the interactive environment. For example, all the string methods, as well as other information, are printed in response to this command:

```
>>>help(str)
```

You can also get help on your own classes in essentially the same way. The generic help message for a new class is rudimentary and not a great deal of help. For example, let's create a Cat class and get help on it.

```
>>>class Cat:
    pass

>>>help(Cat)
Help on class Cat in module __main__:
```

```
class Cat(builtins.object)
 |  Data descriptors defined here:
 |
 |  __dict__
 |      dictionary for instance variables (if defined)
 |
 |  __weakref__
 |      list of weak references to the object (if defined)
```

This help message may not tell you much, but it does tell you three things: 1) Cat is now a recognized class, 2) classes in Python 3.0 implicitly inherit from a root class called object, and 3) Python keeps a data dictionary for each class, although you generally don't have to worry about this dictionary.

You can ensure that your classes and methods have much more informative help messages by adding *document strings* to your classes. These serve the same purpose as comments, but as a bonus, they report information in response to the **help** command.

A document string is placed on the first line of a class, method, or function definition—right after the header. Observe normal indentation.

For this next example, I put all the code in normal font, except for the text that consists of documentation strings (*doc strings*). Note the indentation of these strings.

```
>>>class Cat:
    '''This class provides a data record for a feline
    creature.'''
    def __init__(self, name, age):
        self.name = name
        self.age = age
    def speak(self):
        '''This produces a feline noise.'''
        print('Meow!)

>>>help(Cat)
```

If you type all of this in correctly, then the environment responds with help that adds the strings in quotes just shown, documenting the class itself as well as the purpose of the speak method.

Remember the following syntactic rules for doc strings:

▶ The doc string must be the first statement after the beginning (header) of the definition.

▶ Normal indentation rules apply. The doc string must be indented under the heading of the definition, just as any statement would.

▶ That indentation requirement applies only to the first physical line within the doc string. However, the cleanest style is to continue the indentation of the first line.

▶ You can use any kind of quotation marks. However, the literal quote marks (''') enable you to write doc strings that span any number of physical lines. Literal quotes can also be started and ended with *three* double quotation marks (""").

Remember that you can write doc strings for ordinary functions as well. You can also write a doc string for the entire file, which can be useful if the file is a module that will be imported by other files.

Note ▶ If you create an object as an instance of a particular class, then you can apply the help function to the object, and you'll get similar help information. Here's an example:

```
c = Cat('Fluffy', 12)
help(c)
```

These statements would result in printing help for the Cat class.   ◀ Note

16

Function Typing and "Overloading"

One of the most convenient features of the C++ language is that it provides *overloading*—you can write different functions that initialize (construct) an object, but do it different depending on what kind of data is being used to initialize.

To accomplish the same result in Python, here's what you do:

1 Test the type of an argument that's passed to a function.

2 Take a different action depending on what this type is.

There are multiple ways to test the type of a data object. The preferred way is shown here:

```
isinstance(object, type_name)
```

This expression returns **True** if the object is an instance of the indicated type. You can experiment with this function from within the interactive environment.

```
>>>s = "Ain't we got fun?"
>>>isinstance(s, str)
True
>>>n = 1.5
>>>isinstance(n, int)
False
>>>isinstance(n, float)
True
```

Here's a simple example using **isinstance**. If the argument used to initialize the object is an instance of the string type, **str**, then the function uses the **__init__** method to convert the input to an int before storing the value.

```
class MagicNum:
    def __init__(self, arg):
        if isinstance(arg, str):
            self.num = int(arg)
        else:
            self.num = arg
```

In terms of pseudocode, we can summarize the action of this initialization function as

If arg is an instance of the string class, str.

    Convert it to integer (int) format and assign to self.num.

Else,

    Assign the value of the arg directly to self.num.

There's another way to test a data item's type before proceeding to use it. However, it is not recommended as strongly as **isinstance**, because this other approach does not account for inheritance relationships, a feature we're going to look at later in this chapter.

```
if type(my_thing) == str:
    # Do whatever is appropriate for strings
```

This technique has the advantage of being more readable, so you can be forgiven for preferring it. However, this expression evaluates to **True** only if the type of my_thing matches str—the Python string type—precisely.

Finally, there's an advanced technique called *duck typing*, discussed in the upcoming interlude.

What Is Duck Typing?

Duck typing is something that many C++ programmers regard as blasphemy, but Python programmers look at favorably. If it walks like a duck and quacks like a duck, etc., then it's a duck.

   In other words, duck typing means you don't even bother with testing an object's type directly. You infer what a type is by testing what you can do with it.

Most modern programming languages, such as C++, are strict about typing so that a function never even gets passed an argument unless its type matches the declaration. Class inheritance creates some latitude here; for example, you may pass an object to a `DogClass` argument (for example) if the object has that class or any class derived from `DogClass`. But that still imposes a certain amount of discipline.

   Python is the perfect duck typing language because it freely permits passing of any objects at any time regardless of type but then uses exceptions at run time to give feedback on what operations an object supports. The try and except keywords enable you to respond to situations in which an operation is not supported.

   So, in Python, here's how you might engage in duck typing:

```
try:
    val = thing.quack()
except TypeError:
    # Do something else
```

   This code does not test the type of "thing" explicitly. It just uses **try** and **except** to implicitly ask whether the `quack` method can be called without error. If so, then the program assumes that "thing" has the right type. If the `quack` method is not supported, then you can ask the program to do something else.

Variable-Length Argument Lists

Using variable-length argument lists is a technique that's necessary to the upcoming example. Fortunately, Python makes this feature easy.

A function or method definition that uses a variable argument list has this syntax:

```
def function_name(*args):
    statements
```

Note that the argument name, **args**, can be any valid name, but by convention, Python programmers most often use **args** in this context.

If you're a C or C++ programmer, that little symbol, the asterisk (*), will look quite familiar. But don't get too excited. Forget everything you know about the asterisk in C.

This syntax turns out to be very easy to use if you've followed this book up to now. Where ***args** appears in an argument list, it means that all the arguments passed are packed into a list—which, inside the definition, you refer to as args.

The following example will show how simple this is. It just prints out all its arguments.

```
def print_them_out(*args):
    for thing in args:
        print(thing, '\t')
```

Or let's say you want the arguments separated by hyphens. Here's an even slicker example:

```
def print_them_out(*args):
    my_str = '--'.join(args)
    print(my_str)
```

Let's assume this second definition is in use. Then the following function call

```
print_them_out('John', 'Paul', 'George', 'Ringo')
```

produces this result:

```
John--Paul--George--Ringo
```

You should be able to see how args is being used here (and remember, you can use another name for **args** if you really want, although I don't recommend that). **args** is a list of arguments used in the function call. That enables the caller of the function to pass as many values to the function as he or she chooses.

The full syntax is actually more flexible than that. Here is the more complete syntax:

```
def function_name(fixed_args, *args):
    statements
```

This syntax indicates that you can begin the argument list with any number of "regular" or "fixed" arguments. When the function is called, arguments are assigned to their corresponding parameters (fixed_args) until those arguments are accounted for. Any arguments not assigned to a fixed arg are packed into the list represented by args.

Here's an example:

```
funct(10, 20, 30, 40, 50)

def funct(a,  b,   *args)

args = [30, 40, 50]
```

Here's an example of how this feature might be used in a definition:

```
def print_them_out(n, *args):
    print('There are', n, 'band members.')
    my_str = '--'.join(args)
    print(my_str)
```

And here's a sample function call:

```
>>>print_them_out(4, 'John', 'Paul', 'George', 'Ringo')
There are 4 band members.
John--Paul--George--Ringo
```

But in this case, an easier and more reliable approach is to read the length of the list directly and not involve an additional argument. After all, this is Python!

```
def print_them_out(*args):
    print('There are', len(args), 'band members.')
    my_str = '--'.join(args)
    print(my_str)
```

Example 16.1. *PointN Class*

With all these tools in place, it's now possible to write a PointN class that supports points of any number of dimensions.

In writing such a class, it is desirable to give the class user the option of passing a list of numbers directly, or alternatively, simply listing all the numbers individually.

```
a_list = [10, 20, 34.5, 0]
pt1 = PointN(a_list)
pt2 = PointN(1.5, 33, 5, 100)
```

Ideally, the class should support both approaches to initializing a multidimensional point.

---

pointn.py

```python
class PointN:
    '''General-purpose multidimensional point class.'''
    def __init__(self, *args):
        # If first arg is a list...
        if isinstance(args[0], list):
            self.the_list = [i for i in args[0]]

        # Otherwise, process all the args as a list.
        else:
            self.the_list = [i for i in args]
        self.list_len = len(self.the_list)

    def __str__(self):
        al_list = [str(i) for i in self.the_list]
        return 'point(' + ', '.join(al_list) + ')'

    def __add__(self, other):
        ''' Add two points together & return a point.'''
        new_list = []
        n = min(self.list_len, other.list_len)
        for i in range(n):
            new_list.append(self.the_list[i]
                            + other.the_list[i])
        return PointN(new_list)

pt1 = PointN(1, 2, 3, 4)
a_list = [10, 10, 10, 10]
pt2 = PointN(a_list)
print('pt1 is', pt1)
print('pt2 is', pt2)
print('Sum is', pt1 + pt2)
```

After all this code is entered and executed, if everything has been typed in correctly, you should see the following printed:

```
pt1 is point(1, 2, 3, 4)
pt2 is point(10, 10, 10, 10)
Sum is point(11, 12, 13, 14)
```

How It Works

The __init__ function of the PointN class makes a straightforward use of the variable-argument feature. With this class, we assume that the user initializes an instance in one of two ways: by giving any number of numeric arguments or by giving just one argument—but that argument contains a list of numbers.

Therefore, the __init__ function checks the type of the first argument; if it is a list, then all the elements of that list are copied to an instance variable, self.the_list.

If the second argument is not a list, then all the elements of args are copied to this variable. The action is essentially the same in either case. It's simply a matter of whether the values are copied from the first argument (args[0]) or from all the arguments (args).

```
def __init__(self, *args):
    # If first arg is a list...
    if isinstance(args[0], list):
        self.the_list = [i for i in args[0]]

    # Otherwise, process all the args as a list.
    else:
        self.the_list = [i for i in args]
    self.list_len = len(self.the_list)
```

Note that list *copying* is used here rather than variable assignment. This is by far the safest approach. You should want the PointN object's internal values—self.the_list—to live as long as the object exists; you shouldn't want them to be tied to changes made somewhere else.

The __str__ method, which returns a string to be printed, is simple. Once you realize the object's values are permanently stored in self.the_list, it's an easy matter to print them.

The __add__ method is in some ways the most interesting, although we'll improve on it in the next section. The method assumes that the "other" object to be added is another object of the PointN class. We therefore add each pair of corresponding values (the Nth element in one object and the Nth element in the other) to produce a new PointN object.

16

Note that the built-in **min** function is used to get the minimum of the dimension sizes of the two points involved; otherwise, with two points of different dimensions, the code would raise an exception.

```
def __add__(self, other):
    new_list = []
    n = min(self.list_len, other.list_len)
    for i in range(n):
        new_list.append(self.the_list[i]
                        + other.the_list[i])
    return NPoint(new_list)
```

Optimizing the Code

The current version of the **__add__** method, although it works, is not the most "Pythonic" solution. With preferred Python style, we want to avoid indexing where possible, preferring to operate on "iterables" as a whole.

The Python **zip** function takes two lists and produces a hybrid list, containing a list of tuples. Each tuple contains an element from the first list and an element from the second. Here's an example:

```
>>>coll_a = [1, 2, 3]
>>>coll_b = [10, 20, 30, 40]
>>>coll_c = zip(coll_a, coll_b)
>>>coll_c
[(1, 10), (2, 20), (3, 30)]
```

Note that the size is the minimum of the two input lists, which is what we want. Using the **zip** function, we can write a better **__add__** method for two points.

```
def __add__(self, other):
    hy = zip(self.the_list, other.the_list)
    new_list = [i[0] + i[1] for i in hy]
    return NPoint(new_list)
```

Isn't this a short, simple, elegant solution?

EXERCISES

Exercise 16.1.1. Write a **__sub__** method for the NPoint class and test it. This method should take two NPoint objects and return a third object in which each element is generated by subtracting corresponding point values.

Exercise 16.1.2. Write a **__mult__** method for the NPoint class and test it. In addition to the self argument, the method should take a single numeric argument, n, and multiply each element by n, producing (val1 * n, val2 * n, val3 * n....). Then return the result.

Exercise 16.1.3. Does the class get a "free" test for equality or do you have to write an __**eq**__ method? Why or why not?

Exercise 16.1.4. This one is for the truly ambitious! Write an is_linear function that takes three points and returns **True** or **False**, depending on whether the three points line up in N-dimensional space. The solution is to calculate the difference (using __sub__) for p2 – p1, and the difference for p3 – p2. Now, all three points are linear if and only if one of these "deltas" (differences) is a strict multiple of the other difference. Determining this last condition is not trivial, however, as you need to avoid dividing by zero. Also, remember to return **False** if the two NPoint objects don't have the same number of dimensions (points).

Inheritance

Gobs of material have been written about inheritance, but in this chapter, I'm going to reduce it to its basic idea, which is simple in theory:

✱ | **When one class inherits from another, it automatically gets the methods and attributes of that parent object—which it may either maintain or override.**

A class inheriting from another is said to *subclass* the other class, which in turn becomes the superclass or parent class. The basic syntax for subclassing is

```
class class_name(base_class):
    class_definitions
```

What exactly gets inherited in Python?

▶ In Python, all methods are inherited, including special methods such as __**init**__ (unlike C++, in which constructors are not inherited). Be careful, though: if you override __**init**__, you may need to call the parent's class version of that method.

▶ All class variables are inherited.

▶ But instance variables are a different matter, and here it gets a bit complicated. In Python, instance variables attach to instances, not classes; therefore, they are not necessarily inherited. However, if you use __**init**__ or some other method to create those variables, then that behavior is inherited as well, assuming you do not override __**init**__.

The great advantage of subclassing is that you can potentially save yourself from writing the same code over and over. I'm going to start with a simple example, but one that involves several classes.

▶ The `Pet` class stores basic information for each pet: name, breed, and age.

▶ The `Dog` and `Cat` classes each inherit directly from the `Pet` class. The `Dog` class adds a method, called `play`; and the `Cat` class adds a method called `snooze`.

▶ Finally, the `Puppy` class inherits from the `Dog` class and adds an instance variable: `favorite_toy`.

The important point is (as with all object-oriented languages) the `Dog`, `Cat`, and `Puppy` classes all inherit all the methods and variables created in the `Pet` class so that code (at least in theory) does not have to be written again, so attributes defined in `Pet` are shared everywhere in this hierarchy. Here is a figure that illustrates the relationships:

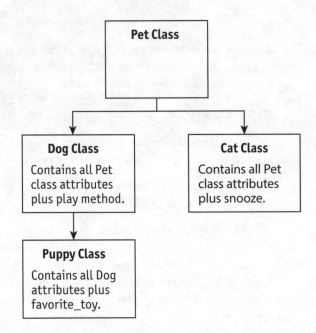

Here's how this class hierarchy might be coded:

```
class Pet:
    '''Parent class for Dog, Cat, etc.'''
    def __init__(self, name, breed, age):
        self.name = name
        self.breed = breed
        self.age = age
```

```
class Dog(Pet):
    '''Dog class — adds play() method.'''
    def play(self):
        '''Dogs just want to have fun.'''
        s = ''
        while not s or s[0] not in 'Nn':
            print(self.name, 'fetches the ball!')
            s = input('Wanna play again? (Y/N) ')

class Cat(Pet):
    def snooze(self):
        print(self.name, 'opens an eye slightly.')
        for i in range(5):
            print('Snooze.')

class Puppy(Dog):
    def __init__(self, name, breed, age, toy):
        Pet.__init__(self, name, breed, age)
        self.favorite_toy = toy
```

Most of this example is straightforward if you just remember the one basic rule: subclasses automatically inherit all the methods of their superclasses.

But there are some fine points, even in this simple example.

First, inheritance can be either direct or indirect. In this case, Puppy inherits directly from Dog, but it not only gets the play method, which originated in the Dog class; it inherits all the attributes of the Pet class (the *grandfather class*) as well.

Descendant classes inherit all parent-class methods, including the **__init__** method, so it isn't always necessary to write new **__init__** methods.

However, sometimes it's useful to call an ancestor class version of a method. The Puppy class does that so that it doesn't have to do all the initialization itself. It calls its "grandfather's" version of **__init__** to initialize everything but the favorite_toy variable.

The way to call another class's version of a function is to use the dot (.) notation.

```
class_name.method(self, args)
```

The Fraction Class

Now let's graduate to a more practical example. One of the more practical ways to use inheritance—although you do have to show some extra care—is to inherit and extend classes provided by Python itself.

One of Python's most useful extended classes is the Fraction class. It requires the following **import** statement:

```
from fractions import Fraction
```

Here's a sample session using this class.

```
>>>a = Fraction('1/2')
>>>b = Fraction('2/3')
>>>print('Total is', a + b)
Total is 7/6
```

Wow, do you see the usefulness of this class? It can add two fractional numbers, such as 1/2 and 2/3, and produce the correct result precisely and reliably—a result that floating-point formats can sometimes get right, but with a high risk of errors.

Consider that floating-point format, which is based on binary radix, cannot really hold a figure like 1/3 or 1/7 precisely. If you execute an operation such as 2/7 + 5/7, you may get the right answer (1.0), but there is no guarantee that such operations will always be right. Rounding errors may creep in. But a Fraction class can hold rational numbers such as 1/3 with absolute precision.

In this next example, I'm going to show how to add new capabilities to this class.

Example 16.2. *Extending the Fraction Class*

If you experiment with the Fraction class, you'll find that it can perform calculations such as 1/2 + 2/3. But this produces 7/6 as the answer, when we instead might want to get a *proper* fraction, namely:

1 1/6

The correct strategy is to override the **__str__** method. However, it's not quite that easy; a few other modifications need to be made as well.

```
pfraction.py

from fractions import Fraction

class PFraction(Fraction):
    def __str__(self):
        n = self.numerator
        d = self.denominator
        i = n // d
        int_str = str(i)+' ' if i > 0 else ''
```

pfraction.py, cont.

```
            n = n % d
            n_str = str(n)+'/'+ str(d) if n > 0 else ''
            return int_str + n_str

    def __add__(self, other):
        f = Fraction.__add__(self, other)
        return PFraction(f)

f1 = PFraction('1/2')
f2 = PFraction('2/3')
print('The result is', f1 + f2)
```

When run, this code will print

```
The result is 1 1/6
```

Note that we get this result rather than the "The result is 7/6" answer.

How It Works

The Fraction class maintains numerator and denominator instance variables, as well as performing internal operations so that given any mathematical operation, these variables will reflect the correct value of a fraction.

We don't want to mess with these. Let the methods in the class do their thing. The only thing we want to change, ideally, is the **__str__** method, although we'll find that other changes need to be made as well.

The overridden **__str__** method works by, first of all, assigning self.numerator and self.denominator—two instance variables created in the Fraction class—to the variables n and d, for convenience.

```
            n = self.numerator
            d = self.denominator
```

Assuming these values produce an improper fraction, we can reduce to a "proper fraction" by performing the following operations:

▶ n // d (integer division) will give us the integer portion.

▶ n % d (modular division) will give us the adjusted numerator.

So, we're done, right? Not quite. If no changes are made to the **__add__** function, then the program prints

```
The result is 7/6.
```

This would mean the PFraction class did nothing different at all! But why?

The explanation is if the **__add__** method is not overridden, then when two PFraction objects are added, the base_class method, **Fraction.__add__**, gets executed. This is as we ought to expect.

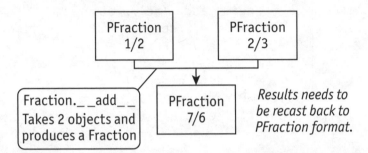

But the **Fraction.__add__** method returns a Fraction, not a PFraction object. So when we add two PFraction objects, we get a Fraction object. And therefore when we print it, we get the old printing behavior as well.

The solution is to override the **__add__** method. We want the base class, Fraction.__add__, to do its thing. But then we want to change the type of the return value so that we end up with a PFraction object. Only then will we get the **__str__** behavior we want.

```
def __add__(self, other):
    f = Fraction.__add__(self, other)
    return PFraction(f)
```

Remember, this overridden method doesn't change any behavior by itself. All it does is recast the type of the object being returned to **PFraction**, so when this object is printed, it will use PFraction's **__str__** method.

It's as if the code is saying, "Go ahead and use the base-class version of __add__, but don't forget to return a PFraction object."

Note ▶ In addition to built-in methods **__add__**, **__mult__**, **__div__**, and so on, Python also recognizes corresponding methods such as **__radd__**, **__rmult__**, and **__rdiv__**, which are useful if you want to define how to add objects of different types. For example, if you want to define how to add pfract1 to fract1, where the types are PFraction and Fraction, respectively, then you need to define **__radd__** so that the following expression can be evaluated:

```
fact1 + pfract1
```

Note that in this case, pfract1 is on the right side. This is a situation in which defining PFraction.__radd__ is useful.

◀ Note

EXERCISES

Exercise 16.2.1.   Write a calculation program that prompts for input in the form of a fraction and continues until the user enters a blank space. Then print the total of all the fractions, in PFraction form.

Exercise 16.2.2.   Look at the solution devised for the **__str__** method of the PFraction. Then apply the same solution to other operations, by overriding the **__sub__**, **__mult__**, and **__div__** methods.

Exercise 16.2.3.   Override the **__init__** method so that if the first argument is a string of the form "2 1/3", it parses the string into the form (n, d) and then passes those two numbers to the base-class method, Fraction.__init__. If the first argument is a string that does not contain an embedded space, pass it along to the base-class method. If there are two arguments instead of one, then just pass them along to the base-class method.

Class Variables and Methods

Instance variables, it should be clear by now, are variables whose values are attached to individual objects. Although all instances can (and usually should) have a common blueprint, each will maintain its own values. Instance variables are not shared.

A class variable is a variable that *is* shared among all members of a class. This is an advanced technique, and you may go a long time in your Python career before you ever really need it.

A common example is an automatic counter that keeps track of how many instances you've created. Let's call this variable num_dogs. To create this as a class variable, I simply make an assignment to it, directly under the class header. Let's assume a rudimentary Dog class.

```
class Dog:
    num_dogs = 0
```

Not that interesting, is it? But I access this new value by using class name combined with the dot notation.

```
>>>Dog.num_dogs
0
```

I can also access it through any of the objects of the class, in a similar manner.

```
>>>d = Dog()
>>>d.num_dogs
0
```

But within methods of the class, do not refer to class variables as **self.**_variable_. Instead, use the syntax _class.variable_. Here's a complete example, with the key lines in bold:

```
class Dog:
    '''Dog class illustrating a class variable.'''
    num_dogs = 0
    def __init__(self, name, breed, age):
        self.name = name
        self.breed = breed
        self.age = age
        Dog.num_dogs += 1
```

With these additions (remember, marked in bold), the class will now behave the way we wanted: it will keep track of how many dogs have been created. Here's how to demonstrate this feature from within the interactive environment:

```
>>>my_dog = Dog('Toodles', 'Poodle', 5)
>>>yr_dog = Dog('Masher', 'Doberman', 7)
>>>Dog.num_dogs
2
```

The environment correctly reported that two `Dog` objects have been created.

A class may also support class methods and static methods, which are similar: they are shared by all instances of a class and do not apply to individual instances. The difference is that static methods take no additional argument at all, whereas class methods take an additional argument referring to the class itself.

Static methods have the following syntax:

```
@staticmethod
def method_name(args):
    statements
```

I'll show an example of such a method in Example 16.3.

The syntax for class methods is similar. The difference is that the extra argument (which by convention is **cls**) provides a convenient way to call other methods of the same class, as **cls.**_method_.

```
@classmethod
def method_name(cls, args):
    statements
```

Instance Variables as "Default" Values

Still not convinced that class variables are worth learning? They have still more uses, in addition to the `count` variable shown in the previous section. These other uses include

▶ Defining constants that are useful to the class generally, such as `pi`.

▶ Defining default values for instance variables.

For example, suppose we have a `Circle` class, which includes a `get_area` method for calculating the area of that circle.

```
class Circle:
    pi = 3.14

    def __init__(self, r):
        self.r = r

    def get_area(self):
        return Circle.pi * self.r * self.r
```

Here's an example of the class in use:

```
r = 2
c = Circle(r)
print('For circle of radius', r, '...')
print('area is', c.get_area())
```

This prints an answer of 12.56.

The limitation here, of course, is that 3.14 is a very rough approximation of pi, and we might like to use a much more precise approximation: 3.14159265.

Let's try to do this by changing the value of pi on the object itself. Python allows this, and it seems, at first, to work. You can demonstrate this feature from within the interactive environment.

```
>>>c.pi = 3.14159265
>>>print(c.pi)
3.14159265
```

But if you rerun `get_area()`, the result doesn't change; it's still 12.56. The explanation is that the `get_area()` method specifically referred to the class variable `pi`, not the instance variable.

```
        return Circle.pi * self.r * self.r
```

Remember that you assign a value to `c.pi`, it creates a new instance variable...just as in a function, if you assign a new value to a variable, it creates a new local.

So if you create other `Circle` variables, you'll see the value of pi hasn't changed.

```
>>>new_circ = Circle(2)
>>>print(new_circ.pi)
3.14
```

What happened was that the statement

```
c.pi = 3.14159265
```

created an instance variable attached to the object `c`, and that in turn has no effect on other objects, such as `new_circ`.

If you want to change the class variable itself, and not add an instance variable, remember to use the class name.

```
Circle.pi = 3.14159265
```

This statement will change the value of the class variable `pi`, which in turn will affect other `Circle` objects.

When Python comes across an expression such as `c.pi`, it looks for an assignment to `pi` in this order: instance variable name, class variable name, and any inherited names from the base class.

How Python resolves expressions such as *obj.var*

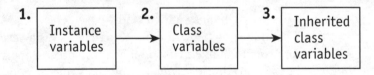

Example 16.3.   *Polygon "Automated" Class*

In the following example, a great deal of work is "automated" by being placed in the base class, `Polygon`, which is ideally how you should want to use inheritance when possible.

Normally, when you create polygon classes such as `Square`, `Circle`, and so on, you'd have to write code—either in the class or outside the class—to get the value of each side (or in the case of circles, the radius). You'd also need to write a function that calculated such things as area of volume.

In this example, both those basic functions are automated...by being performed in the base class.

```python
class Polygon:
    '''Base classes for polygons and solids.'''
    pi = 3.14159265

    @ staticmethod
    def get_area(factors, sides, cfacts):
        ''' This method prompts for values of all
            sides and returns area or volume.
            Factors is a list indexing all the sides;
            'sides' is a list of strings, cfacts are
            constants multiplied into the result.'''
        data = []
        for name in sides:
            x = float(input('Enter ' + name + ': '))
            data.append(x)
        prod = 1
        for i in factors:
            prod *= data[i - 1]
        for i in cfacts:
            prod *= i
        return prod

class Square(Polygon):
    def __init__(self):
        self.a = Polygon.get_area([1,1], ['side'], [])

class Rectangle(Polygon):
    def __init__(self):
        self.a = Polygon.get_area([1,2],
                    ['height', 'width'], [])

class Sphere(Polygon):
    def __init__(self):
        self.v = Polygon.get_area([1,1,1],
                    ['radius'], [Polygon.pi, 4/3])

print('The area of a square...')
a_square = Square()
print('The area is the square is', a_square.a)
```

```
print('The area of a rectangle...')
a_rect = Rectangle()
print('The area of a rectangle is', a_rect.a)

print('The volume of a sphere...')
a_sphere = Sphere()
print('The volume of the sphere is', a_sphere.v)
```

How It Works

The subclasses that appear in this example include Square, Circle, and Sphere. All each of these subclasses do, upon initialization, is to call the class function, get_area, which is inherited from Polygon. But each calls the get_area method with different arguments, supporting an endless variety of shapes and solids.

Although different words are used for the input data—*side*, *length*, *width*, *radius*—and so on, the process of prompting the user for this data is repetitive. That's why it can be automated. And the process of calculating area (or volume, as the case may be) is just a matter of multiplying together the right list of values. The get_area method uses list arguments to determine what information to multiply together.

```
prod = 1
for i in factors:
    prod *= data[i - 1]
```

The data list was filled out by an input loop before this loop is executed. This loop then takes that data and multiplies it together according to the one-based index numbers in the factors list.

Therefore, a factors list of [1, 1] combined with a sides list of ['side'] causes the following calculation to be made:

```
Area = side * side
```

Likewise, a Rectangle object passes a factors list of [1, 2], combined with a sides list of ['height', 'width'], multiplies together *two* factors, not one.

```
Area = height * width
```

Finally, all the numeric values in the cfact list are multiplied directly into the result. So a factors list of [1, 1, 1] combined with a cfact list of [pi, 4/3] calculates the result as

```
V = radius * radius * radius * pi * 4/3
```

Throughout this example, note that all references to the class variable, pi, as well as the class method, get_area, are qualified with a reference to the Polygon class.

```
class Sphere(Polygon):
    def __init__(self):
        self.v = Polygon.get_area([1,1,1],
            ['radius'], [Polygon.pi, 4/3])
```

EXERCISES

Exercise 16.3.1.   Add the following shapes to the program, remembering to subclass from Polygon: pyramids and cylinders. (Each has its own volume formula that you can easily look up online.)

Exercise 16.3.2.   One limitation of Example 16.3 as it now stands is that each subclass object ends up storing area/volume only, with access to no other data. Solve this problem by revising get_area to return the information in the factor and name arguments; then, store that information in subclass objects. Doing so will enable each object to have extensive information about the polygon or shape.

Exercise 16.3.3.   Ask yourself: does get_area have to be written as a class method? Could it have been written as an instance method? If so, what efficiency, if any, is gained by having it written as a class method?

Interlude

OOPS, What Is It Good For?

Object-oriented programming (OOP)—or as I like to say, object-oriented programming systems (OOPS!)—has for decades been among the biggest topics in computer programming. It was once seen as the solution to every problem; now it's seen as a convenient way to package certain kinds of code.

In particular, although OOPS is not equivalent to event-based programming, or graphical user interface (GUI) programming, all these models are in harmony. Think about it: a window or a command button is very much like a self-contained object, which you can send messages to in the form of method calls.

I've always liked that model…thinking of objects as independent entities that sit there and send messages to each other.

▼ *continued on next page*

Interlude

▼ *continued*

Object orientation is almost too well supported in Python. Inheritance is easy, with no protected variables. Polymorphism is automatically supported. This means that every object can have its own implementation of the `print_me` method, for example, and an object's own version of the code (not the caller's) will always be executed.

In these last two chapters, I hope I've shown some cases in which the class-object syntax is useful, even necessary: this includes situations in which you need a data-record type and situations in which you need a customized data type. Still another good use for OOP occurs when you have repetitive code that can be put in a base class and then inherited by subclasses.

But OOPS has a drawback in Python. Because variables are not declared and have no type except that of the data assigned at run time, Python is less self-documenting than other languages (although you can make up for that with extensive comments). When you assign an object, what class is it? Who knows? This can make reading another programmer's code a nightmare, especially if this person likes to write lots of classes.

You might be better off sticking to built-in types and consistent naming conventions. For example, `my_str` should be a string, and `a_list` should be a list. Simple variables, such as a, b, and c, should be **int** or **float**. I've tried to stick to that standard in this book.

Chapter 16   *Summary*

Here are the main points of Chapter 16:

▶ In Python, documentation strings serve the same basic purpose as comments but also provide automatic help text from within the interactive environment. Place a string right after the heading of a class, function, or method definition while observing standard indentation. You can also place it at the beginning of a file to provide information on a module that has been imported.

▶ You can test the type of an object at run time, by using either the **isinstance** or **type** functions. The first—which is preferred because of how it cooperates with inheritance—returns **True** or **False**.

```
if isinstance(my_dog, Dog):
    print('I am a dog.')
```

- You can treat a series of N arguments as a variable-length list by including an asterisk.

```
def print_the_out(*args):
    print('First arg is', args[0])
    print('Second arg is', args[1])
    print('There are', len(args), 'args total.')
```

- Inheritance is realized through subclassing in Python. The following syntax causes *new_class* to automatically include all the methods and class variables of *base_class* (although the methods may be overridden):

```
class new_class(base_class):
    definitions
```

- Remember that **__init__** is a true initialization function. This makes some aspects of inheritance easier. In particular, the **__init__** function is automatically inherited but may be overridden.

- A subclass may call any method in the base class by referring to the base class explicitly and using the dot notation (.).

```
class Dog(Pet):
    def __init__(self, name, breed, age, toy):
        self.toy = toy
        Pet.__init__(self, name, breed, age)
```

- Class variables are defined directly under the class header rather than from within a method. Class variables are shared by all members of the class and are always referred to with the syntax *class_name.var*, rather than *object_name.var* or **self**.*var*.

16

Conway's Game of Life

How do you get to Carnegie Hall? Practice, practice! Now answer this: how do you become a programmer?

The answer is to practice on what I call "real projects." That's why I focused on Tic-Tac-Toe in Chapter 14. Playing a perfect strategy—even for this simple game—is far from trivial. It required serious mastery of Python fundamentals, as well as creative decision-making.

In this chapter, I'll apply Python tricks introduced in the last few chapters to an even more ambitious project: Conway's Game of Life, which simulates living cells! That this entire program can be written in 100 lines (38 if you take out the comments and blank lines!) is remarkable. The strategy of this chapter is

▶ Develop a general-purpose matrix class

▶ Print out a matrix as a series of blanks and Xs

▶ Create the full Game of Life program

Interlude

The Impact of "Life"

The "Game"—which is more properly called a *simulation*—has its origins back in the 1940s when John von Newman, the legendary mathematician and game theorist, invented a set of rules for a "self-reproducing machine" that used complex rules played out on a grid.

The British mathematician John Horton Conway came up with a way of simplifying Von Newman's rules, producing the Game of Life we know today. A 1970 issue of *Scientific American* contained an article by Martin Gardner, explaining the rules and presenting some of the more interesting patterns.

▼ *continued on next page*

▼ *continued*

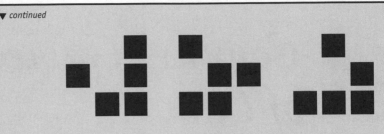

I was very young at the time, but I remember reading that article. Personal computers were not yet on the market, so the Game could only be played by painstakingly working out alternating generations on a chessboard... first with blue chips, then with red chips. Research institutes, of course, could use mainframe computers to run the game, but other people had to do it the hard way. Even then, it was fascinating.

Martin Gardner's article on the Game had immediate impact. It single-handedly created the field of *cellular automata*—which seeks to understand cell behavior as if each were a little machine. And it made John Horton Conway famous overnight.

After the advent of personal computers in the late 1970s, the Game of Life became even more popular—among programmers. I knew at least one programmer I worked with told me that when he could write the Game of Life in a new programming language, then he knew he "had finally cracked the language."

The Game of Life was the first serious program I wrote in C. At that time processors were so slow that I needed to use every trick I could to optimize speed, eventually ending up with a program 40 or 50 times faster than the one I started with. Some of my optimizations were specific to the C language, but other insights influenced the version I present here.

Game of Life: The Rules of the Game

The Game consists of a grid (of whatever size you like) in which every position is either "alive" or "empty"—that is, dead. This makes everything comparatively simple.

The rules are

▶ For each and every position in the grid, count up the number of neighboring positions that have living cells. Diagonals are counted, so there are at most eight living neighbors and as few as zero.

▶ If there are fewer than two neighbors, the current position has a "death" event: if there is a living cell at this position, it's erased. This is the Starvation Rule.

▶ If a cell has exactly two neighbors, keep the cell as it is: if it was empty, it stays empty; if it was living, it continues to live. This is the Maintenance Rule.

▶ If a position has exactly three neighbors, this is a birth event. Three neighbors is the "ideal" condition, indicating a perfect environment. Action: turn the cell to living if it is currently empty.

▶ If a position has more than three neighbors, this is also a death event. If there is a cell at the current position, turn it off. This is the Overpopulation Rule.

This may sound like a lot of rules but turns out to be incredibly simple. When you synthesize these rules, using the techniques I use in this chapter, there are actually only two.

N = NEIGHBOR COUNT FOR A CELL POSITION	ACTION PERFORMED
N < 2 or N > 3	Death event. Set corresponding cell in Life matrix to OFF. (Famine and Overpopulation Rules.)
N == 3	Birth event. Set corresponding cell in Life matrix to ON.

That's it! We need no other rules to process the next generation... just generate a "neighbor-count" matrix from the current state (the "Life matrix") and then set positions in the Life matrix to ON or OFF as summarized by these two rules.

For N equal to 2, no action is taken at all: cells that are already ON are left on, and cells that are OFF are left off. N equal to 2 is a *no op*.

The next figure illustrates how these rules would be applied to a "blinker" pattern, which oscillates between two states.

▶ An X in the first graphic shows a living cell in the old generation.

▶ The numbers in the second graphic show the neighbor counts, superimposed on the living-cell information. It includes the values in the corresponding cells in the Neighbor Count matrix; the little wedges show the living cells from the old generation, so you can see the information combined.

▶ An X in the final graphic shows the position of a living cell in the *new* generation.

17

The numbers in the middle picture are the neighbor counts. Remember that a count of 3 causes a birth event, and a count of 1 causes a death event. A count of 2 maintains the status quo.

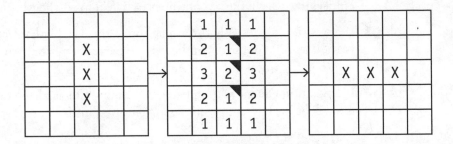

Here's another illustration: the stable square. This pattern has "birth" events only where living cells already exist. And it has "death" events only where positions are empty. Therefore, this pattern goes from one generation to the next without changing...until some foreign cells invade its territory, which can happen.

As these figures illustrate, the key to a super-efficient algorithm for the Game of Life—the one we'll be using in this chapter—is to have two matrixes: one for state of the game and another for neighbor counts.

Generating the Neighbor Count

So, given two matrixes—one that contains the current state of the game and another dedicated to holding neighbor counts—how do you count neighbors?

I've found that the most efficient way to do this is not to count up the neighbors of each individual cell, even though that's the more obvious approach. Let's say we have a Life matrix 40 columns by 20 rows, which is 800 cells. You could do the following:

For each of the 800 cells,
  Count up all 8 neighbors

This approach works, but it's inefficient. It examines each of the 800 cells, and then for each cell, it accesses all 8 of its neighbors. This requires a grand total of 800 times 9, or 7,200 separate cell accesses.

My approach takes advantage of there rarely being more than 5 or 10 percent density in the Life matrix.

For each living cell in the Life matrix,
  Increment the count for all surrounding cells in N.C. Matrix

The current state of the Life matrix is used to "populate" the Neighbor Count matrix. The beauty of this approach is that where cells are empty, the program does almost nothing. Living-cell density above 5 or 10 percent is rare, so this approach constitutes a big win in terms of efficiency and execution speed.

For example, if a living cell is found in the Life matrix at point (2, 2), then Neighbor Count elements are incremented in the following positions:

▶ On the row above: (1, 1), (1, 2), (1, 3)

▶ To either side: (2, 1), (2, 3)

▶ One the row below: (3, 1), (3, 2), (3, 3)

Here's how the operation looks in graphical terms. Remember, the living cell is located in the Life matrix, but incrementing is done to cells in the Neighbor Count matrix.

There's a twist here. If the Life-matrix cell is on an edge or in a corner, then the results "wrap" to the other side. I'll return to that technique later and show how wrapping is implemented.

Design of the Program

The overall flow of the program is fairly simple.

> *Get N from the user,*
> *For 1 to N times,*
> > *Print out the Life Matrix.*
> > *Reset Neighbor-Count Matrix to all 0's.*
> > *Populate Neighbor-Count matrix.*
> > *Use Neighbor Count to generate next generation of Life, using the two rules.*

The main work of the program comes down to these steps: (1) print the Life matrix, (2) populate the Neighbor Count matrix, and (3) create the next generation in the Life matrix by using the two rules stated in the previous section.

The first thing to do is to create a generic `Matrix` class that knows how to perform a number of useful operations. This will simplify the rest of the programming to be done later.

This `Matrix` class will be used to generate the two matrixes:

▶ `life_mat`, which holds the current state of the game

▶ `nc_mat`, which holds all the neighbor counts

Example 17.1. ## The Customized Matrix Class

Here's the code for the `Matrix` class. Although I've included certain methods that will be especially useful in the Game of Life application, this is to a large extent a general-purpose class; you could reuse it with other applications.

For each method, I've supplied a doc string that summarizes what the method does.

```
lifemat.py

class Matrix2D:
    ''' General-purpose 2-d Matrix class for Life.'''

    def __init__(self, rows, cols):
        ''' Init matrix to rows times cols. '''
        self.grid = [[0] * cols for _ in range(rows)]
```

lifemat.py, cont.

```
            self.rows = rows
            self.cols = cols

        def get_cell(self, r, c):
            ''' Get value at cell r, c. '''
            return self.grid[r][c]

        def set_cells(self, n, *args):
            ''' Set any number of cells to n. '''
            for r, c  in args:
                self.grid[r][c] = n

        def inc_cells(self, *args):
            ''' Increment any number of cells by 1 each. '''
            for r, c in args:
                self.grid[r][c] += 1

        def set_all_cells(self, n=0):
            ''' Set any number of cells to n, default 0. '''
            for i in range(self.rows):
                for j in range (self.cols):
                    self.grid[i][j] = n
```

How It Works

Each of these methods will prove useful in the program. For example, we'll use **__init__** and set_cells to create and initialize the Life matrix to a starting state.

Chapter 13 introduced the technique for creating multidimensional lists, and that technique is used here, in **__init__**:

```
    self.grid = [[0] * cols for _ in range(rows)]
```

The get_cell and inc_cells methods will do most of the work of the program. During the main loop, we'll use get_cell to find out whether a position in the Life matrix is on or off. Then we'll use inc_cells to populate adjacent positions in the Neighbor Count matrix.

The set_cells and inc_cells method both use the variable-length-argument feature introduced in the previous chapter.

```
    def set_cells(self, n, *args):
        for r, c in args:
            self.grid[r][c] = n
```

Any number of arguments are packed into ***args**. This definition requires a little explanation. We assume each argument is a tuple, of the form (r, c). The loop reads one tuple at a time, but it reads that tuple directly into the variables r and c.

Here's an example of a call to this method, preceded by a statement creating the matrix.

```
my_mat = Matrix2D(20, 20)
my_mat.set_cells(5, (0,0), (0,1), (0, 2))
```

This method call sets each of the first three cells of the top row to 5. The first argument, 5, is passed to n, and the tuples (0, 0), (0, 1), and (0,2) are read into r and c during each iteration of the loop. First r and c are 0 and 0; then r and c are 0 and 1; and then finally they are 0 and 2.

EXERCISES

Exercise 17.1.1.   Place this class definition into a file and then add a few lines of code of your own to test the class. First, make some calls to set_cells and inc_cells to put some information in the matrix. Then print out some of these values, one at a time.

Exercise 17.1.2.   Repeat Exercise 17.1, but this time print out *all* the values in the matrix, one row at a time.

Moving the Matrix Class to a Module

If you want to reuse a class in multiple programs or if you just want to break your program into manageable chunks, called *modules*—in which each module occupies a different source file—you can move class definitions into separate modules.

There are just a few steps required to do this:

1 Move the class definition place into a file with a .py extension. Place this file in the same directory that the rest of your program will reside in. Let's say the name is lifemat.py for the sake of illustration.

2 Although the file name has a .py extension, the module name should not include it. In this case, the module name will be lifemat.

3 For a program to use the class definition, place an important statement at the beginning of the main program. Here's an example:

```
from lifemat import Matrix2D
```

Example 17.2. *Printing a Life Matrix*

The first major task in the program is to print out the Life matrix nicely, printing not numbers but some character chosen specifically to represent a living: this might, for example, be an X.

Writing this code shouldn't be difficult, but keep in mind that a border should be printed between generations and smooth, fast printing is achieved by making as few separate calls to **print** as possible.

```
lifeprint.py

# Import from the file lifemat.py in the same dir.
from lifemat import Matrix2D

rows = 20
cols = 40
life_mat = Matrix2D(rows, cols)
life_mat.set_cells(1, (1,1),(2,2),(3,0),(3,1),(3,2))
border_str = '_' * cols    # Create border string.

def do_generation():
    print(border_str + '\n' + get_mat_str(life_mat))

def get_mat_str(a_mat):
    disp_str = ''
    for i in range(rows):
        lst=[get_chr(a_mat,i,j) for j in range(cols)]
        disp_str += ''.join(lst) + '\n'
    return disp_str

def get_chr(a_mat, r, c):
    return 'X' if a_mat.get_cell(r, c) > 0 else ' '

do_generation()
```

17

How It Works

Despite the number of physical lines involved, this example is simple. All it does is create a Matrix2D object, turn some cells on in the matrix, and then print it.

The first statement imports the class from another source file. The statement assumes that there is a file named `lifemat.py` located in the same directory as the rest of the code.

```
from lifemat import Matrix2D
```

The next few statements create a series of global variables, including the matrix itself, `life_mat`; they also initialize the matrix by turning five of the cells on.

```
rows = 20
cols = 40
life_mat = Matrix2D(rows, cols)
life_mat.set_cells(1, (1,1),(2,2),(3,0),(3,1),(3,2))
border_str = '_' * cols    # Create border string.
```

Note that even though these statements create a series of global variables, the **global** statement never needs to be used with any of the functions; this is because (as you'll see) none of the functions in this program ever assigns new values to them. Individual values within the matrix are changed—which is fine, because lists are mutable—but the variable itself, `life_mat`, is never again the target of an assignment after it is declared.

The statement that creates the border string is noteworthy, because it uses the multiplication operator (*) to repeat a character, creating one long string.

```
border_str = '_' * cols    # Create border string.
```

The key function in this example is `get_mat_str`. It creates a string consisting of spaces and Xs corresponding to all the empty and living cells, respectively, in the matrix.

```
def get_mat_str(a_mat):
    disp_str = ''
    for i in range(rows):
        lst=[get_chr(a_mat,i,j) for j in range(cols)]
        disp_str += ''.join(lst) + '\n'
    return disp_str
```

You could print the matrix one row at a time; you could even do it one character at a time. But remember that in Python, making many calls to **print** greatly slows down the application. Therefore, the efficient approach is to build up one long string—newlines included—that contains the entire matrix.

This could have been done through concatenation and nested loops. The more obvious way to create this string (especially if you're programming background is in C, C++, or another language), would be to use the following block:

```
for i in range(rows):
    for j in range(cols):
        if life_mat.get_cell(i, j) > 0:
            out_str += 'X'
        else:
            out_str += ' '
```

However, the approach I use here takes advantage of Python features, specifically, list comprehension and the **join** function, enabling the program to do in two lines what would otherwise take more.

```
lst=[get_chr(a_mat,i,j) for j in range(cols)]
disp_str += ''.join(lst) + '\n'
```

The efficiency of this approach is not limited to the number of lines. By making use of the **join** method, this code is much more efficient than building strings through concatenation. The approach used here builds a full row at a time by doing the following:

1 For each character in the current row, generate either an X or a blank by calling the get_chr function and place it in the list of strings named lst.

2 Then use the **join** method to put all these individual characters into a single string, and append a newline.

Finally, the current row is concatenated onto strings representing other rows. This approach does use some string concatenation, but not nearly as much as the more obvious approach.

The get_chr function uses the trinary, "conditional" operator to select either an X or a blank. This operator is supported in Python 3.0 but not 2.0. If you're using Python 2.0, you could use the following code instead:

```
def get_chr(a_mat, r, c):
    return [' ', 'X'][a_mat.get_cell(r, c) % 2]
```

EXERCISES

Exercise 17.2.1.   Revise Example 12.1 so that it makes even heavier use of the **join** function. A correct solution must create a list in which each element is a string containing all the characters for a row. Those strings should then be joined, using a newline (\n) to separate one row from another.

Exercise 17.2.2.   The program does not have to print Xs. It can just as easily print capital Os, or any other character. Revise the code so that it prints the character contained in the variable ch, which can be set earlier in the program.

Exercise 17.2.3. Using a piece of graph paper as an aid, design a much more complicated pattern, set those cells with set_cells, and then print out that design. For example, you could print out a happy face.

The Famous Slider Pattern

Some patterns die off after a few generations. Other patterns are stable, never changing unless they are "invaded" by a foreign pattern. But the most interesting patterns oscillate through a series of states.

The famous "slider" pattern is one of those that oscillates between several states. But it's more interesting than that...it moves in one of four directions. The slider is not the only pattern that does all that, but it's probably the simplest.

The following figure illustrates how to process one generation of a slider. During each generation, there are always five living cells, but they move—as a group—to the right in this case. Eventually this pattern will move downward as well.

Remember that a neighbor count of 3 is a birth event; a count of 1 or 4 is a death event. 2 means "Keep the status quo."

In the full program shown next, I initialize life_mat to contain a slider, but you can experiment with lots of other patterns and combinations of patterns. For example, sometimes two sliders will collide and annihilate each other. Or they may create a stable colony. It's fun to watch a grid of multiple sliders zipping around the board and causing collisions.

Example 17.3. # The Whole Game of Life Program

Here is the entire program, except for the definition of the Matrix2D class, which I import from a separate module.

```
life.py
```

```
# Import from the file lifemat.py in the same dir.
from lifemat import Matrix2D

rows = 20
cols = 40
life_mat = Matrix2D(rows, cols)
nc_mat = Matrix2D(rows, cols)    # Neighbor Counts
life_mat.set_cells(1, (1,1),(2,2),(3,0),(3,1),(3,2))
border_str = '_' * cols    # Create border string.

# Helper functions for printing state of matrix.

def get_mat_str(a_mat):
    disp_str = ''
    for i in range(rows):
        lst=[get_chr(a_mat,i,j) for j in range(cols)]
        disp_str += ''.join(lst) + '\n'
    return disp_str

def get_chr(a_mat, r, c):
    return 'X' if a_mat.get_cell(r, c) > 0 else ' '

# Do Generation function.
# Print the current state of life_mat, and then process
# one generation.

def do_generation():

    # Print the current 'Life' state.
    print(border_str + '\n' + get_mat_str(life_mat))

    nc_mat.set_all_cells(0)

    # Populate nc_mat, but 1) looking at each living
    # cell in life_mat, and for each, increment all
    # surrounding positions... in nc_mat. Use % op
    # to implement "wrap around" at edges & corners.
```

▼ continued on next page

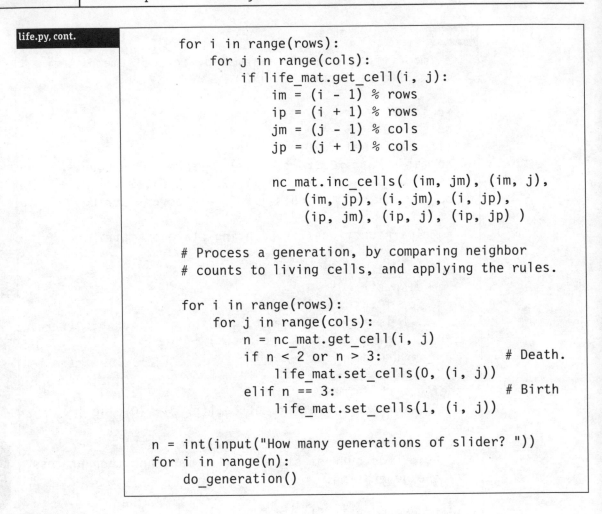

life.py, cont.

```
        for i in range(rows):
            for j in range(cols):
                if life_mat.get_cell(i, j):
                    im = (i - 1) % rows
                    ip = (i + 1) % rows
                    jm = (j - 1) % cols
                    jp = (j + 1) % cols

                    nc_mat.inc_cells( (im, jm), (im, j),
                        (im, jp), (i, jm), (i, jp),
                        (ip, jm), (ip, j), (ip, jp) )

        # Process a generation, by comparing neighbor
        # counts to living cells, and applying the rules.

        for i in range(rows):
            for j in range(cols):
                n = nc_mat.get_cell(i, j)
                if n < 2 or n > 3:                    # Death.
                    life_mat.set_cells(0, (i, j))
                elif n == 3:                          # Birth
                    life_mat.set_cells(1, (i, j))

    n = int(input("How many generations of slider? "))
    for i in range(n):
        do_generation()
```

How It Works

The do_generation function does most of the action in this program. When you understand do_generation, you'll understand the program.

The first thing it does is to print the current status of the Life matrix, life_mat. I explained how this works in Example 17.2.

The next thing it does is reset all the counts in the Neighbor Count matrix, nc_mat, to zero.

```
        nc_mat.set_all_cells(0)
```

The next part is more interesting. The Neighbor Count matrix is "populated" by looking at each living cell in life_mat but then incrementing surrounding cells—not in life_mat itself but in the corresponding nc_mat cells.

First, however, the program has to deal with the "edge" problem. If a cell is on the bottom row, for example, attempting to access positions below it would cause an indexing error.

There are several solutions, but I prefer the one in which the bottom "wraps around" to the top, the top "wraps" to the bottom, and so on. Here's how it's implemented:

```
im = (i - 1) % rows
ip = (i + 1) % rows
jm = (j - 1) % cols
jp = (j + 1) % cols
```

Essentially, i and j are the current row and column, respectively; **ip** and **im** are 1plus and minus the current row number, and jp and jm are 1 plus and minus the column number.

By using remainder division (%), also called the *modulus operator*, we effectively get the left edge to wrap around to the right edge, and so on. For example, assume the current column is 0. Subtracting 1 and applying remainder division produces cols-1, the right edge.

The effect is wonderful. It causes the program to view the Game of Life board as *finite yet unbounded*, very much as most physicists today regard our physical universe. That means theoretically, if you traveled in a straight line in any direction, eventually you'd come back around to where you started. How is this possible? Because according to Einstein, space is curved, so an explorer in space would eventually come back to her starting point, just as Magellan's ships did when they went all the way around the earth.

Now, with ip and im calculated (plus or minus 1 from current row) and jp and jp calculated (plus or minus 1 from current column), the corresponding neighbor cells in the Neighbor Count matrix are incremented.

```
nc_mat.inc_cells( (im, jm), (im, j),
    (im, jp), (i, jm), (i, jp),
    (ip, jm), (ip, j), (ip, jp) )
```

The last step is to examine the neighbor counts, stored in nc_mat, and use them to determine where birth and death events happen in the game-state matrix, life_mat.

```
for i in range(rows):
    for j in range(cols):
        n = nc_mat.get_cell(i, j)
        if n < 2 or n > 3:                  # Death.
            life_mat.set_cells(0, (i, j))
        elif n == 3:                         # Birth
            life_mat.set_cells(1, (i, j))
```

EXERCISES

Exercise 17.3.1.   This version of the Game of Life creates several data objects outside of any function; they are therefore global variables, yet there is no use of the **global** keyword. Why is this or isn't this correct?

Exercise 17.3.2.   Without removing the five initial cells that constitute the "slider" pattern, add a "stable box" pattern somewhere to the Life matrix. Remember that this is a pattern of just four cells that form a square. With this pattern added, you should be able to watch the slider zip around the grid until it finally runs into the box and destroys it. Or, it may form some completely new pattern.

Exercise 17.3.3.   Currently the game produces one generation after another without delays or pause, so you don't get a good look at any given state. Slow the game down by prompting the user in between each generation. If the user presses Enter or types Y, process the next generation. If the user enters N or n, then quit.

Exercise 17.3.4.   Slow down the game—this time not by waiting for user input, but through an arbitrary delay device. More specifically, put in a loop that counts to some large number in between generations.

Exercise 17.3.5.   Right now the game always starts with a single slider on the board and nothing else. Revise the game so that it starts by asking the user to enter as many cell coordinates of the form (r, c) as she likes. You can do this either by repeatedly prompting the user for a cell—with an empty string signaling she's done—or by letting her enter any number of coordinates on one line. The best solution combines both these techniques, because one line may not be long enough to enter all the coordinates desired. Write this solution as a single function that can be called from the main program.

Exercise 17.3.6.   If you look at the overall program size, including the definition of the Matrix2D class itself, *the total number of lines of code* is longer because it defines this class. However, there are other considerations. First, the Matrix2D class may be profitably used by other programs. Second, the main program is easier to write and easier to follow as a result.

To convince yourself of this, rewrite the loop that increments cells in the nc_mat class. Instead of making nc_mat an object of type Matrix2D, write nc_mat as a simple two-dimensional grid without making it into a class. You should find that the code you have to write is much longer and more cumbersome.

Does "Life" Create Life?

When the *Scientific American* article appeared in 1970, the Game of Life promised to change the way that everyone thought of biology. In that, I think it was only partly successful.

Many scientists, mathematicians, and computer scientists saw great promise in the field of study, *cellular automata*, that the Game of Life created. Traditionally, biologists, chemists, and others thought of biology as entirely a top-down endeavor.

First, observe behavior on the macro level, the level of everyday reality. Try to explain this behavior by analyzing the underling building blocks—that is, organic chemistry. Understand the chemical laws in terms of its basic laws. From there, analyze those laws in terms of even smaller building blocks—atoms, molecules, and elementary particles.

Eventually, you were supposed to have explained the entire universe.

The Game of Life suggested that a *bottom-up* approach might work as well or better. With this approach, you experiment with individual cells programmed to follow some set of rules. Then see if you can find the *right* rules, and the *right* group of cells, to simulate the behavior we see all around us. If you could do that, then you might have discovered the hidden secrets of nature.

How successful is the Game of Life at simulating our reality? If you try the program in this chapter, you'll see that some patterns, such as the "slider," look promising.

And there are much more sophisticated patterns, such as a slider "gun" that every few generations launches a new slider and sends it on its way. That's an example of a pattern that is both self-sustaining and endlessly expanding, because it generates a never-ending supply of new colonies sent off to infinity.

However, there is some reason to be skeptical. After I wrote my first computerized version of Life, I experimented with it for some time. And I found that the vast majority of patterns degenerated into stable (and therefore boring) patterns such as square blocks, or they died out.

Yet it's been shown you can use Life to build complex machines, such as a slider gun. You can also—and this is especially interesting to computer scientists—build a Turing machine, a device that, in theory, can solve any problem a digital computer can solve.

But here is where I think patterns in Conway's Game of Life fail: in a very complex pattern involving tens of thousands of cells, it seems to me that having even a single extra or a single missing cell makes the entire

▼ *continued on next page*

Interlude

▼ *continued*

machine fail. Can the computerized Game of Life ever achieve the robust-
ness of real life, in which a stray cell (let's say, a virus or cancer cell) is
"cleaned up" by the rest of the body without causing the whole thing to
collapse?

That remains to be seen. It might be a clue as to how real life really is
different.

Chapter 17   *Summary*

Here are some of the important points utilized in Chapter 17—even though
many of them were introduced earlier:

▶ *Cellular automata* is the field of coming up with a set of simple rules that can
be programmed into individual "cells" and then watching what happens as
they interact.

▶ In designing and implementing complex programs, it's often helpful to classes
that do most of the work of the program, or at least much of it. If you can do that,
then the main program may be much easier to write and understand as a result.

▶ The class can then be placed in a separate module and used by any program
that needs it.

```
from lifemat import Matrix2D
```

▶ Remember that two-dimensional arrays require some special syntax to build
successfully; you either need to list comprehension or nested loops. (This idea
was first introduced in Chapter 13.)

```
self.grid = [[0] * cols for _ in range(rows)]
```

▶ Remember that the fewer individual calls you make to the **print** function, the
faster your output will be in Python. String-concatenation and the string join
method are both helpful in this regard, but the latter is preferred by the most
experienced Python programmers.

▶ Therefore, use **join** whenever you can. For example, the following statements
work by creating a list of strings, in which each string is a character returned
by get_chr; that function returns either an X or a blank. A call to the **join**
method then combines all these one-character strings into a single string.

```
lst=[get_chr(a_mat,i,j) for j in range(cols)]
disp_str += ''.join(lst) + '\n'
```

▶ The multiplication operator (*) can be used to generate characters over and over again. We've already seen how useful this is when creating a list, as in a two-dimensional grid. But you can also use this technique to create a border string, which consists of a series of underscores:

```
border_str = '_' * cols
```

▶ Remember that to use variable-length argument lists, include the special ***args** argument. (This technique was first introduced in the previous chapter.)

```
def inc_cells(self, n, *args):
    for r, c in args:
        self.grid[r][c] += n
```

Advanced Pythonic Techniques

Python is a big language. In this chapter, I introduce you to some of Python's more advanced features—features that you don't necessarily have to learn to be productive but can be used to do some amazing things. This chapter explores

▶ Generators

▶ Properties

▶ Decorators

Generators

Python is based largely on the concept of *iterables*. You can create your own iterables within Python, which in turn can be used within **for** loops as well as other contexts.

But what exactly is an iterable?

The idea is simple. Return to the car factory example from Chapter 15, "Classes and Objects I." But this time, the factory can produce only one car at a time, and it does so only when an order has been placed.

next!

As soon as the car dealer places an order for a car, the factory fulfills it. What happens when the factory runs out of materials and can't produce another car? It says, "Out of stock," and the car dealer accepts there are no more cars.

To create your own iterable, replace a **return** statement with the following:

```
yield value
```

Remember how easy it is to print Fibonacci numbers? Here's one away to do it:

```
def print_fibos(n):
    a = b = 1
    while a <= n:
        a, b = a + b, a
        print(a)
```

To make this function into a generator—and therefore an iterable—just replace the call to the **print** function with a **yield** statement.

```
def gen_fibo(n):
    a = b = 1
    while a <= n:
        a, b = a + b, a
        yield a
```

The gen_fibs function stops executing as soon as yield a is reached. At that point, it sends back the value of a, and then it suspends operation until called again. Unlike an ordinary function, this generator saves the value of all local variables.

All the local variables are saved. Therefore, when the user says, "Give the next number," the generator yields a larger number in the series. Here's another example:

```
for num in gen_fibos(1000):
    print(num)
```

What would be the advantage of replacing this approach—using an ordinary function—with the use of a generator?

One advantage is that you can represent a "virtual sequence" in a very small space.

For example, the following generator produces odd numbers. You couldn't hold the entire sequence of all the odd numbers in memory at the same time; it would be infinite. But you can process any quantity of these numbers as long as you deal with them one at a time.

```
def gen_odd_num():
    i = 1
    while True:
        yield i
        i += 2
```

Exploiting the Power of Generators

You can use a generator anywhere Python syntax calls for an iterable. This includes **for** loops. The call to gen_odd_num is an iterable, and here I place it in bold for emphasis.

```
for i in gen_odd_num():
    print(i)
    if i > 1000:
        break
```

You can also combine a generator with the **in** and **not in** operators. Assuming that gen_fibo is defined as in the previous section, what do you think the following does?

```
55 in get_fibo(55)
```

Give up? Here's another clue. This use of gen_fibo returns **True** or **False** in the interactive environment, depending on the input.

```
>>>55 in get_fibo(55)
True
>>>56 in gen_filo(56)
False
```

The answer is the generator, along with the **in** operator, becomes a slick way of testing whether any given number is a Fibonacci number.

Note ▶ Note that this version of the generator, gen_fibo, has an argument that limits how long the generator runs before it stops. Otherwise, assuming it did not find 55 or 56, it would run forever.

◀ Note

18

You can think of an iterable as something you can get the "next" of. In fact, **next** is a built-in function that can be applied to any iterable.

```
next(iterable)
```

So, we ought to be able to make repeated calls to next and the gen_fib() generator to get as many Fibonacci numbers as we want, one at a time.

```
>>>next(gen_fibo(100))
2
>>>next(gen_fibo(100))
2
>>>next(gen_fibo(100))
2
```

Oops! What happened? We should've gotten the first three Fibonacci numbers that the generator produces. Instead, we got the first number, three times.

Each separate invocation of gen_fibo(100) starts a new instance of the generator—thereby starting over. The solution is to create a new instance only once. We can do that by assigning the name gen_fibo(100) to a name and then reusing the same instance.

```
>>>my_gen = gen_fibo(100)
>>>next(my_gen)
2
>>>next(my_gen)
3
>>>next(my_gen)
5
```

What happens if you set the limit very low and keep iterating until you go past the end?

```
>>>my_gen = gen_fibo(3)
>>>next(my_gen)
2
>>>next(my_gen)
3
>>>next(my_gen)
Traceback (most recent call last):
  File "<pyshell#122>", line 1, in <module>
    next(my_gen)
StopIteration
```

Python raises a **StopIteration** exception in these situations. This exception is usually handled internally, as an end-of-loop indicator. Alternatively, you can handle this exception yourself, using **try** and **except** keywords, catching the **StopIteration** exception.

Example 18.1. ## A Custom Random-Number Generator

Some of the most useful of all generators are random-number generators, which Python supplies through the **random** module. It's used in game programs and simulations.

There are several reasons you might want to write your own. Maybe you don't trust the standard version. Or maybe someone has hacked into the

Python code, and you want your program to use a randomization scheme that hasn't been hacked yet.

Here is a "homemade" random-number generator you can use yourself:

```
rand_gen.py

   from time import time

   def gen_rand():
       p1 = 1200556037     # Prime number 1
       p2 = 2444555677     # Prime number 2
       max_rand = 2 ** 32
       r = int(time() * 1000)    # Get time in millisecs.
       while True:
           n = r
           n *= p2
           n %= p1
           n += r
           n *= p2
           n %= p1
           n %= max_rand
           r = n
           yield n
```

Given this definition, you can use the following loop to simulate a 100-sided die, rolled 10 times:

```
my_gen = gen_rand()
for i in range(10):
    print(next(my_gen) % 100)   # Roll 100-sided die.
```

Here's some sample output. Your results, of course, will vary.

```
4
76
25
16
78
93
10
76
69
23
```

How It Works

The goal is to generate *pseudorandom numbers*. To achieve anything resembling randomness, you need to have an appropriate *seed* to begin the sequence. System time is ideal for this purpose. For that reason, the program uses the **time** module.

```
from time import time
```

The **time** module supports several functions, but the one needed here is the **time** function itself, which returns the number of milliseconds since a particular date.

```
r = int(time())
```

The generator, gen_rand, takes this seed and performs a series of mathematical transformations on it. Not just any transformation will do. For reasons explained later, this random-number "engine" makes use of two large prime numbers, p1 and p2.

```
p1 = 1200556037
p2 = 2444555677
```

You may wonder where I got these prime numbers. That's easy. I used Python itself! First, I created an is_prime function that efficiently tests whether a particular number is prime.

```
def is_prime(n):
    sqrt_n = int(n ** 0.5)
    for i in range(2, sqrt_n + 1):
        if n % i == 0:
            return False
    return True
```

I then wrote a function called get_next_prime that—given a target number—returns the first prime number that is larger than the target number I input.

```
def get_next_prime(n):
    while True:
        if is_prime(n):
            return n
        n += 1
```

Finally, I entered a couple of large numbers, got the two prime numbers I wanted, and plugged them in the program as p1 and p2. By replacing them with your own prime numbers, you in effect create your own random-number generator.

The generator needs to produce random numbers in a consistent range. The range of integers is theoretically infinite. Therefore, to restrict ourselves to a 32-bit range, the generator uses remainder division.

```
n %= max_rand
```

where `max_rand` had been set at the beginning of the function.

```
max_rand = 2 ** 32
```

The statements that make use of the generator restrict output to an even smaller range, by again using remainder (modular) division. For example, applying the operation % 100 produces numbers, equally distributed, in the 0 to 99 range, just as % 6 would produce numbers, equally distributed, in the 0 to 5 range.

```
my_gen = gen_rand()
for i in range(10):
    print(next(my_gen) % 100)
```

EXERCISES

Exercise 18.1.1.   Using the sieve of Eratosthenes, as explained in Chapters 5 and 6, create a generator for prime numbers. First, generate the primes up to N, where N is an argument to the generator; yield one of these primes at a time by stepping through the set; and then combine this generator with the **in** operator to determine whether a given number is prime. Note: This technique is incredibly slow for large numbers, so don't use it for help in the exercises that follow!

Exercise 18.1.2.   Using the techniques I just showed in "How It Works," obtain two large primes in the range of one to four billion. Then substitute these numbers in for p1 and p2, rerun the exercise, and see if the results still seem acceptably random.

Exercise 18.1.3.   Can you improve the quality of the generator by arbitrarily selecting *four* large primes and putting them in the code?

Exercise 18.1.4.   Use the random-number generator in Exercise 18.1 to simulate the roll of two six-sided die. Roll these "dice" ten times. Do these rolls appear random?

Interlude

How Random Is "Random"?

Given that everything that happens inside a computer is deterministic— for a particular state of the computer, what each instruction does is absolutely predictable—how is randomness possible even in theory?

▼ *continued on next page*

Interlude

▼ *continued*

Randomness is impossible inside the computer itself but may be introduced by interaction with some outside physical device. In the case of the random-number generator used here, the random element is provided by the system time, which is always changing.

But despite the system time changing too fast for a human to predict, it's not good enough by itself.

What we need is a technique in which small differences in system time cause large differences in the next number in sequence so that the numbers produced will vary all over the range, in this case, a minimum of 0 and a maximum of 2 to the 32nd power.

Random Numbers:

0199637412743300
2482681660386877
1489637365552079
6820133556430219
173...

The mathematical transformations used by the generator, `gen_rand`, produce a series of pseudorandom numbers. Why pseudo? It's because the sequence, by its very nature, is deterministic. But random-number engines are thought to have the practical effect of randomness, for a couple of reasons.

First, the combination of system-time seed with the mathematical transformations makes it difficult to predict the first number generated by the sequence.

Second, the repeated use of modular division makes it extraordinarily difficult to "reverse engineer" the sequence based on output alone. For example, an output of the dice-rolling experiment (Exercise 18.1.4) might be 5. But how did we get there? The number of different states that could've resulted in the generation of "5" is astronomical.

Of course, 5 itself is not produced in isolation; it is part of a sequence, and the weak spot of any pseudorandom generator is this: does a subtle pattern emerge that a sufficiently smart mathematician could detect? Specialists working with mainframe computers can sometimes "crack" a pseudorandom-number generator unless it is very, very good.

What makes a good generator? Clearly, the more transformations, the better; but time is not a limitless resource even in the digital world.

Equally important is the quality of transformations. You should see that transformations based on small numbers, or numbers that are not

▼ *continued*

Interlude

prime, are poor. Let's say that you did modular vision by 2 or a multiple of 2, for example. Repeated division by 2 would tend to weed out even numbers, therefore causing a bias toward odd numbers. Conversely, multiplying by 2, or any multiple of two, would cause a bias toward even numbers.

A better approach is to alternately multiply, and use modular division with, large prime numbers. Primes are frequently used in randomization and encryption schemes.

Back in the days before personal computing, companies such as the RAND Corporation used to print large books full of nothing but random numbers. They were necessary for anyone running a simulation or playing a game that demanded true randomness. Another technique—occasionally still used—for people who play games by post (that is, ordinary mail) is to look at the last digit in the Dow Jones Industrial Average the next day.

What those examples should illustrate is that 1) random numbers are useful, and 2) human beings are poor generators of random numbers. A human, told to write down 1,000 random numbers, would do a poor job because they would try too hard to avoid patterns. A subject would not write down "9999," for example, even though a truly random sequence not only can produce this pattern, it's nearly inevitable that it will produce it.

Properties

When Microsoft first introduced Visual Basic 1.0 (it was just called Visual Basic then) and I headed up the documentation team, I came upon my first sight of a *property*:

```
MyFrame.BackColor = Blue
```

From the beginning, I knew it was revolutionary. Gone were the long lists of obscure arguments one had to use in programming the Windows SDK. Instead, here was an altogether new syntax. The simple declarative statement `MyFrame.BackColor = Blue` was a kind of imperative statement; that is, it *did* something.

What the statement did in this case was to set the background color (`BackColor`) of a frame to blue. When Visual Basic (VB) executed this statement, it turned the background color of the frame to blue without any further effort on the VB programmer's part.

18

But underneath the covers, properties are driven by two hidden methods:

▶ A *"getter" method*: This method is called whenever there's an attempt to get the attribute, for example, a statement of the form value = object.property.

▶ A *"setter" method*: This method is called whenever there's an attempt to set the attribute to a value, for example, any statement of the form object .property = value.

The setter and getter methods are what make properties work. The attribute itself does not necessarily have to exist at any physical location. All that matters is that the setter and getter methods are called as needed. These methods can do any additional work you need, such as changing color or redisplaying something on the screen.

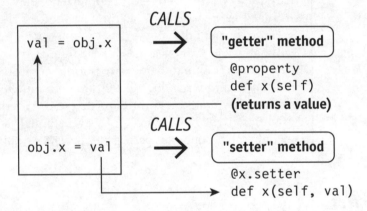

When you use getter and setter methods, you typically (but not always) include both a setter and getter for each property in your class.

Getter Methods

To write a getter method for a property, place the following definition inside a class:

```
@property                         # "Getter" method
def property_name(self):
    statements

    return value
```

A getter method is automatically called when the user of the class tries to get the value of the named property. Here are examples for properties named a, b, and c:

```
class MyClass:
    def __init__(self):
        self._a = self._b = self_c = -1

    @property          # "Getter" for property a
    def a(self):
        return self._a

    @property          # "Getter" for property b
    def b(self):
        return abs(self._b)

    @property          # "Getter" for property c
    def c(self):
        return self._c % 2 == 0
```

Each of these "getters" would be invoked in a statement such as this, where my_obj is an instance of MyClass:

```
print my_obj.a
```

In the case of the property named a, the value of _a (a private version of a) is returned exactly as is. In the case of the property named b, the absolute value of _b is returned. Finally, in the case of the property named c, **True** or **False** is returned, depending on whether the value of _c is even or odd.

Note ▶ The variables _a, _b, and _c are instance variables like any other, except that the underscore (_) suggests they are meant to be private. *Double-underscore* names, such as __a, __b, and __c, enforce privacy by *mangling* the names. Any references to these names, from outside the class, are automatically changed during run time into cryptic (altered) versions of themselves. The effect is to make these names private to the class, for all practical purposes.

◀ Note

18

Setter Methods

Setter methods are the flip side of getters. To write a setter method for a property, place the following definition inside a class:

```
@property_name.setter          # "Setter" method
def property_name(self, new_value):
    statements
```

A setter method is automatically called when the user of the class tries to set the value of a property. Here's an example:

```
my_obj.a = 100
```

Here are examples for properties named a, b, and c. In these examples, we assume that the corresponding getter methods do nothing but print the underlying value (_a, _b, or _c) and that we rely upon the setters to adjust the values.

```
@a.setter                # "Setter" for property a
def a(self, new_a):
    self._a = new_a

@b.setter                # "Setter" for property b
def b(self, new_b):
    self._b = abs(new_b)

@c.setter                # "Setter" for property c
def c(self, new_c):
    self._c = max(new_c, 100)
```

These methods set the property values for properties a, b, and c, respectively. Note that the properties don't set instance variables a, b, and c, but rather private variables _a, _b, and _c. Each of these methods sets the value differently.

Putting Getters and Setters Together

Getters and setters are typically written in pairs. There are some exceptions, however; if you want a property to be read-only, then write a getter but not a setter.

Here's a simple example that has property b that is always zero or positive, no matter what the class user attempts to assign to b:

```
class MyClass:
    '''Demonstrates a property, b, that is always
        non-negative.'''

    def __init__(self, new_b):
        self.b = new_b  # Invoke "setter"

    @property            # "Getter" for property b
    def b(self):
        return self.__b

    @b.setter            # "Setter" for property b
    def b(self, new_b):
        self.__b = abs(new_b)
```

Let's examine these in reverse order. First, the setter acts as a filter for the property. The absolute value of the argument is assigned to the private variable, __b; therefore the property will never have a negative value. If the user of the calls assigns a negative value to the property, it's changed into a positive.

```
>>>my_obj = MyClass(-5)
>>>my_obj.b
5
```

What about the getter? In this case, all it does is return the value stored in __b.

The __init__ method must set the value of property b, because otherwise, the first time you referred to my_obj.b, you'd get an error. However, the __init__ method does not set the value of __b directly, which it could have done.

```
self.__b = abs(new_b)
```

Instead, the method leverages the work done in the setter method, by causing the setter method to be called.

```
self.b = new_b
```

Example 18.2. *Multilevel Temperature Object*

Another use for properties is to encapsulate a *virtual* value, which is a value that's never stored in memory but is calculated on the fly. For example, suppose you wanted a temperature object that can be set in either Fahrenheit or Celsius—but stores only one value.

The temperature has only one value at any given time, but it can be read in one of two ways. To implement this behavior, we create a ctmp (Celsius) property.

18

```
multi_temp.py

class Temperature:
    ''' This class is a Temperature object that stores
        just one value, but represented two ways.
        ftmp is an inst. variable, ctmp a property.'''

    def __init__(self, ftmp=32.0):
        self.ftmp = ftmp
```

▼ *continued on next page*

`multi_temp.py, cont.`

```
    @property                # ctmp "getter" method
    def ctmp(self):
        return (self.ftmp - 32.0) / 1.8

    @ctmp.setter             # ctmp "setter" method
    def ctmp(self, ctmp):
        self.ftmp = ctmp * 1.8 + 32.0

my_tmp = Temperature()
my_tmp.ctmp = 0
print('0 C. is', my_tmp.ftmp, 'F.')
my_tmp.ctmp = 100
print('100 C. is', my_tmp.ftmp, 'F.')
my_tmp.ctmp = 50
print('50 C. is', my_tmp.ftmp, 'F.')
my_tmp.ftmp = 86
print('86 F. is', my_tmp.ctmp, 'C.')
```

This program, when run, produces the following output:

```
0 C. is 32.0 F.
100 C. is 212.0 F.
50 C. is 122.0 F.
86 F. is 30.0 C.
```

How It Works

This class has some interesting uses. It could be used in a situation in which two groups of meteorologists are working on a project, but each group is using a different scale.

It would be inadequate to have an object with separate instance variables for Fahrenheit and Celsius, because there'd be no way to keep the two variables in sync. But this class—which makes ctmp into a property and not a separately stored value—solves the problem by calculating one of these values (ctmp) "on the fly" while storing ftmp in memory.

There's only one instance variable, ftmp, and it stores Fahrenheit temperature. Suppose you set the ctmp property.

```
my_tmp.ctmp = 100
```

The ctmp setter method is called, and the value 100 is passed to this method.

```
@ctmp.setter
def ctmp(self, ctmp):
    self.ftmp = ctmp * 1.8 + 32.0
```

The value is converted and then stored in ftmp as 212.0. Likewise, any operation expressed in Celsius (ctmp) is translated into Fahrenheit (ftmp) before being stored.

EXERCISES

Exercise 18.2.1.   Do the following statements both work? Why or why not?

```
my_tmp.ftmp += 10.0
my_tmp.ctmp += 10.0
```

And if they do both work, do they have the same effect? Why or why not?

Exercise 18.2.2.   Use the Temperature class of Example 18.2 to get a list of Fahrenheit temperatures and convert this as efficiently as possible to a list of equivalent Celsius temperatures.

Exercise 18.2.3.   Rewrite the Temperature class so that ctmp, the Celsius temperature, is the instance variable and ftmp is a property. (This actually makes more sense because for most of the world, Celsius is the standard scale; therefore, it's more efficient for most people to use Celsius as the default unit.)

Exercise 18.2.4.   Write a class that maintains a distance value, but measured in two different ways: inches and centimeters. Create inch as an instance variable and cent as a property—or vice versa.

Exercise 18.2.5.   Write a class that has an instance variable, x, but it is restricted to the range 1 to 100, inclusive. Settings below 1 are automatically converted to 1, and settings above 100 are converted to 100.

Exercise 18.2.6.   Write a class in which both ftmp and ctmp are properties so that you can restrict both of them to temperatures that are physically possible. Specifically, neither should ever go below 0 on the Kelvin scale ("absolute zero"). This temperature is −459.67 on the Fahrenheit scale and −273.15 in Celsius. The relationship between ftmp and ctmp should be retained, as it is throughout Exercise 18.2.

The physics of absolute zero, by the way, are fascinating. The temperature is in principle not achievable, but scientists have come within a billionth of a degree.

Decorators: Functions Enclosing Other Functions

Next we set sail to the rocky shores of *decoration*, which has a reputation for being difficult. But if you do need to write decorators, you can use the code in this chapter as a template.

To understand decoration, start with how Python enables you to define nested functions, that is, functions inside of other functions. Here's an example:

```python
def outer(n):
    print('I am in outer.')
    def inner():
        print('I inherited', n)
    inner()
```

The function outer can then be run.

```
>>>outer(4)
I am in outer.
I inherited 4
```

Note carefully what happened. The outer function defined the inner function, called `inner`. After the outer function created this inner function, it executed inner by calling it.

```
inner()
```

We can diagram the process as follows:

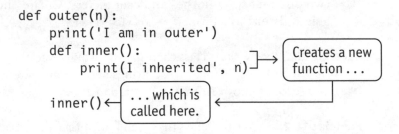

Now we're going to add a twist. Functions, in Python, are objects just like any other. They can be assigned to names and even returned…by other functions. The difference between data objects and function objects is that functions can be called.

For example, from within the function named `outer`, we could have done this, assigning the function to the name `f` and *then* calling it:

```python
f = inner   # The name 'f' now an alias for inner.
f()         # Call 'inner' by using the alias.
```

Now things are going to get more interesting. Consider the definition of outer again, this time, with a new feature. This version of outer returns inner as its return value.

```
def outer(n):
    def inner_func():
        print('I inherited', n)
    return inner      // Return this new function!!
```

If you now execute outer, it doesn't seem to do anything.

```
>>>func = outer(10)
```

But actually, outer did something important. It created a new function—passing along an argument, n, to it—and then returned this new function. The new function was assigned to the name func. So the name func can be used to call the newly defined function.

```
>>>func()
I inherited 10
```

Now, there is one more thing to add, and we're ready to add decoration. A function can both return a function and take a function as an argument. So you can write this:

```
def outer(f):
    def inner():
        print('I am doing extra stuff.')
        f()
        print('Doing more extra stuff.')
    return inner  // "outer" returns NEW function!
```

The effect of the function outer is now to take a function argument, f; *build a new function around it*; and return that function. For example, define some function, f1.

```
>>>def f1():
    print('Hi!')
```

Now pass this function to outer(), which returns a new function that does everything f1 did but does more. The result—the new function—is assigned to the name g.

```
>>>g = outer(f1)
```

Now g is an alias for the newly created function (which we could also call the "wrapper" function). You can use g to call this function as often as you like.

```
>>>g()
I am doing extra stuff.
Hi!
Doing more extra stuff.
```

Here's another example. We can use `outer()` to create a wrapper around any function and then assign the result to the name g; g then names this new function, and we can call it.

```
>>>def print_nums():
    for i in [1, 2, 3]:
        print(i, '   ')

>>>g = outer(print_nums)   # Create new function around
                           #   print_nums, assign to g.
>>>g()                     # Call this wrapped function.
I am doing extra stuff.
1   2   3
Doing more extra stuff.
```

Any function we "wrap" will do what it did before, but it will also print a message before and after execution. We can even re-assign to the old function name! Here's an example:

```
>>>print_nums = outer(print_nums)
```

Okay, this is weird. Is the function name, `print_num`, being reassigned to a new version of...*itself*? Yes, that's exactly what's happening. Now we can execute this new function.

```
>>>print_nums()
I am doing extra stuff.
1   2   3
Doing more extra stuff.
```

Okay, that's a lot to digest, so let's diagram the process up to this point:

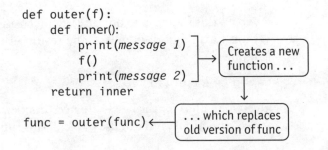

The key point here is that the name func, which started out referring to a simple function, now refers to a more elaborate version of itself—the function we started with.

Python Decoration

Decoration reassigns a function name to a "wrapped" version of the original function. These actions are useful for debugging and performance testing, as you'll see. Let's revisit the example in the previous section, but this time I'll use more meaningful names.

```
def my_decorator(f):
    '''Take an ordinary function, create a new version
        called wrapper, and return this new function.'''

    def wrapper():
        print('I am doing extra stuff.')
        f()
        print('Doing more extra stuff.')

    return wrapper    // Return the "wrapper"!
```

The decorator creates a new function...and returns it. We assign it to the name of the original function. We can do the same thing for any functions we choose!

```
func1 = my_decorator(func1)   # Wrap func1!
func2 = my_decorator(func2)   # Wrap func2!
func3 = my_decorator(func3)   # Wrap func3!
```

The final stage is to apply the decoration syntax. This syntax generates a line similar to each of the three lines above. Then it reverses the order. Consider the following lines of code:

```
@my_decorator                      // New syntax!
def hello():
    print('Hi!')
```

Python translates this into

```
def hello():
    print('Hi!')
hello = my_decorator(hello)  // This is the key line!
```

Here is the syntax display that summarizes how decorators work:

```
@decorator_name
def func(args):
    statements
```

This translates into

```
def func(args):
    statements
func = decorator_name(func)
```

But what if the function to be decorated has arguments? And what if it returns a value?

The argument problem is solved by passing the list of arguments, represented by *args, back to the wrapped function. We also pass **kwargs to take care of named arguments.

```
def my_decorator(f):
    def wrapper(*args, **kwargs):
        print('I am doing extra stuff.')
        f(*args, **kwargs)
        print('Doing more extra stuff.')

    return wrapper
```

You should recall from Chapter 16, "Classes and Objects II," that ***args** is a list of all the arguments passed to a function. wrapper becomes the new function, and it takes the list of arguments; these function are now passed back to f, the wrapped function.

The other change is to make the wrapper return the same value, if any, that f does.

```
def my_decorator(f):
    def wrapper(*args, **kwargs):
        print('I am doing extra stuff.')
        value = f(*args, **kwargs)
        print('Doing more extra stuff.')
        return value

    return wrapper
```

Now the return value of the function object, f, is *also* returned by wrapper(). If f has no return value, the value **None** is returned by default. Let's diagram this final version.

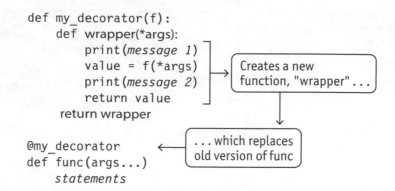

```
def my_decorator(f):
    def wrapper(*args):
        print(message 1)
        value = f(*args)
        print(message 2)
        return value
    return wrapper

@my_decorator
def func(args...)
    statements
```

Creates a new function, "wrapper"...

...which replaces old version of func

Example 18.3. *Decorators as Debugging Tools*

Now we're ready to apply a decorator to a practical use, namely, printing function diagnostics each time a decorated function is called. But just to be clear, let's restate what decoration does:

> ✳ A decorator re-assigns a function name to a "wrapped" version of the original function. The wrapped version does everything the function did but does additional things as well.

If you've ever had to debug a complex program, you realize it's useful to know which functions were called when and what values were passed to it. It would be nice to have an easy way to add such diagnostics to a function. The following code shows how to do that:

diagnostics.py

```
from time import time

def diagnostics(f):
    def wrapper(*args, **kwargs):
        print('Executed', f.__name__, 'at', time())
        value = f(*args, **kwargs)
        print('Exited  ', f.__name__, 'at', time())
        print('Arguments:', args)
        print('Value returned:', value, '\n')
        return value
    return wrapper
```

▼ *continued on next page*

18

```
@diagnostics
def print_nums():
    for i in range(4):
        print(i, end='\t')
    print()

@diagnostics
def calc_hypotenuse(a, b):
    return ((a*a + b*b) ** 0.5)

print_nums()
print (calc_hypotenuse(3, 4))
```

Here's some sample output:

```
Executed print_nums at 1492177491.831115
0       1       2       3
Exited    print_nums at 1492177492.31574
Arguments: ()
Value returned: None

Executed calc_hypotenuse at 1492177492.803701
Exited    calc_hypotenuse at 1492177493.000599
Arguments: (3, 4)
Value returned: 5.0

5.0
```

This output shows the diagnostics decorator working successfully on two different functions, print_nums and calc_hypotenuse. Examining the relative time stamps in this case shows that arithmetic calculations, even those involving exponentiation, are fast.

How It Works

The diagnostics function is the decorator: it takes a target function, f, as an argument; then it builds a wrapper function around f and returns the wrapper as the new function.

Then the @diagnostics syntax says, "Re-assign the function name to refer to this wrapper function." Remember that the syntax is equivalent to

```
print_nums = diagnostics(print_nums)
```

Therefore, the name `print_nums` is re-assigned to refer to the *wrapped* version of `print_nums`. The wrapped version does everything done before but also prints diagnostics.

Example 18.3 uses a couple of advanced features, introduced earlier in this book. First, the **time** function is imported from the **time** module. This function returns the number of seconds that have elapsed from a particular date, expressed in a fixed-point format. It's used to determine when function execution began and ended.

```
print('Executed', f.__name__, 'at', time())
value = f(*args, **kwargs)
print('Exited  ', f.__name__, 'at', time())
```

The expression `f.__name__` displays the name of the function: **__name__** is an attribute that every function has.

Finally, `args` accesses a list of argument values. The expression ***args** indicates a list of arguments of indefinite size. Referring to **args** gets the actual list. If there are no arguments, this statement just prints an empty list.

```
print('Arguments:', args)
```

EXERCISES

Exercise 18.3.1. Revise the example so that it prints the difference between the two time stamps (start and stop) rather than printing out the time itself. Also, rename the decorator as `timer`.

Exercise 18.3.2. Use this timer to compare sieve timings. Compare the speeds of the sieve of Eratosthenes run on numbers up to 1,000, for the functional version (Chapter 5), the list comprehension version (Chapter 6), and the set-comprehension version (Chapter 12).

Exercise 18.3.3. Revise the decorator so that it displays named arguments used in a function call, if any. You should be able to do that with the following statement, which should print any named ("keyworded") arguments in the form of a data dictionary.

```
print('Keyword args:', kywrds)
```

Chapter 18 *Summary*

Here are the key points of Chapter 18:

▶ To build your own iterable in Python, write a generator function. Instead of returning a value, the generator uses a **yield** statement.

```
yield x
```

▶ The state of the generator is saved and reused when it's invoked again. The current values of all local variables are preserved.

▶ Once you instantiate a generator function, do not instantiate it again unless you want the generator to start over. Instead, save it once and then reuse.

```
my_gen = gen_fibo(1000)
print(next(my_gen))
print(next(my_gen))
print(next(my_gen))
```

▶ Although a property looks and behaves just like an instance variable, its implementation is different. You support a property by adding two special methods: getter and setter for each property.

▶ The getter method for a property is called when the user of a class tries to get the value of the property. A getter has this syntax:

```
@property
def property_name(self):
    statements
    return value
```

▶ The setter method for a property is called when the user of a class tries to set the property's value. A setter has this syntax:

```
@property_name.setter
def(self, new_value):
    statements
```

▶ A decorator takes another function as argument (let's call it f), defines a new function around the old one (f), and finally returns the resulting function.

▶ The following statement causes the new version of the function (the "wrapped" function) to replace itself, that is, the original function.

```
function = decorator(function)
```

▶ The @decorator syntax provides a more readable version of the same thing. Preceding a function definition with @decorator causes the function name to be replaced with the wrapped version of the same function.

```
@decorator_name
function_definition
```

▶ In Python, functions have attributes, just as other objects do. You can use the __fname__ attribute to get the name of the function at the time it was defined.

```
print(f.__name__)
```

Python Operator Precedence Table

Operators in Python expression are evaluated in the order shown here, for Python 3.0:

OPERATOR	DESCRIPTION
func(args)	Function call
collection[*begin* : *end* : *step*]	Slicing
collection[*index*]	Indexing
object.attribute	Property or member access
num ** *num*	Exponentiation
~*int*	Bitwise NOT
+*num*, -*num*	Plus/minus sign
*, /, %, //	Multiplication, division, remainder division, integer division (when operation is between two numbers); also multiplication of lists and strings: *list* * *n*
+, –	Addition and subtraction (when operation is between two numbers); also *str* + *str* produces string (or list) concatenation
int << *n*, *int* >> *n*	Left and right bit shifts
int & *int*	Bitwise AND
int ^ *int*	Bitwise XOR
int | *int*	Bitwise OR
in, not in, is, is not, <, <=, >, >=, <>, !=, ==	Comparisons; each produces Boolean value (true/false)
not *val*[a]	Boolean NOT
val and *val*[a]	Boolean AND
val or *val*[a]	Boolean OR

a. The *val* may be almost any kind of value; Python will apply the operation bool() to convert before applying to conditionals—within, say, if or while. See notes that follow.

Other notes:

a Where operators are at the same level of precedence, they are evaluated left to right.

b Parentheses override precedence rules.

c The special symbol = (not to be confused with ==, which is test for equality) is part of assignment-statement syntax and is not an operator.

d With combined assignment-operator symbols (+=, *=, /=, etc.), the entire expression on the right is evaluated and then the assignment operator applied, regardless of precedence. For example, if x starts out as 12, then the statement x /= 3 + 9 sets x to 1, but the statement x = x / 3 + 9 sets x to 13.

e Assignment-operator symbols include +=, −=, *=, /=, //=, **=, <<=, >>=, &=, ^=, |=. In each case, x op= y is equivalent to x = x op y; but note d applies.

f As mentioned in Chapter 4, the Boolean operators apply short-circuit logic. If the first operand is true, the operator **and** returns the second operand. If the first operand is false, the operator **or** returns the second operand. Otherwise, the first operand is returned without evaluating the second operand.

g To determine whether a value behaves as true or false, Python applies a Boolean conversion, **bool()**. For numeric values, zero is "false." For collections, an empty string or collection is "false." For most types, **None** is "false." In all other cases, the value behaves as if "true." (Comparisons, such as n > 1 always return **True** or **False**, which are fixed values.)

By combining the last two rules, you should be able to see why Python responds as follows:

```
>>>print(None and 100)
None
>>>print(None or 100)
100
>>>print(not(''))
True
```

Summary of Most Important Formatting Rules for Python 3.0

This appendix explains the most common ways to use the **format** method for string objects, which provides an easy way to print data in nicely structured columns.

1. Formatting Ordinary Text

Ordinary text in a format specification string is printed as it appears. This includes all text except for curly braces, {}, and the content between them.

2. Formatting Arguments

Use curly braces, {}, to indicate arguments. This example

```
'{} plus {} is {}!'.format(4, 6, 10)
```

prints the following:

```
4 plus 6 is 10!
```

3. Specifying Order of Arguments

$\{n\}$ is a zero-based index into the argument list. This example

```
'{2} {1} {0}'.format(10, 20, 30)
```

prints the following:

```
30 20 10
```

This feature—order specification—can be combined with any and all of the rules that follow. If so, the ordering number appears to the left of the colon (:).

4. Right-Justification Within Field of Size N

By default, numeric values are right-justified within a print field of indicated size *n*; other text is left-justified by default. Here is the general syntax for right justification:

```
'{:>n}'.format(arg)
'{:n}'.format(arg)        # Numeric data assumes
                          #  right justification.
```

This example

```
'ab{:>10}ab'.format('1234')
```

prints the following:

```
ab      1234ab
```

5. Left-Justification Within Field of Size N

Non-numeric values, by default, are left-justified within a print field of specified width *n*. But you can always specify left-justification by using <.

```
'{:<n}'.format(arg)
'{:n}'.format(arg)        # Non-numeric data assumes
                          #  left justification.
```

This example

```
'**{:<10}**'.format('Hello')
```

prints the following:

```
**Hello     **
```

6. Truncation: Limit Size of Print Field

Specifying a number to the right of a decimal point gives a limit to the size of the argument to be printed. This example

```
'{:.4}'.format('abcdef')
```

prints the following:

```
abcd
```

7. Combined Truncation and Justification

Put the field size to the left of the decimal point, and put the limit on the length of the printed item to the right of the decimal point. This example

```
'##{:12.4}##'.format('abcdef')
```

prints abcd but left-justifies it in a field of 12 spaces.

```
##abcd        ##
```

8. Length and Precision of Floating-Point Numbers

The width and precision specifications, which, respectively, specify print-field width for floating-point numbers, as well as precision (number of positions displayed to the right of the decimal point), has this syntax:

```
'{:width.precisionf}'.format(number)
```

Right justification is the default for numeric fields, so it's not necessary to specify right justification (>) if you want it. This example

```
'{:7.3f}'.format(3.1415962)
```

prints the following:

```
  3.142
```

To produce this result, Python examines the third digit after the decimal point and rounds it upward.

Either width or precision may be omitted. A decimal point is required for the latter. Note that number (the value to be printed) may be an integer, but it will be printed in floating-point format.

9. The Padding Character

If a leading zero or other character appears just before the print-field-width specification, that character becomes the padding character for the print field. This example

```
'{:07.3f}'.format(3.1415962)
```

prints the following:

```
003.142
```

Glossary

attribute: A named quality attached to an object. For example, for a Dog class, every Dog object might have the attributes breed, name, and age, the first two of which are strings and the third of which is a number. In Python, attributes are usually instance variables or properties.

Each attribute has a value as well as a name, and each is accessed as *object .attribute_name.*

base class: A class that another class inherits from; also called a superclass. See also *superclass.*

bitwise operations: An operation applied to individual bits of a number (which must be in integer format). For example, the integers 14 and 9 can be represented as binary-radix expressions 0b1110 and 0b1001, respectively. The expression 0b1110 & 0b1001 applies binary AND (&) to these operands, resulting in 0b1000.

Although Python does not support everything that C does—in particular, it has no pointers—it supports the bitwise operators.

Boolean: A value intended to be limited to two values: **True** and **False**. However, the Boolean operators **and**, **or**, and **not** work with Python values generally and treat a value as "true" or "false" as appropriate. For example, all nonzero numeric values are treated as if true; a zero value is treated as if false. The special value **None** is treated as false.

Note that empty collections and strings are treated as false; collections and strings with a size greater than zero are treated as true.

Such a true/false value determines the behavior of an **if** or **while** statement. See the notes to Table A.1 for more information.

callable: Essentially, a function. A callable is created whenever Python manages to correctly execute a **def** statement—that is, execute it without syntax errors. A variable can become a callable through assignment to a function: *new_name = existing_function.*

Until a callable exists (through definition), it may not be executed. Once it is defined, it can be called through the syntax *name*(*args*). There is no forward-reference problem in Python provided that all functions are defined before any are executed.

class: In essence, a programmer-defined or language-defined type. The `class` keyword is used to define new types (that is, programmer-defined types). A class can define any number of methods, as well as static and class variables. Once a class is defined, it can be used to define any number of instances, which are called *objects*.

class variable: A variable shared by all objects of the same class.

collection: A series of data objects tightly organized together, with a group name. In most collections, including strings, lists, and dictionaries, individual elements can be accessed through a key or index.

Collections are important to computer programming in general, and Python in particular, because they permit you to have units of data ranging in size from very small (such as [1, 2, 3]) to extremely large; for example, [0] * 1000000 creates a list that's a million units in size!

comment: Text that is placed in a program but is skipped over by the Python interpreter. In general, the purpose of a comment is to make the program more readable to a human looking at the code (but note that you can place any text in a comment you choose). In Python, a comment consists of text from the comment sign (#) forward to the end of the physical line.

control structure: A statement or loop that determines what to do next. Such structures include code constructed with the **if**, **for**, and **while** keywords.

decorator: A function that takes a target function as an argument and then returns an enhanced version of this same function, usually called a *wrapper* function. The wrapper function does everything the old target function does, but it may do other things as well, such as print out diagnostics and timing information. Once a decorator is defined, you can then wrap any number of functions. This example

```
@my_decorator
(Definition of a_func)
```

is translated by Python into the following:

```
(Definition of a_func)
a_func = my_decorator(a_func)
```

This last line means, "Reassign the name a_func to refer to the new (wrapped) version of itself."

dictionary: A collection in the Python language that organizes information around key-value pairs; each such pair is a *tuple*. Within a given dictionary keys must be unique, and each key is associated with a value. (Values, however, need not be unique.) For example, a database for storing numeric grades could be realized as the following dictionary:

```
grades_dist = {'Bob' : 4.0, 'Nancy' : 3.5, 'Sid' : 3.5}
```

The names—which are keys in this case—must be unique with regard to each other, but Sid and Nancy both have a grade of 3.5.

first-class object: A data (or function) object that has attributes, can be assigned to a name, and can be returned by a function definition. You can query a first-class object for information about itself. In Python, unlike most other computer-programming languages, functions are first-class objects. This is why decoration is possible.

floating point: A numeric value that can hold a fractional portion. For example, 3.75 is a floating-point value and 3 is not. Although the details of numeric operations are hidden from Python programmers (generally speaking), it's important to know a few basic facts about numeric storage. Internally, floating-point and integer formats are completely different, but Python takes care of executing an expression such as `3.75 - 3`, by promoting 3 to floating-point format. All that is handled automatically for you, the Python programmer.

However, it's worth knowing that in Python, the positive and negative range of integers is actually greater than the range for floating-point numbers. Furthermore, Python storage of very large floating-point numbers (5 times 10 to the 75th power, for example) causes a loss of precision so that adding 1 to such a value has no effect. For this reason, if you have a choice and don't need to store fractional portions, use integer values. Another alternative is to use the **fractions** module and its **Fraction** class, which can store numbers such as one-third with absolute precision.

Note that expressions with a decimal point (.) are stored in floating-point format even if they currently have no fractional portion. `1.0` is stored in floating-point format.

for loop: A control structure that executes a block of statements, each time applying the statements to a different value within a collection. In other programming languages, the **for** loop is based on a sequence of numbers (for example, 1 to N). In Python, the **for** loop is based primarily on the idea of iterating through a collection.

A **for** loop can be combined with the built-in **range** function to iterate through a series of numbers (such as index numbers). However, experienced Python programmers iterate through collections rather than index numbers most of the time.

function: A subunit of the program that takes inputs and (optionally) produces outputs. The existence of functions enables a programmer to take a "divide and conquer" approach to accomplishing programming tasks, rather than having to put everything in one big undifferentiated sequence. The key concept is that once you write a function, you can execute it (or rather call it) any number of times.

Python functions have some interesting quirks. First, you define a function by using the **def** keyword. Second, a reference to a function does not have to exist until the function is actually called. The practical effect is that as long as you define all your functions before calling any of them, you can write them in any order you choose and ignore forward-reference problems.

Finally, functions in Python are first-class objects, which means that certain information is always available, such as function name. Note that you can assign a function to any name you want—and even later assign a new function to the same name (which is what makes decorators possible).

generator: A function that yields a new value each time it's called. Unless restarted, a generator retains its state, including the value of all local variables. (See Chapter 18, "Advanced Pythonic Techniques," for more information.) A generator can be used as an *iterable*.

global variable: A variable with a value that's shared by multiple functions so that changes to the variable by one function are recognized by all the functions that can "see" the variable in its global form. Global variables enable communication between functions (although passing arguments and returning values is an alternative technique). To create a global variable, either place it in module-level code, outside all functions, or else declare it **global** within a function and then assign a value to it.

The most important rule regarding global variables is this: if a function is going to assign a value to a variable that needs to be global, make sure that the statement **global** *variable_name* is included at the beginning of the function.

If a variable x is used, but there is no local version of x, and if there is no assignment to x, then the global version of x is automatically used—if it exists.

grounded division: See *integer division*.

IDLE: The Python interactive development environment. Although Python may also download another (less interactive) basic environment, IDLE is the environment you should prefer, and many mini-exercises in this book are designed to be followed with IDLE.

immutable: A data type that cannot be changed. Strings, for example, are immutable, as are tuples. However, the name of a string (but not its internal data) can be *reassigned to a completely new string* at any time. Therefore, the following statements might seem to break the rule of immutability for strings, but actually they do not break this rule at all; the second statement shown here re-assigns `my_str` to refer to a completely new string.

```
my_str = 'Brian'
my_str = my_str + ' Overland'
```

index: A numeric selector for an element within a list, string, or tuple. In Python, indexes are zero-based rather than one-based. Therefore, the first element in a collection is referred to as *collection_name***[0]**.

infinite integer: The capability of integers in Python to store incredibly large numbers (both positive and negative)—limited only by the physical capacity of the system.

inheritance: The ability of a new class—called the *subclass*—to automatically inherit all the attributes and methods of another class—called the superclass—except those that the subclass overrides.

instance: An individual data value or data object that has a clearly defined type (or class) but has its own values. For example, you might define a `Dog` class, but individual instances might be named `fido`, `rover`, and `skippy`, and each of these `Dog` instances has its own data values.

instance variable: A value attached to an object. Two objects of the same class share the same general design, but each will have its own individual instance variables, with their own values.

Note, however, that you can use a class's **__init__** method to assure that objects of the same class share a common list of instance variables. Even then, however, each object will maintain its own values.

integer: A numeric value that can store positive, negative, and zero values, as long as those values do not include a fractional portion. Integers are absolutely precise, because adding 1 to an integer always results in a distinct value, and there are never rounding errors. Integers in Python are "infinite" in range, in the sense that the only limits to integer range are those imposed by what the system can support. You can, for example, create integers in excess of a google (10 to the 100th power).

integer division: Division between two numbers in which the result is rounded down to the nearest integer, and the fractional portion, if any, is thrown away. (The remainder, however, can be found through modular, or remainder, division.) Integer division in Python 3.0 is specified by // instead of /.

iterable: A collection, or a generator, that produces a series of values in a particular order; these may be processed one at a time or viewed as a series. The concept of iterable is fundamental to Python, because a number of control structures (such as the **for** loop) depend on it. Even text files in Python are considered iterables, as you can read one line at a time.

key: A data value that works like an index into a Python *dictionary*. But whereas an index is numeric, the keys to a dictionary can be built around some other type. Those types must be immutable and "hashable"; this enables strings and tuples, but not lists, to be used as keys.

keyword: A reserved word that has special meaning to the Python language, such as **if**, **not**, **def**, and **for**. You cannot use these words to name your own variables. Also, Python supports "passing by keyword," in which you specify an argument's name along with the value you are passing. (These are two different uses of the word *keyword* that have little to do with each other.)

list: An ordered collection in Python in which elements are accessed by zero-based indexes. A list is *mutable*, meaning that its elements can be modified. A list in Python can do almost everything that an array in C or C++ can do; however, it can do a great deal more. For example, Python lists support many built-in methods such as **min**, **max**, and **sort**. Moreover, you can grow or shrink a list without any negative consequences, subject only to the physical limits of the system. Python lists are the major replacement for the array feature of other programming languages.

list comprehension: A technique for building a list by compressing the effects of a **for** loop into a single statement. A simple example is the following, which builds a list of square numbers out of another list. The result is a list of the first five square numbers: [1, 4, 9, 16, 25]. For more information, see Chapter 6, "List Comprehension and Enumeration."

```
num_list = [1, 2, 3, 4, 5]
square_list = [i * i for i in num_list]
```

local variable: A variable seen by only one function at a time. For example, each function can have its own variable named **amount**, and changes to **amount** in one function have no effect on the value of amount in any other function. In Python, variables are local by default. See also *global variable*.

loop: A control structure that repeats a set of statements over and over, until some terminating condition is reached. In a **for** loop, for example, the loop completes after the end of a collection (or other iterable) is reached.

magic method: A method that has special meaning to Python and is automatically executed under certain circumstances, such as **__init__** (initialization) and **__add__** (addition).

matrix: A two-dimensional list. The successful creation of such lists are non-obvious in Python and require a special technique. See Chapter 13, "Matrixes: 2D Lists," for more information.

method: A function defined inside a class. By defining methods, you give a class and its instances the ability to *do* things, rather than just passively store data. Unlike ordinary function calls, a method is called with the *object.method(args)* syntax.

modular division: Modular (or remainder) division returns the remainder from the division of two numbers. This operation is surprisingly useful in a large number of applications. For example, modular division by 2 (N % 2) always returns a 1 or 0; depending on this result, you know whether N is odd or even.

mutable: A mutable object is changeable; more specifically, its elements, if any, can be changed. For example, changes to a string (immutable) are not legal, whereas changes to a list (mutable) are.

```
my_str = 'hello'
my_list = [5, 6, 3]
my_str[0] = 'H'   # ERROR! Strings are immutable
my_list[1] = 9    # Fine; lists are mutable
```

object: A data object, or other item, that has a definite value and can also have attributes. An instance of a class is an object; but many other elements of a Python program are also objects, although you don't always need to know that. (For example, in Python, functions are objects.)

When you first start learning about classes and objects, it may be easiest just to think of an object as an instance of a class.

object orientation: An approach to programming and design, in which data and functions are organized tightly together into units called *classes* and in which objects are instances of classes. Object-oriented programming tends to be more data-centric than programming that does not use object-oriented techniques; such traditional methods tend to develop data structures and functions separately.

In Python, object orientation is deeply built into the structure of the language, even though you don't necessarily have to create your own classes. The better you understand object-oriented concepts, however, the deeper will be your understanding of Python, especially as everything in Python is an object.

Personally, I prefer the name object-oriented programming systems and its acronym, OOPS!

one-based indexing: An indexing system that begins with 1, and in which name[1] is the first object. Python itself exclusively uses zero-based indexing rather than one-based indexing.

polymorphism: One of the fundamental properties of object orientation, as well as being a universally supported aspect of Python. With polymorphism, every class of every object may define a method with the same name, but

Python will always ensure that the method executed is the one attached to the object's class. This may not sound like much, but it's very important. For example, every class may define an **__add__** method, but each class can customize this method so that it makes sense for the particular type of data you're working with. The important point is that the correct version of **__add__** is always called when the program is run.

In Python, you don't have to do anything special to support polymorphism.

property: An attribute of a class that looks like (and is used in the same way as) an instance variable but may have a far more sophisticated implementation. You implement a property by writing "getter" and "setter" methods; these methods are automatically called when someone tries to get or set the value of a property. A property doesn't even have to correspond to any particular place in memory; it may be a value calculated "on the fly." See Chapter 18, "Advanced Pythonic Techniques," for more information.

reference: Essentially, what a variable name is in Python. A variable does not have any attributes of its own. Any valid name may refer to any kind of data at any time: string, list, number, dictionary, etc. You give a variable attributes by assigning it to refer to a particular object. Otherwise, it has none.

In theory, many names may refer to the same data object. Changes made through one variable are reflected by all the others.

For this reason, it's important to develop a consistent naming scheme. For example, in this book, `_str` is the suffix used for most strings, and `_list` is the suffix used for most lists.

remainder division: See *modular division*.

set: A collection in Python similar to a dictionary, except that it has keys only and no "values." The important characteristic of a set is that it contains N unique elements. For any given value, it is either in the set or not in the set. Python supports all the traditional operations on sets, such as union and intersection.

Unlike lists—in which order is significant—sets contain values without distinguishing between sets of different ordering. For example, {1, 2, 3} is equivalent to {3, 2, 1}. Also note that because elements in a set are always unique, sets may be more efficient for applications in which you don't want duplicate values to accumulate when you add elements to the collection.

set comprehension: A technique similar to *list comprehension*, except that it can be used to create sets.

slicing: A technique in Python enabling you to efficiently select subsets of strings and lists. The general syntax is `collection[index1 : index2]`. This selects all elements beginning with `index1` (using zero-based indexing) up to but not including `index2`.

string: A packed series of text characters (usually human-readable characters) that can form a word, phrase, or sentence. When the program is run, these characters can be displayed to the end user. You can specify a string by enclosing it in single quotation marks, double quotation marks, or triple quotation marks (which are used for literal quotations). The beginning and ending quotation marks, however, must match each other. Examples of strings include

```
'Brian'
"Mike"
'''Tell the teacher we're surfing!'''
```

superclass: A class from which another class—a subclass—inherits all the members, including all methods, even initialization.

symbol: Generally variable names, as opposed to keywords. I also use *symbol* briefly in Appendix A to discuss operator symbols.

tkinter: A graphical user interface (GUI) package that is automatically downloaded with the standard Python release. This package includes support for drawing, selecting fonts and colors, and using event-driven, rather than purely procedural, programming; the package also supports window management and creation of standard controls, or *widgets*.

tuple: An organized collection similar to a list, except that it is immutable (unchangeable) and does not support all the same methods that lists do. In Python, when you want to use a list, but it will never be changed, manipulated, or sorted, it is often sufficient—and more efficient—to use a tuple instead. Note that tuples can be indexed, so that the first element of a tuple is *name* **[0]**.

type: A general class of data. The type of an object determines the precise format in which information is stored; but a type in Python may also have many other attributes, such as the type name. For example, all strings have the type **str**. Types in Python include **int**, **float**, **complex**, **str**, **list**, **dict**, **tuple**, **set**, and user-defined types, called *classes*.

variable: A name assigned to refer to a piece of data (or possibly a function). There are no data declarations in Python, and variable have no attributes. The type associated with a variable is determined by the data or function assigned to it.

Note that in Python, a variable is created through an assignment (or alternatively, through the implicit assignment that occurs within a **for** loop).

For this reason, it's particularly important in Python to use consistent naming conventions that suggest how a variable is intended to be used. Or, rather, this is important if you want your programs to be readable by humans.

widget: A standard screen element—such as a label, command button (or just *button*), text box, or canvas—supported by tkinter, which supports 21 different kinds of widgets.

wrapper function: A function built around another function. For example, a typical wrapper prints out the name of a function and its arguments; but it also executes the target function itself (the "wrapped" function).

Through the process of *decoration*, the wrapper can be made to replace the target function so that every time the target function is called, it's really the wrapper that gets called.

zero-based indexing: An indexing scheme in which the first element is name[0], not name[1]. Python itself uses zero-based indexing exclusively in all situations; however, it is possible for your programs to adopt one-based indexing and then translate it into "Python-ese" by subtracting 1.

Index